Penny Postcard

My Mother's Life

Janet Lee

ARPress
ILLUMINATING IDEAS
EMPOWERING VOICES

ARPress
45 Dan Road Suite 36
Canton MA 02021

Hotline: 1(800) 220-7660
Fax: 1(855) 752-6001

Ordering Information:
Quantity sales. Special discounts are available on quantity purchases by corporations, associations, and others. For details, contact the publisher at the address above.

Printed in the United States of America.

ISBN-13:   Paperback   979-8-89676-202-7
           eBook   979-8-89676-203-4

Library of Congress Control Number: 2024925218

With special thanks to my cousin, Debbie Gregg, without her I'm not sure I would have gone through with writing my book.

Prolouge

This is the story of my mother's life.

Some of her life was so terrible it's almost more than you could imagine, but then some was so wonderful it will make your heart sing with happiness.

First of all, she was born in a barn—literally. Stella Mae Attebery was born in Stanton, Texas, the sixth of twelve children. She was always very beautiful as a child and grew into an even more beautiful woman, with an amazing figure.

Her mother was a wonderful woman, who married at age fifteen to a man who she thought was a good man, I'm sure. Maybe he was for a while, but it didn't take long for her to find out she was married to a drunk who only wanted to keep having kids—plenty of them to pick cotton, fruit, or whatever work he could find for them to do to keep him in whiskey money. As the boys got older, he let them go to school some, so as not to get in trouble with the law. My mother said she was only able to go to school on days when there was absolutely nothing he could find for her to do to make money. Her dad said girls didn't need schooling since they were only good for having babies and working.

Mom had a sister two years older than she, who was mentally off because some of her older brothers had swung her around and dropped her on her head, which caused a brain injury. Birdie became very mean because of the injury as she got older. Mom said when she was about six or seven, Birdie tried to drown her in a pond. After that Birdie had to be watched carefully. Birdie died at the age of nine from diphtheria.

Mom loved all her brothers and sisters very much because they tried their best to protect her when her dad got drunk and mean. She said her daddy was only nice to whoever was the baby at the time.

Her oldest brother, Al, was ten when she was born, and her oldest sister, Lola, was eight. J. E., as he was always called, was six, and then came Preston, age four, and Birdie, whom I spoke of earlier. Maxine was two years younger than my mother, and then two years later along came Bill (called W. K. for some reason). I don't understand what the thing with the initials was back then. Well, J. E. was named after his dad, James Edward, so they had a reason. Two years after Bill came Joyce, and then two years later along came Velma. Then I think it was about three years before Garner was born, and about the same before, last but far from the least, Kenneth was born.

Mom's daddy was always really mean to the boys and made them work all the time. One time on a really cold day, the pipes froze up in the house they were staying in, and he made J. E. go up on the roof with him. He told J. E. to hold on to the pipe while he put the wrench on the other one to loosen it. When he told J. E. to let go of the pipe, J. E. said he couldn't get his hand loose, so his dad took the wrench and hit him over the knuckles so hard that he screamed in pain; he pulled his hand loose, ripping off some of the skin.

Mom said that was just one of the many terrible things he did over the years. He regularly came home drunk and hit her mama and yelled and hit any of the kids who he didn't think were doing just what he thought was right. Every one of the kids ran away from home as soon as he or she was old enough.

Al, being the oldest, ran away and got a job on a farm not too far away. His daddy had no idea where he was, but Al made sure news got to the older kids and his mama so that she wouldn't worry about him. All the kids loved their mother so much, and it just killed them that there was nothing they could do to help. If they tried, they got a beating, and their mama just got it worse. Their father said she was raising the kids to show no respect. How could anyone possibly respect a horrible drunk who abused his wife and children constantly?

J. E. and Preston weren't too far behind Al; they ran away at about fifteen and thirteen after their daddy beat Preston on his naked back with a heavy wire until the blood was running down his legs. They both decided they'd had enough, threw a couple of things together, and took off quietly in the night, leaving a secret note with Stella, knowing she would get it

Janet Lee

to their mama without the old man knowing about it. They both lied about their ages and went into the army. My uncle Preston was so handsome, and he looked so much like my mom; I guess that's why he was my favorite. Out of twelve children, they were the only two with beautiful black hair.

Most of the kids had light to medium brown hair. And Maxine and Joyce both had fiery red hair. Velma and Kenneth were little towheads. Strange how twelve kids from the same mama and dad can be so different.

But I am getting way ahead in this story. I just wanted to get the kids' ages and names out there first. Now I think it's best to let Mama take over and tell her story in her own words.

CHAPTER 1

Daddy's Cruelty

Daddy was extra hard on me—maybe because I made it a point to study and read anything I could get my hands on. Then I was smart enough to argue about things I thought weren't right. I had a hard time keeping quiet about it. My daddy once hit me so hard I flew across the room and hit my head so hard on the baseboard that it bled very badly, but he kept hitting me. My mother, even though she feared him terribly, picked up a hammer and hit him over the head with the claw; it stuck in and made him pass out. They called whatever doctor they knew, and he came and sewed up my head and put medicine on all the other wounds. Then he had my daddy thrown in jail. He was so drunk that he didn't even know what had happened. Daddy got out of jail after only a short while, considering how badly he had hurt me, but he remembered none of it, and I guess no one ever told him. Thank goodness—for my and Mama's sake!

The various times when he was thrown in jail were the happiest times all of us children ever knew. We were free to talk and have fun and play like other children with a normal dad.

One day Maxine and I decided to go swimming in a nearby pond. We had no swimsuits, so we just took off our clothes and laid them on a tree. After a while some young boys came along who we had never seen, so we hid behind a bush. We couldn't help but giggle a little after the boys were leaving, but our giggles were a bit too soon; the boys heard us and then looked around and saw our clothes.

They yelled, "You're going to have to come out if you want your clothes," and they were laughing so hard it frightened Maxine and me so badly that we started crying and asked the boys to please leave and not take our clothes away or our daddy would beat us really bad. We knew it was wrong to lie, but if our daddy hadn't been in jail, it would not have been a lie.

I guess the boys felt sorry for us because they left without the clothes. We were so very glad and dressed quickly. Anytime we ever had a chance to swim again, we made sure our clothes were hidden really well and kept a close watch out for more strangers. It was always a different pond or stream we were in, as we were always moving to wherever work could be found.

I was very young, around ten or eleven, when I heard all the whispers and knew that my daddy was messing around with Mama's younger sister Willie Mae. When she became pregnant, Mama's daddy had him thrown in jail for rape, and then he paid a man in town to marry Willie Mae so her baby wouldn't be a bastard. My mama was so angry that she changed Joyce's name, which had been Willie Joyce. She changed it to Jonnie Joyce. But Joyce was all she was ever called, so I never saw the point. Anyway, my daddy was in jail again. He got out way too soon, considering the charge, but I guess it was because my grandpa wasn't the sheriff in that town, so he didn't know about his early release.

We moved around a lot, and Mama said it was because Daddy wanted to keep her away from her family. He wouldn't ever let her get in contact with them. He didn't stay in contact with his own family either for a long time, and when he finally did contact them, his mother had died, and his daddy had remarried. Mama had heard that her mama and dad had also died a couple of years back. How terrible it must be to love your parents and never get to see them or even go to their funerals! The grandparents on both sides were fairly well off, and both grandpas were sheriffs. That's probably why Dad wanted to be away from them all, especially after the Willie Mae episode. He didn't want to let them know what a worthless drunk he had become or how terribly he treated his family.

Daddy had four brothers and sisters that I know of. His two oldest sisters were very beautiful. In the only picture I ever saw of his family, the other girl and boy were just young kids, probably ten or twelve. They were all dressed so fancy, especially when compared to what we were used to wearing. I only remember seeing them once in person, and then the grandma was very nice to us. I don't think the grandpa was there.

The next time we moved, it was to somewhere in Arizona. We lived in a camp of tents—big rows of tents, all alike, with dirt floors. We slept on old cotton mattresses on the ground. Mama cooked what little food we had outside on a campfire. There were six of us at home at the time: myself, Maxine, W. K., Joyce, Velma, and the youngest, Garner. We were always hungry and had to wear the same clothes for a week sometimes. But Mama always kept everything as clean as she could. She swept the hard dirt floors every day, and it always seemed so strange that dirt floors could look so shiny and clean. Mama worked so hard; it broke my heart to see how sweet and wonderful she stayed after all she had been through. When Daddy was home, I don't remember a day that he didn't slap her around for some ridiculous reason or another. If we tried to stop him, we got it too, and Mama just got beat on worse.

It had been drizzling rain for a week, and there was no work. Daddy was drunk and had been for a week or more. There was always money for whiskey, but none for food or clothing.

CHAPTER 2

California Bound

There was a Mr. Jones in the camp whom Daddy had made friends with. He was just as vulgar and nasty as Daddy.

Mr. Jones came to our tent one morning and was calling for Dad, but he was dead to the world, sleeping off his drunk.

Mama raised the tent flap and asked him to come in. Most women would have cursed and spit on him, but not my mama; she was too good and kind to be cruel to anyone.

Mr. Jones said, "Mrs. Attebery, I've heard there is lots of work in California, and I'm heading out there soon. I have plenty of room for you folks if you want to go."

Mama told him we would go. Mama never did anything without asking permission from Dad, but she did that time. Mama and us older kids packed up the few things we had. Then we rolled Daddy on to the ground, rolled up the old cotton mattresses, and loaded them on the truck. Next,

Daddy was boosted up on the truck, still half asleep and drunk, not knowing what was going on and caring less. So we were off to California. All of us kept singing, "We're going to California, where you sleep out every night."

There was the Joneses and their teenage boy, a young couple with a little baby, and then the eight of us on the truck. It rained off and on all the way to California. If it wasn't raining when we stopped at night, we threw down our mattresses and slept outside. If it was raining, we slept a very cramped night huddled together with the only tarp stretched over us as best we could.

As we neared Los Angeles, it was raining really hard, and the tarp leaked.

I just remember all the little ones crying and saying, "Mama, we're hungry; Mama, we're cold." My poor Mother! I can imagine how she must have felt, wanting to do her best for her children, but unable to have much say about anything.

The woman with the little baby just cried and prayed. She took all their clothes out of her big trunk and put the baby down in the trunk to stay dry.

I asked Mama, "What's that woman crying for?" and Mama said she was afraid her baby was going to die.

When we got into Los Angeles, it was flooded, and the water was up to the bumper of the truck. We crossed a bridge, and there were parts of houses and pieces of furniture floating down the river. After crossing the bridge, we parked. While we were sitting there, another bridge down the way washed out also. It was so cold, and I kept thinking, Where's all this California sunshine I've always heard of?

The Salvation Army took us in, and we had clean, warm beds and plenty of food to eat. They even gave us all some secondhand clothes and shoes that fit. We were all so proud of our new things. As far as we were concerned, we felt like we had brand-new things.

I don't know for sure how long we stayed there, but Daddy worked and finally saved enough money to buy an old car.

We moved again, this time into another row of tents. All of us that were old enough worked in the orchards, picking prunes. Mama tried to send Joyce to school, but all the other kids laughed at her and called us "old prune pickers." Joyce cried so hard Mama finally gave in and let her stay home.

Daddy started drinking again and said he hated California. He griped, "I'll get out of this place if it's the last thing I do. I was shanghaied here, and I'll never come back." I heard him curse and rant for hours so many times about how he was shanghaied to California.

Soon we had enough money to get started back to Texas. Daddy and Mama both had been born and raised in Texas. We got as far as Avondale, Arizona, before we found a place to stay for a while. Daddy drank all the way, driving from one side of the road to the other, scaring us all to death. He stopped at every town to find a bar so he could have another drink or two, leaving us all crowded in the old car.

In Avondale we got on relief and lived in a government camp. The camp was rows of tin buildings with concrete floors. We ate what the government wanted to give us, which was better than what we were used to. Daddy worked just enough to have whiskey money. That's all he ever cared about. I think every one of us kids hated him by the time we were old enough to walk and talk. He was such a horrible, smelly person that I can't imagine poor Mama having to sleep with him; Daddy was always drunk and always saying he wanted more babies. She always smelled so clean and fresh. They couldn't have been any more different.

After a while, we started out for Texas again, and again Daddy started out drunk. When he came to Coolidge, Arizona, he had to stop for a round in all the bars again, and he again left us sitting in the hot car for who knows how long.

It took a lot to make Mama mad, but she was furious, worrying that all us kids would get heatstroke and die. It had to be upwards of 110 degrees, and she was really mad seeing how terrible it was on us kids. She got out of the car, went to the sheriff's office, and told him what Daddy was doing and had always done.

The sheriff arrested Daddy and threw him in jail—forever I hoped.

Well, we were rid of him again for a while, but not much better off, because not a one of us knew how to drive a car.

Mama saw a young man who looked nice walking down the street and asked him if he could help us. He said he knew a big cotton farmer who always needed hands. He drove us there, and we were hired as cotton pullers. We had done this way too many times in Texas, so we knew how—that was for sure. The farmer had a tent for all of us to live in.

CHAPTER 3

The Courtship

Clarence Rader, the nice young man who took us there, had the tent next to ours. He was a bachelor and was very nice. He took us to town on Saturdays to buy groceries. I fell in love with him immediately. Clarence was thirty-five and I was just sixteen, but that didn't matter to either of us. If you didn't know his age, you would probably guess he was maybe twenty-five at the most. He was so handsome, and he was just the sweetest man you could ever find—and so very kind, especially to the little kids. He would buy candy and gum for us, which we had never had before. I could already tell that this was the man I wanted to spend the rest of my life with and to raise a family of our own with. I hoped he felt it too.

In about two weeks, Mama decided she had better go see Daddy. We all begged her not to, but I think she was afraid of what might happen if she didn't go. We all refused to go except the little ones; Velma and Garner had to do what Mama said. Well, Velma loved Mama so much she always did what Mama wanted her to do anyway.

So Mama, Velma, and Garner went to the jail to see Daddy. He put on a really good show and promised to be better. He even cried and tried to get Mama close enough to kiss her. (Yuck! It makes me want to puke to think about it.) He said to Velma, "Come over here and give your daddy some sugar." Tears filled her eyes, and he kept saying, "Don't you love your daddy anymore?"

I'm sure she wanted to say, "I hate you and always have," but she didn't.

He said again, "Come over here and give your daddy a kiss."

She was so afraid of him that she finally stepped forward and let him kiss her a real quick peck, moving away very fast. She just stood there looking at the floor or the men in other cells while Mama talked to Dad.

Daddy said, "Mama, don't you want me to come back to you when I get out?"

Mama said, no, she didn't.

Then Daddy said to the kids, "Well, you want your daddy home, don't you, Velma?" He reached through the bars really quick and grabbed Velma and pulled her to him. "Don't you want your daddy home again?"

She was so afraid of him that she nodded her head yes. She looked up at Mama with big tears in her eyes and saw that Mama's eyes were full of tears also.

Poor Mama, it seemed like all she did anymore was to pray and cry, except when she was back to working so hard she couldn't think of anything but the pain in her bleeding hands. She cried and worked and cooked and prayed, but I never heard her complain. All the older kids picking cotton had the same blood all over their hands when they finished work for the day. I swore when I could get away from all this, I never wanted to see a cotton patch again.

Daddy was let out of jail in about two months. Velma was playing out in front of the tent one day, and she looked up and there he was. After Daddy got home, we all had to work harder. If any of us didn't pull almost as much cotton as he did, we got a really bad thrashing with a big cotton stalk.

Every chance I got after work, I ran off to meet Clarence somewhere we had decided upon. I loved him more every day. He was the most special and smartest man I'd ever met.

He told me all about his large family and how much he loved them all and missed them. They were all over in Oklahoma, where he was from. He was the oldest of eight children by his mother who had raised him.

His real mother was a Cherokee Indian, and after she married his dad, they fought all the time about her sleeping on the nice big featherbed mattress he bought her when they got married. Almost every morning when he woke up, she would be down on the floor with a blanket she had brought with her. He would yell at her to get back in bed.

A couple of months after Clarence was born, she took him one day while his daddy was at work and went back to the reservation.

I guess the Indian tribe moved around a lot, and it took his daddy almost a year to find where she was. He would stay out far from the reservation and watch for her to see which teepee she lived in. After he was sure no one was in there with her but the little baby boy, who was walking by then, he waited until everyone in the tribe seemed to be in their teepees sleeping; then he went to the back of her teepee and quietly put a slit large enough for him to get in and out quickly with his son.

That was the last his dad ever saw of her until Clarence was home from college on a break. When he had to go back to school, he took his daddy aside and asked him if he knew where his Indian mother was. His daddy told him that last he'd heard, she was living way out in the country. He told him where to get off the train and that he would have to walk a couple of miles on a dirt road; it should be the only house there.

So Clarence did exactly as his dad told him, and sure enough, there was a little house out there all by itself. He went up to the door and knocked; there was no answer, but he heard a lot of rustling around inside so he knew someone was in there. He waited another minute, listening to the strange noises inside. Then he knocked again, really hard this time—twice.

Finally, a young boy opened the door.

He asked if Minnie was home, adding that she was his mother by T. L. Rader.

Immediately she came to the door and said, "Come in, Clarence."

It seems they all saw his Texas A& M uniform and thought he was a fed or something like that; they were hiding some equipment, because they made moonshine.

He only stayed for a short while, saying that he had to get back or he would miss his train back to college.

She hugged him, and he could tell by the look on her face that she was proud of him.

That was the last time he ever saw her. He said he had no idea how many kids she had by now since she was still very young and also very pretty still.

He also told me he had been married before to a woman for nine years. She had worked as a manager in a big J. C. Penney store and made good money, so she decided she didn't want any children. He said they had talked about how much he wanted a bunch of kids after they were married. He also worked and also made very good money, and she liked spending all that money so much, she just decided she didn't want any babies to take care of. She sounded like a very selfish woman to me, and Clarence confirmed she was, so they agreed to get a divorce.

Clarence had graduated from Texas A&M University with an engineering degree at the top of his class, but this was the beginning of the depression and work was hard to come by. He wanted to get away from Oklahoma for a while, so he had been hopping trains and finding work here and there and leaving whenever he wanted to. Being a bachelor made this possible, but he said he always gave whomever he was working for at least a week's notice. That showed me what a good, respectable man he was. He said he was seeing the country and wanted to go to California.

One day we were sitting in Clarence's car necking, and my little brother, W. K., found us and saw that Clarence's hand was up my top.

W. K. ran home and said to Mama that Clarence was playing with Stella's titties. He got his butt swatted hard, and nothing was ever said to Clarence or me.

It was a good thing Daddy wasn't home, but if he had been, I am sure W. K. was smart enough not to say anything in front of the old man, as we all called him when he wasn't around. They all knew that their daddy hated Clarence, because he said Clarence was sniffing around Stella. That's why we had to sneak around really carefully. I hated to think of what would happen if Daddy ever caught us. I tried to stay as far away from him as I could except when I was working. We only had short moments together.

One early evening when we knew the old man had gone to town, we met in our favorite place, way out on the other side of a big cornfield. No sooner had we got in the car than Clarence kissed me several times. Then he pulled out a ring and proposed to me. Of course, I said yes. We sat there making plans that Clarence would leave for California right away so he could find work there and start sending me money to run away and take the bus to California, so we could marry right away. Clarence had already given his boss a week's notice.

We all knew that Daddy had said we were leaving soon to get back to Texas. I had already written to Lola and told her of our plans; I asked her if Clarence could send money to her house for me every week to save until I had enough to leave for California. He wasn't sure what kind of job he could get or how much it would cost to get a place to stay. But he planned to send just as much as he possibly could. We were both so excited to marry and start a family of our own. I knew Lola would be happy for me, as she was for any of her siblings to be able to get away from that monster that actually called himself a father. He didn't know the meaning of the word.

Daddy came home drunk again and said we were leaving the next day really early because he had gotten into a fight in the bar in town over who had paid for the last round and who owed. Daddy knew he owed, but he was broke and said the guys might be showing up there early to get their money. He went to the farmer and told a big lie about getting news from his family that his daddy was real sick, he had to get home to Texas, and they needed him back right away. So the farmer paid him what we were owed and told him how sorry he was. Daddy could really put on a charming act—and what an actor he was when he needed to be. It was sickening to watch him being so nice, when he was just never that way. The only time I'd seen him being nice was way back when we'd stopped at his dad's place. I guess he didn't want his father and siblings to know what a real terrible person he was to his wife and children.

I had no way to tell Clarence what was happening. I racked my brain and decided to just write a note really quickly and throw it in his tent explaining what had happened so he would understand why I hadn't shown up at our special place. I had already asked him to keep my ring safe, and he understood what Daddy might do if he ever found my ring. He had already warned me, if my daddy ever hurt me again, he would kill him, and I believed he just might if Daddy hurt me as bad as he had many times before.

CHAPTER 4

Scurrying out of Texas

While it was still dark, we all rolled up the mattresses, put our meager belongings in the car, and off we were for Texas. For the first time, Daddy wasn't drunk and just drove and drove. He was so set on getting to Texas. I still think a lot more went on in that bar than Daddy said. He wasn't that afraid over a round of drinks. I had never seen him act so strangely. I think he must have killed someone, but we'll never know. Except for stopping for bathroom breaks and long enough for Mama to fix us something to eat real quick, then sleeping when it got dark, Daddy actually drove straight through to Texas.

We were very close to Dallas, so I begged Daddy to let me go to Lola's house. It had been so many years since I had seen her. Maxine begged too, so he finally gave in. We were going to try to hitch a ride, but he said he would drive us. I don't know what happened—he had never been nice before for no reason—but we weren't going to worry about that now. Thinking back, I don't think he knew exactly where

Lola's house was, and that was probably the reason. He sure didn't want Maxine and I to get away from him. We were two of his best workers. The two oldest had left, of course.

Lola, her husband, and their two daughters lived in a beautiful house in Fort Worth, just about twenty miles from where we had stopped, and Daddy found a job. It was doing something that they only needed him for, so the kids were all going to get a break, at least until Daddy found some work for all of us. Daddy said he'd wait in the car until we found out if it was okay with Lola that we spend a couple of days there. (I think there was a switch somewhere back in Arizona because this was not my daddy.)

Maxine and I just stared at each other, then got out of the car and ran to the house to ring the bell. Lola answered and was so excited to see us, almost as excited as we were to see her. We hadn't seen her since she had left home to marry at eighteen. We told her what Daddy had said, and she said, of course she would love to have us there so we could meet our nieces and they could get to know their grown-up aunts. I only wish Mama could have been there too, but there were the four little kids to take care of, plus Daddy sure wasn't going to let his main slave leave—no one could change that much.

While we were there, Lola cooked a feast for us. She told us to go find the guest bedroom at the back of the house and put our things in there, and we could wash up and change our clothes if we wanted to in the bathroom right down the hall from our bedroom. We did and then came back to the kitchen. She was even baking a delicious cake; we had never in our lives eaten like that before.

Her house was so big and so beautiful. We were so happy that one of us got out and had a wonderful life. I told her all about Clarence, and she was so happy for me. She received my letter the next day, but it was so much nicer to tell her all about my wonderful man in person. She said she would be happy to save the money he sent for me. But even better, she said the lady down the street three doors was looking for a housekeeper. And she would pay me well, because she was a very generous person and made a very good wage—and best of all, she was nice too.

Lola's husband, Henry, was on the road so we didn't get to meet him, but we just loved Glenda and Joyce. They were such refined young little ladies and obviously adored their mother. Lola said they adored their daddy too, but he worked driving a large cattle truck and was gone sometimes for weeks. The money was really good, and he always said he had a family to support; Henry didn't want Lola working and away for even part of the day from the girls. Lola had left home at eighteen to marry Henry. Daddy had no choice as she was of age. She had met him while in town one day, and like Clarence and me, it was love at first sight. Truly, sometimes, you just know these things at once. She said he was such a good man and a wonderful father to Glenda and Joyce. They missed him so while he was on a long haul.

The next morning after getting the girls off to school, we went down the street and talked with the lady. She said she would need me every day except the weekends, and I assured her I was a hard worker and she wouldn't be disappointed. We told her all about Clarence, so that she knew it wasn't a permanent thing. In the meantime, she could be still looking for someone else. The best part was my pay. She offered me sixty dollars a week. She said that knowing my daddy (through talks with Lola) and things we had talked about during our conversation, she knew he would be taking my paycheck just like he always took all the money we all made picking cotton, fruit, or whatever work we did. So Mrs. Harvey said I could tell Daddy that I'd gotten a job making forty dollars a week, and she would give the other twenty to Lola for my travel money.

I was so excited I wanted to see Clarence and tell him right away, but all I could do was write a letter and send it to the post office box where Clarence said he would check regularly.

When Daddy came for Maxine and me, we told him about my job and asked if he could take me to Lola's on Sunday nights and pick me up on Friday nights. He was drinking again. I could smell him even from outside the car, so I had no idea if he was falling for it or not. He just sat there a minute and then said he would pick me up at Mrs. Harvey's, so he could get my check. I asked him if I wasn't going to be allowed to have any of it. He snarled and said, "We'll see." I knew what that meant!

The next Sunday night, he dropped me off at Lola's, and I started work Monday morning. I really worked my butt off so my new employer was happy with me. When she came home, she said she had never seen her house sparkle like that. I was a happy girl.

By the end of the week, I received a letter from Clarence. He wrote so beautifully and was so very romantic. He had just found a job at a construction company that paid pretty well, but they held back a week. I didn't understand what that meant, but Lola explained it to me. He also said places to stay were pretty expensive there, so he was sleeping in his car for a while. Then in the next letter, he said that sleeping in the car didn't work there, because the cops patrolled and said it was loitering, so he had to get an apartment. It was just one room with a small bath and little kitchen. But it would be large enough for us both for a while until he could save more money.

I was a little down because I had hoped I could get away from Daddy before he exploded again.

Daddy picked up my check on Friday, and Mrs. Harvey was furious, according to what Lola told me on Sunday. But Daddy was very happy to have a big night on the town. I felt sick.

CHAPTER 5

A Plan is Hatched

On Monday morning, Mrs. Harvey said she had thought of a way I could leave sooner for California. She said when Daddy came for my check on Friday, she would tell him she was short of money this week, and she would pay both weeks the next Friday. Of course, the plan was to give me both weeks' money on Friday morning, and I could take off. With what money Clarence had sent and the forty dollars that Lola was saving for me, I should be able to get a bus to Carmel, California, where Clarence was working, and have plenty to stay the night somewhere if I got too tired sitting on the bus.

Friday came, and Daddy was told the lie; he was not happy at all. His plans for the weekend were spoiled. I cried and said it wasn't my fault. I guess I was learning how to act also.

Late the next Thursday night, Daddy was really drunk, and he came to Lola's for me. He thought something wasn't right. Lola told him I was sleeping at Mrs. Harvey's because

I had to be at work early the next day. He said he was going down there and get me, and Lola told him he couldn't be disturbing Mrs. Harvey that late. He said, "The hell I can't; you just watch me."

As he staggered down the street, Lola woke me up and said, "Honey, you have to throw all your clothing in your bag right now." She grabbed all the money she had and said she was so sorry she hadn't expected this; she was going to the bank the next morning early to get what Clarence had sent and her $40, plus Mrs. Harvey was going to have her $120 the first thing in the morning. She said she had Clarence's address somewhere from one of the first letters he sent, and she would send it all plus the hundred and twenty from Mrs. Harvey for the past two weeks, but she said I had better get out the back door and over the fence quickly before Daddy came back. She would call down and explain to Mrs. Harvey. She told me how to get to the Greyhound Station and said I should have enough for a bus ticket, with some left over, she hoped.

Well, Mrs. Harvey, being the smart woman that she was, refused to open the door and said if Daddy didn't leave, she was calling the police immediately. That scared him off a little, but he went back to Lola's and told her I'd better be ready tomorrow and have the whole eighty dollars, which was what he thought was due.

I was so scared that my daddy might follow me, and there was no telling what he would do to me if he caught me at a bus station. I made it to the station and stayed way in a corner for a while until I figured it was safe. Then I went and bought a ticket for Carmel, California. Just the thought of being with Clarence made me so happy all of a sudden. After buying the ticket, I only had four dollars left. I'm sure Lola had no idea what a bus ticket would cost; she had given me all she had to give at that hurried moment. I figured I would just stay on the bus and get off just to go to the bathroom and get a tiny bit to eat, enough to keep me alive until I reached Carmel.

The bus left in two hours. I thought of going back to Lola's or Mrs. Harvey's to see if they had any more money, but I was afraid my daddy might be hanging around watching. I sure wished that I had the time to make some sandwiches and get some fruit and things like that. Lola always had loads of food in the house. She was such a good wife and mother, as well as a very good sister. She had helped me so much. I felt like I would never be able to repay her.

When the bus arrived and I got on, I finally took a deep breath and felt I was home free. On my way to see Clarence, I was filled with excitement. The miles seemed to go so slowly. I hadn't realized that the bus stopped in almost every town and let out people and waited for people to be picked up. I was getting so hungry, but decided to wait for one more food stop. It was several hours before the next food stop. I got off the bus and got a sandwich and an apple. I decided I'd better drink some water. The sandwich wasn't very good, but at least my stomach wouldn't be growling the rest of the day. The apple was a little mushy, but again, I just thought of being with Clarence, and that made even my mushy apple good. I didn't think I had enough money to get off for another food stop, so I just made up my mind that I was going to stay full and not think about food. I'd only think about Clarence.

The whole next day, my stomach kept growling, and it was so embarrassing, but I just smiled if someone looked at me; most of the time I tried not to make any eye contact.

CHAPTER 6

Always Trusting the Lord

The next town they stopped in, a sweet little older lady got on; to my surprise, the lady came to the back and sat down next to me. She introduced herself. Her name was Hazel Roberts, and I told her I was Stella Attebery. We talked a while, and I told her I was going to Carmel, California, to meet my fiancé. She thought that sounded so romantic. I said, "Oh, Mrs. Roberts, I think so too." Then she stopped me and said, "No more of that Mrs. Roberts." She was going to California too, and since we were going to be traveling buddies for quite a few days, no more formal stuff; she was just Hazel. We quickly became great friends.

She had been in Texas visiting her son, his wife, and her three little beautiful granddaughters. Now she was going to Los Angeles to visit her daughter and her husband. They were expecting their first baby in a few weeks, and she was staying with them for a while to help out. She said she felt so fortunate to have such wonderful in-laws who loved having her at their homes. Some of her friends said their children were married to people who didn't like them visiting.

I told her that my mother was always going to be welcome at my home, and she knew Clarence felt the same way. His parents would always be welcome also. I told her we both had large families, so there was just no telling how often we would have visitors dropping in, which was fine. I didn't want to go into all the gory details, but I told her about our daddy being mean and how we all left home as soon as we were old enough. So I had brothers I hadn't seen in years, and I hoped somehow to get word to them where I was. I knew J. E.'s and Preston's addresses in the army. They had written to my mama, and I tore off the return address and stuck it in my bag, so I could write them some day. I never dreamed at the time that I would be having such great news to tell them.

I hoped someday I could find Al too. He was always such a funny character when Daddy wasn't around. He could make us all laugh for hours when we had evenings without Dad. There were a lot of happy memories in my head about all the precious times we had just sitting around with Mama and her reading her Bible to us. The Lord was always with us, she had said. Sometimes that was hard to believe when we went through some of the horrors that we'd been through. But I still always believed anything Mama said to us.

As I sat there with my mind wandering through the good times, Hazel had drifted off to sleep, and I decided that was a good idea. I laid my head over on my side and went to sleep right away.

When I woke up, Hazel said to me, "Honey, you must be starving; your poor little tummy was just growling all the time you slept." I said that I would be fine. Hazel reached down and pulled up her big basket. She opened it up, and I never saw so much food in one basket. It was so perfectly packed and arranged that it held lots.

She took out a sandwich of chicken salad and offered it to me. I told her I couldn't eat up her food, and she said she wouldn't be able to eat all that even if she were on that bus for two more weeks, so I took it. As I bit into it, I couldn't help making a humming sound because it was just so good. She told me her daughter-in-law put it all together because it was such a long trip, and she thought someone else might be hungry also; this way Hazel would have enough to share.

Now I knew Mama was right when she said, "The Lord will always take care of you." I bowed my head and thanked God right then. We had so much fun talking. I felt like it should have been like that with my mama, but poor Mama had to work so much, she never had much time to talk one-on-one with us. There were so many kids and so much for her to do. My heart broke, thinking what a sweet, wonderful mama she was. When Daddy wasn't around, she tried her best to show us how much she loved us all. It's just that she still had to work so hard wherever we were.

I dozed off thinking about my mama, instead of Clarence like I usually did. I guess it was because I knew I would be with him before I knew it.

When I woke up, Hazel was sleeping. I closed my eyes and tried to go back to sleep, but my mind just wondered about all the things that Clarence had talked about that we would be doing when we got married. I could hardly stand the wait. But it would only be a few more days, I hoped. The drivers never gave me a straight answer when I asked. One driver would say, "It depends." Then the next day there would be a different driver, and he'd say about the same thing, except he would add it depended on how many people we had to pick up at each town, and at each town, they might add another stop for the bus. I got so many tiring answers, but they were just doing their jobs.

After an hour or so, Hazel woke up, and we continued with our talks. She had just two children and would spend time with each for a while. She still had her home in Chicago, and her sister, who was also a widow, lived there with her. They got along so well. Her sister had one son, and he lived close to them in Chicago. He was so good about fixing any little thing that was needed. He had been married, but his wife died in childbirth. I thought that was just the saddest thing I'd ever heard.

I told Hazel about the time my mother had a baby too early and it died. I remember her asking my younger brother W. K. if he would go find a small blanket to wrap the tiny baby in, and then she asked him to dig a hole as deep as he could to bury the baby. Then the three of us went and said a prayer over the grave, and Mama cried so hard.

I said, "I guess no matter how many children you have, they are all important to you." Hazel assured me that was true. I had never ever told anyone that secret before, except Maxine. We told each other everything. I would miss my brothers and sisters very much, but I knew how much family meant to Clarence too, and we would always have room for family to visit.

Another day passed, and we munched on good things from her basket. We had finally left New Mexico, and we were in Arizona. It was so very hot, we hated to get out for bathroom breaks. But you have to go when you have to go. We laughed about it. At least when the bus was moving and all the windows were down, we had the wind making a good breeze. We had to keep them closed mostly at night because the bugs would eat us up alive. So we just tried to sleep and not think about the bugs. We noticed when it became night in Arizona that there were not as many bugs there. Maybe it was too hot even for them.

I thought we were bound to get to Nevada the next day since there didn't seem to be as many towns we were stopping in—thank the Lord. We just went through a very small area of Nevada, and then, finally, we were in California. It was so hot there; I think the temperature was even hotter than Arizona. Hazel said we were going through the desert part of California and it would get better. I think it had to have been 120 degrees when we got to this place called Barstow. You could hardly breathe.

When we got to Bakersfield, Hazel had to change buses because she was headed down south to Los Angeles. I was sure going to miss her. She had made all these days so much nicer, plus she fed me all the time. I felt terrible, but she kept showing me all the things still in there to eat. She even insisted on leaving me some fruit and another sandwich of ham and cheese.

"I must be the luckiest girl in the world to have met you, Hazel," I told her. We both hugged and cried when she got off the bus. It was going to be lonely the next day, but then I would be with Clarence—my one and only love for the rest of my life; I knew this without a doubt.

As we were pulling away from Bakersfield, I could see Hazel standing there waiting for her bus. We both waved and threw kisses to each other. I had come to care so much for this woman in just a matter of days. it's strange how some people affect you. She had probably saved my life. I really don't know if I would have made it four long days more with nothing to eat, especially with all the heat. I would have had no money to even buy drinks. I only had maybe thirty-five cents left; I hadn't counted it for fear Hazel might try to give me money too, and I had taken so much from her already. I hoped sweet Hazel would not have to wait too long for her bus to come. They were sure never right on time.

When we got to Sacramento, I counted my money and had enough for a Coke. It tasted so good—not like I had ever had many, but this one had to be the best. Now I knew it would not be more than a couple of hours before I got to Carmel and to Clarence. My excitement grew with each minute, I think, if possible. Finally I heard the driver say, "Next stop, Carmel." They were the most beautiful words I'd heard for a long time.

I got all my things together and waited as patiently as I could. As soon as the bus stopped, I almost ran off. I looked around, and everything seemed so crowded all of a sudden. I guess my mind hadn't ever gotten this far; I just took it for granted that when I got to Carmel, all things would fall into place. I would go to the construction company and ask for Clarence Rader, and that would be it. He would be there, and we would get married.

Well, as I walked around and asked a few people where the construction company was, no matter who it was, they said, "What's the name of the company?" I had never thought about there being more than one since I had, for most all my life, lived in towns where almost everyone knew one another and where things were, as there weren't many things to look for: a grocery store or a hardware and feed store, a bank and a gas station, a jail, and a few farmers—and most everyone knew their names. I felt completely lost and had no idea what to do.

As I sat on a bench for the longest time, I finally thought, Stella Attebery, you are smarter than this; think of something. Then it came to me: I would go to the police station. They could surely help me. I knew I looked at least nineteen, so that is what I would tell them. When I got there, I made sure I steadied myself and tried hard to appear calm and like I knew exactly what I was doing. When I got there, I thought I did. Wrong! I am sure Clarence would have told me all the things I needed to do if I had had time to get one more letter and to get another letter off to him letting him know I was coming sooner, but there hadn't been time for that.

CHAPTER 7

Search for Clarence

Anyway, I calmly walked into the police station and asked for someone who could help me find my fiancé. They first asked why I was looking for him and what his name was. I told the officer I was speaking to that I was supposed to come there and my fiancé and I were to be married. I told him that I had decided to come early and surprise him—and that I had no idea how large this area would be. "I am from a little town in Texas, and things are a little easier there." They asked how old I was, and I confidently told them I was nineteen. Then they asked where I expected to find Clarence. I told them he worked at a construction company. They asked me if I knew the name of the company. When I said I had no idea, they told me there were probably at least a hundred or more in the area, with so many other towns almost connected to Carmel.

Then I started to cry. I had finally lost my calm and just didn't know what to do. I explained that Clarence was mailing money to my sister's house, and I was sure that in my next letter from him, he would probably have told me all these things I needed to know, but I didn't know I would need to know them. I was talking so fast and crying at the same time, and the officer asked where I was going to stay until I found him; then I really started crying and told the officer that I had less than ten cents left to my name, so I had no idea what I was going to do. God was there with me again, as I probably had found the most understanding policeman ever made.

As it turned out, the officer was really good friends with the woman who was in charge of the Red Cross for this whole area, and she was always looking for people who were willing to help with making things that the soldiers needed. There were always things to be made. He said it was hard work, but Mrs. Peterson was the best ever to work for. He wasn't positive that she wanted to take someone in to live there for a while, but it didn't hurt to ask. Officer Joe, as he told me to call him, said it would be better to go to her house when he got off rather than to call, if I didn't mind waiting around for an hour or so.

I told him I would just sit out in front and wait. But he said no, I could stay in there and sit on the bench up front. I was so thankful because it was getting a little chilly outside. It was just amazing how different the weather was in just a few hundred miles difference. Clarence had mentioned that I would love the weather in Carmel, and he was sure right. I didn't even own a coat, but I could tell I was going to need one; it was not important now, that's for sure. I was close to Clarence, and that would keep me warm.

35

Officer Joe was ready to go in just a bit over an hour, and I was so excited to maybe have somewhere to stay while I looked for Clarence. When we arrived at Mrs. Peterson's house, I could not believe my eyes. It looked like a mansion that I could only imagine in a dream. It must have been at least three stories high and had the fanciest decorations all over it. I told Officer Joe what I was thinking, and he just laughed. He said it was called a Victorian house, and all that stuff was called gingerbread. He also told me not to worry: everyone felt that way when they saw this house. He said Mrs. Peterson was the richest woman in all the nearby towns, and she was nicer than she was rich.

I asked if she lived there all alone, and he said yes she did, but she always had many people there working for her. Since the war had first started, she had turned many rooms into work areas. They did many different things to help our soldiers and to help families of the soldiers who needed help with food, medicine, and learning how to take care of themselves without their husbands. He had explained as much as he knew, and now it was time to go up to the house and meet Mrs. Peterson.

We walked up to the house. I felt very nervous all of a sudden, not knowing if she was going to want me to stay in this beautiful house. We rang the doorbell, and it made the most beautiful chimes sound. After just a short while, a lady came and opened the front door. Officer Joe asked if Mrs. Peterson was available to talk to company. The lady said she would go ask.

After just a minute, the most lovely older lady, who was dressed like she was going to a party, came to the door and opened it up and hugged Officer Joe. She said, "Get in here out of this cold. Of course I have time for you—always."

He introduced me to her, and then she said, "Let's go into the parlor and sit." She asked the other lady to bring in some tea and cookies. Officer Joe started out telling her all about my story.

Mrs. Peterson looked like she was going to cry, and then she came over and hugged me. She said, "What a beautiful little thing you are, and not hardly old enough to be on your own."

I told her I was nineteen and had lived a very different life than anything like this, so I was much older in years than even my nineteen years. I was so glad I had read books, so I knew a little how to talk with people and sound somewhat intelligent.

Mrs. Peterson picked up my hands and said, "Oh, dear, I can see that you have done very hard labor. I have seen many men that have not had anywhere near the calluses on their hands that your poor young hands have. What in the world have you been doing?"

I didn't want to tell her how really disgusting my daddy was, but I had to say something, so I told her there were many children in my family and to get enough money for food and clothing, we all had to pick cotton or fruit or whatever kind of work we could get. I told her I had left home at eighteen and gone to Fort Worth, Texas, and gotten a job cleaning house for a very nice woman.

Mrs. Peterson looked like she just wanted to pick me up and rock me. I felt a little self-conscious so I tucked my hands away under my dress. Lola had given me several nice dresses, and I was so glad about that now.

After we had some delicious hot tea and even better cookies, Officer Joe finally got on the subject of me and the fact that I had no money and nowhere to stay.

She immediately said, "Well, don't you worry your little head about that. You will stay here with me and learn how to help with all my Red Cross projects."

I wanted to jump up and kiss her, but I just said very ladylike, "Oh, thank you so much; I will work so hard for you. I can clean."

She stopped me right there and said she already had that kind of help. I would be doing things for the Red Cross projects she handled.

It was getting late, so Officer Joe said he had better be getting home to his wife and kids before they thought something had happened to him. He laughed and said they were used to him having late nights sometimes "because you just never know at the police station." He assured me he would help look for Clarence and let me know from time to time what was going on, if anything. He also said not to think it was going to be easy because of so many construction companies and so many little towns nearby. So he said he would spread the word to other stations in the other towns and do all he could do. I felt my heart was going to break, but I really did believe Officer Joe would do as much as he could, and I believed he meant it sincerely.

After Officer Joe left, Mrs. Peterson asked the other nice lady—Annie was her name, and she told her I was Stella— to show me to the nicest room on the second floor, so I could get freshened up before we ate dinner. I was amazed. I figured the tea and cookies were all we would have, since it had been about dinnertime when we got there. I thought dinner was over.

I followed Annie upstairs to the most beautiful fancy room I'd ever dreamed of. I felt like I was in a fairy tale, and all that was missing was my Clarence. My room had its own private bath with a big claw-foot tub. I was told dinner would be in twenty minutes. Annie would come for me to show me to the dining room.

As soon as Annie left, I took off my dress that I had been wearing for about a week. It didn't look dirty because I'd just been sitting on a bus, but I felt dirty and wanted to look fresh. I ran a little water in the tub and washed with the best-smelling soap I'd ever smelled. I soaped up really quick and then rinsed as fast as I could and dried on a big fluffy towel. I couldn't believe this was all for me. I hurried and brushed my hair so it would look as good as it could without having time to wash it.

When Annie came for me, she commented on how nice I looked and how good I smelled. She said Mrs. Peterson was the best to work for and I would love it there. She also whispered that Mrs. Peterson always bought the best-smelling soaps ever. She ordered them from New York, where she bought her hats and a lot of her clothes and fancy things. Annie said most employers wanted their maids to wear uniforms, but Mrs. Peterson said I could wear whatever I felt comfortable in as long as it was a dress and I was always clean. She had other people who came in very early and cleaned the house.

Annie took me to the dining room, which had two large doors that when opened up revealed this unbelievable room. The table was set for just two, but there were twelve chairs, and they had the most beautiful lavender brocade fabric you can't even imagine. I hated to sit on them, but that was silly because my chair was pulled out for me, and Mrs. Peterson was already seated at the head of the table.

My head was swirling from all I had seen already. The walls had a beautiful silk-looking wallpaper, and all the lights were lit with little flames. I had never seen all these things before, and I know Mrs. Peterson could tell what I was thinking. She said that she entertained important people quite often, and so since she loved decorating, she did it well.

Another lady came in and served us soup. She was the cook, and her name was Kathleen, I was told. It was delicious—so much better than anything we ever had to eat; there just was not the money to buy much more than beans and potatoes, and sometimes Mama would make bread, which was a treat.

When Kathleen came to take away the soup bowls, the plates were left, so I knew something else was coming. In a minute she came carrying a large platter of sliced roast beef and creamed potatoes with peas. I could not believe the piece of roast she laid on my plate. And then she added a large serving of the potatoes and peas. It was so tender you didn't even need a knife to cut it, but I used one anyway because I tried to watch what Mrs. Peterson was doing and follow along. Everything was so good, and the yeast rolls with real butter just melted in my mouth. I told her if I ate this way all the time, I would get fat. She assured me I had a long way to go before that.

After all the dishes were cleared, Mrs. Peterson said, "Kathleen, you can bring dessert into the sitting room."

We opened up the doors on the other side of the dining room and went into another room, which was just as beautiful as the last, just a deeper shade of purple. I told Mrs. Peterson purple had always been my favorite color, and she said it was hers too, and Annie's also. She told me she wanted me to feel at home while I was her guest.

When we walked over to the window to look outside, I could see she had a view of the ocean; she said there was always a nice breeze from the water. Oh, it was so pretty, I wished Clarence were there. But he had told me all about the ocean and how, when I got here, we could go swimming in it and walk along the water in the sand, barefoot of course.

My mind was in a whirl; it kept thinking of one thing and then jumping to another. It was all too much, and I'd only

41

seen my room and three others, all so beautiful with the fancy French furniture and gorgeous little tables with the really curved legs. It was all too much.

In a few minutes, Kathleen came in with a tray holding a silver coffeepot with matching cream and sugar. It also had two huge pieces of chocolate cake. I would never tell Lola, but it was even better than hers. I couldn't believe I ate all of it, and so did Mrs. Peterson. I was stuffed to the top. We talked for a while, and then she caught me yawning.

She said, "You have had a long, hard week. You go up and fill that tub with hot water, and make sure you put in some of that bubble bath under the sink. It will soften your skin, and you will sleep like a baby. Don't worry at all about getting up in the morning because I'm leaving early tomorrow for a meeting at a company where I am on the board, so I have to go. Ugh. The meeting usually runs a couple of boring hours." She laughed and said, "Oh, what they would all think if they heard me say that. Oh well; they can't. Ha-ha!" She added, "Just sleep in as long as you want, and if you're hungry when you do wake up, just tell Kathleen what you would like to eat, and she'll bring it to your room. We must pamper you for a day or two till you're rested from your long trip."

I went right up to my room, started my bathwater, then undressed, found the bubble bath, and poured some in. When I got in, I felt like I had died and gone to heaven. The hot water was so relaxing, but the bubble bath made me feel like I was in some exotic spa I'd read about. I must have soaked for at least an hour. When I got out, a fresh towel was hanging there. I dried quickly and jumped into the big bed, which had already been turned down for me. It was so soft and comfortable, I think I fell asleep immediately.

When I woke up the next morning, I opened the pretty drapes and saw that I had a view of the ocean also. How special I felt. I really didn't feel very hungry, so I just made my bed, straightened up everything, and admired how perfectly beautiful my room was. It was decorated in a shade of periwinkle blue. I think that's what it was called. Whatever it was was perfect. I felt like a princess.

When I opened the door to go downstairs, Annie said that they were supposed to bring me my breakfast in my room. So I asked what would be the easiest for them to make. Annie said Kathleen could make anything. There were always fresh pastries she made every morning, and they were heavenly. I told her that sounded delicious, with some tea and a glass of milk if they had it.

I went back to my room having forgotten to ask what time it was. When Annie brought me my tray, I asked the time. She said it was eleven thirty. I could not believe I'd slept that long, but I sure felt good.

Annie said that Kathleen was from Denmark, and that was why she knew how to make the delicious danish pastries. There were about six or seven pastries; they had been warmed, and I had a little bowl of butter to put on them. They were heavenly, and I devoured them before I knew it. Oh, but they were so good, I couldn't help myself. They were pretty small. Now I'm just trying to justify how many I ate. Well, I thought, they brought me that many, so they must have expected me to eat them. I drank my milk and then had a few cups of the good tea. Now I knew I had died and this was heaven.

But I had no Clarence. I wondered all the time how long it would take to find him. Not too long, I hoped. I was a virgin, but Clarence and I had talked a little about that. I couldn't help being just a little nervous about it, but Clarence had assured me he would be gentle and go as slowly as I needed. He was such a gentleman. I sat there staring at the ocean for a while dreaming about my wedding night. Lola had even given me a really fancy little nightgown for my honeymoon. I loved it, and I was sure Clarence would love it too. It was a baby-soft pink and was very low cut to show off my pretty good-size breasts. Clarence had touched them, and it felt so good that I knew our wedding night would be wonderful. Clarence would see me for the first time without clothes, and I would see him. Just thinking about it made me as excited as when Clarence was caressing my breasts. I thought, if it felt that good to just be touching, how special would the rest be? I had never talked about sex with anyone, except Lola a little bit. She told me all brides were nervous and didn't know what to expect, that it would just come natural and everything would be like heaven.

Mrs. Peterson came home about a half hour later, and I went right down when I heard her. I asked what she needed me to start doing. She said we would talk about that tomorrow. Today was for rest and whatever I wanted to do. I really didn't have a clue about what to do. She said, "Go outside; it's a beautiful day, and you will love the beach. Go around to the back of the house, and there's a trail down to the sand." Now I was really amazed: she lived right on the beach—wow!

While walking along the beach in my bare feet, all I could think of was Clarence and how much I wished I could have written him before leaving Texas so he would have been there to meet me and we could have been walking along this beach together. Maybe married already. But I didn't, and all I could do now was to enjoy all these beautiful things that I was experiencing now, here at this magnificent home of Mrs. Peterson, whom I would never have met if it weren't for my traveling mishap. Of course being with Clarence would be better, but now I just had to enjoy what was happening. I lost track of how long I walked. Suddenly I thought I'd better get back in case Mrs. Peterson was ready to tell me what I was expected to do the next day.

When I returned I found Mrs. Peterson out picking a beautiful basket full of the prettiest flowers I'd ever seen for the table tonight at dinner. I wasn't used to seeing so many pretty flowers since we were always in some dirty camp with only dirt and dust to look at. The cotton fields sure never had anything beautiful around them. I asked her what time it was, and she said it was about four o'clock. I hadn't realized I had walked so long just thinking.

Mrs. Peterson said, "Annie said all you had for breakfast was a few pastries. I'll have the cook make you a sandwich so you don't waste away to nothing before dinner."

I asked her what time I should be ready for dinner.

Mrs. Peterson said dinner was usually at six, but we had eaten so late the night before because she was enjoying Officer Joe's visit and his telling of my terrible circumstances.

I told her I would be just fine waiting until dinner and that I was feeling a bit messy after walking along the beach for so long; I would just go up to my beautiful room and get cleaned up for dinner. I then thanked her again for her kindness in letting me stay here at her home.

She said not to give it a thought; she was sure I would be a big help to her with all her Red Cross projects. She said we would have plenty of time to get started talking about all that tomorrow morning.

I asked her if she had an alarm clock so I didn't oversleep again tomorrow.

She told me she would have Annie bring one up to my room a little later and show me how to work it.

I couldn't help myself: I put my arms around her and gave her a big hug. She saw the tears in my eyes and asked if everything was okay. I told her how I felt so guilty enjoying being here and wanting to find Clarence so badly at the same time.

She said, "Don't be silly. Everything you are feeling is absolutely normal; you wouldn't be the sweet naive little young lady that you are if you felt any different."

Then I felt guilty about lying about my age.

She added, The Lord, in his own time, will make sure everything works out just fine; just enjoy what you can to make the best of a bad situation."

I said, "How could I possibly consider this a bad situation, living here in this beautiful house and being treated like a princess?"

She just laughed and said I would start helping out tomorrow, earning my keep.

I told her I would feel better helping her.

We had another amazing meal that night and sat out on the back enclosed porch and had our tea and dessert. No matter how wonderful all this felt, all I could think of was hoping and praying to hear soon from Officer Joe.

Later that evening after my bath, as I put on my nightgown, there was a quiet knock on the door. As always, my heart jumped, but it was Annie with the alarm clock Mrs. Peterson had promised earlier to have her bring up. She sat with me and showed me how simple it was to set. We talked for quite a while, and I told her all about my trip here to this beautiful town, my shock as to the amount of places and people there were, and how I had thought I would just step off the bus and be led to a construction company. She said she felt so sad for me. I told her not to, because I had faith that God would bring Clarence to me in a short time.

Annie held my hand and. like a wise older woman, said she certainly hoped it all worked for me. and she would pray every night for me. She was all of twenty-five, just a few years older than they all thought I was. I felt guilty lying to them all, but I felt if they knew I was just sixteen, they might feel they had to contact my parents in Texas. That would be almost unthinkable having to go back there. I hated to think of the wrath of my daddy. So my lie would have to stay a secret.

The next morning I was downstairs with a work dress on. It was one of the few that Lola had given me to clean house in. Even these were so nice compared to anything that I had grown up wearing. Mrs. Peterson said, "Sit down, Stella, and have a good hearty breakfast." The cook came in with a huge pile of fresh hot biscuits, and Annie followed behind her with a tray of scrambled eggs and three different kinds of jam. Then came some sausage gravy and another large tray of warm danish pastries. I asked if they ate this way all the time. Mrs. Peterson said, "You have to eat well if you're going to work hard." I just knew I was going to blow up, and Clarence wouldn't even recognize me when he was found. I had to keep thinking positive, though.

After breakfast, the doorbell rang, and there were four more ladies who came to see what they could do to help. Mrs. Peterson said, "Come on in; we have plenty of work to get done." I thought I couldn't work with all this food in me. I was introduced to the ladies, and they all were around Mrs. Peterson's age, I thought. They must be friends of hers.

What we started out doing was just rolling up strips of soft cloth for rolls of bandages for the soldiers who were already overseas in the war that was just beginning. They weren't fighting yet, but as Mrs. Peterson said, you couldn't wait until they needed them, or it would be too late by the time they were shipped over there. She said this Hitler guy sounded like a monster from things her friends had told her. All the ladies agreed.

We did this for several hours and started layering them into boxes to be shipped. I was amazed at how many boxes we filled; it had seemed so easy. I had been expecting work. This was not work; it was just chatting and rolling and more of the same. I just knew none of these sweet ladies really knew what hard work was.

After a while we stopped for some tea and ate a couple of the danishes. Oh my, but they were so good and just went down so easy. I could feel myself growing, my imagination I knew, and Mrs. Peterson said. I sure hoped so!

We all went into the kitchen. It was the first time I had been in any of the back part of the house. The kitchen was so big and had so many cabinets and drawers it almost made me cry, thinking of all my poor mama had to do and the little space she had to do it in. What I wouldn't give to see her face if she could walk into this kitchen and be told she had to cook dinner or whatever meal it was. She would think she was in heaven with our Lord already.

I missed her sweet face so much, and my sisters, especially Maxine, and my brother W. K. He was always so small that I felt Daddy just didn't like him, so he was extra mean to him. With me the oldest leaving them at home, I hated to think how Daddy was treating Maxine and W. K. now. Actually I really wasn't too worried about Maxine, even though she would be the oldest. She never seemed to argue with Daddy, so he didn't pay much attention to her one way or another. But poor W. K. would be getting all the anger that Daddy had shown me. It broke my heart just to think of it. Velma was getting old enough, and she was a sassy one, like me, so I hoped they were all right.

Garner being so young, I didn't have to worry about him yet. Daddy was always nice to the baby. It was strange, I thought, because he really didn't have a nice bone in his body; I guess it was just that they weren't old enough to yell at yet or slap around. I cringed at the thought of my last encounter with the old bum. Oh how I hated him, even though Mama always read to us from the Bible and told us hate was a sin. All I could think of was when the Bible was written, they didn't know my daddy.

Anyway, back in the kitchen, we were shown where everything was, and we all started making sandwiches and filling baskets. Some were filling baskets with fruit, and some with slices of pound cake; I was told what it was as I had never seen or heard of a pound cake. It all just went so fast, and with everyone chatting along the way, it just didn't seem like work. Mrs. Peterson told us all we could grab a plate and make ourselves a sandwich out of whichever meats and cheeses we wanted and then get some fruit and a slice of that pound cake and we would all go out on the veranda and eat lunch. What a treat, I thought.

Very few people were on the beach, even though it was June and a beautiful day. Mrs. Peterson said that most people knew this part of the beach was hers, and if we looked down farther, we could see many more people. It still wasn't a lot, I thought, considering it was such a beautiful day. We sat there talking and just enjoying being outside.

All the other ladies asked me all about how I came to be in California by myself at such a young age. I gave them a quick version of my story and heard all their oh mys and poor dears that I tried to change the subject, drawing everyone's attention to a lady walking along carrying a beautiful baby, with one not much older hanging on to her dress tail. It was just so cute. Everyone stared and said the poor lady probably was alone since she was so young; her husband had probably been drafted and was in boot camp being trained to be a soldier, as were most young men about her age.

Then it came right back to me. They asked why my fiancé had not been drafted. I explained that Clarence was quite a bit older than I, and it didn't matter to me at all because we had fallen in love the minute my older sister had introduced us. He was a widower and was friends with my sister Lola and her husband. Clarence had come to California because he had heard there was lots of work for men here and that he could make more money and we could afford to get married sooner. And then I got anxious, and my sister Lola, knowing what a wonderful man Clarence was, helped me get a bus ticket to come out and meet with him sooner, since I had been moping around ever since he had left. Having always lived in Texas, as I did, I thought that finding him would be easy.

I thought that was way too many lies for such a short while, and finally, I said, "Don't we need to get back to work?" Mrs. Peterson looked at her watch and said, "Why, yes, we have had a rather long lunch today. Thank you, Stella. I'm glad someone wants to work around here." We all laughed.

Back in the kitchen, I wondered what we were going to do with all this food now, and of course everyone but me knew. They said we would all go in groups of two to the train station. As the trains stopped, we would give food to the soldiers who were traveling from place to place; since none of them had much money and were traveling to fight for their country, the least we could do was feed them. I wondered how Mrs. Peterson could afford to buy all this food. She must really be rich. A couple of us went to addresses we were given to take food to young women with little children; they could not work outside the home, and they also needed food. None of it seemed like work at all to me; I just felt like one of the other ladies who were all there to volunteer their time.

At the end of the day, the others went home, and Mrs. Peterson said to go up to my room and rest and clean up for dinner. I was not tired, but I went up, took a bath, relaxed in my bubble bath, and changed to a nicer dress for dinner.

Annie came up about five thirty to let me know what time it was. I reminded her she had brought me a clock. She said she felt silly not remembering since it was just last night. I laughed and said sometimes I forget how many days have gone by.

I asked her if I could ask her something on the personal side as far as Mrs. Peterson was concerned. She said she would answer if she knew. I told her I knew I shouldn't be so nosey, but I just couldn't figure out how she could afford to feed all these soldiers and their families every day.

She said, "Oh, that's an easy answer. Mrs. Peterson is a very wealthy widow, but she doesn't have to use her money to do all this. She has large parties for all her other wealthy friends and raises money from all of them to help. Also, every couple of months, she has events; people donate items they don't use anymore or that they just feel like donating; the items are auctioned off, and other rich people bid on them at enormous prices. For the very rich, this is all just a fun way to help with the war that seems sure to happen."

So now I understood a lot better.

Day after day we all did about the same things. Some days there were six or eight ladies who showed up, and sometimes just a few, depending on the other things that had to be done. Everyone had their own lives and families, and it was all on a volunteer basis.

One night at dinner a week or so later, Mrs. Peterson said she had to take me shopping for a new dress. I asked why in the world she would do that. She told me she was having a very large formal dinner the next Saturday night, and she knew I would feel out of place in the very nice dresses that I had. I told her I could just stay in my room, but she wouldn't hear of it. She said almost all her friends had heard about the pretty young lady she had living with her and they were all very anxious to meet me. I felt embarrassed, and I know I was blushing.

The next day we got in her limo (as she called it), and her driver took us downtown; there were so many fancy-looking shops. We went into the first one she told her driver to stop at, and all the salesladies came rushing over to her. They asked what they could bring her, and she told them to bring out everything in their best dresses. Within minutes I had several ladies with tape measures getting all my measurements, and before I knew it, we were walking out of there with several dresses, a beautiful new coat, and a couple of bags full of odds and ends, of which I'd lost track. The dresses were hanging up, with plastic covering them. I had never seen anything like this.

I told her she bought way too much, and she said, "Oh I'm not finished yet, young lady." My mouth was hanging open, and she said I had better shut it or I would catch a fly. We both laughed.

Then her driver stopped at another store up the street a little ways, and she did the same thing. Before I knew it, I had two more dresses, silk stockings, fancy undergarments, and a couple of beautiful pairs of shoes that cost a fortune.

And that's not counting the jewelry she bought to match each outfit.

I would bet all this cost more than my entire family had made all of our lives put together. Mrs. Peterson said she hadn't had this much fun since her husband had been alive and they would go on huge shopping sprees to New York City; he just loved to shower her with everything money could buy. Now without him, she said it just wasn't the same going to buy herself a few new dresses when she needed them. She also took Annie and Kathleen out and bought them things as they needed them. She said, "Now I know what my wonderful husband felt when he did all that for me."

She said her family had been middle class and never really needed anything. When she met her Harry downtown one day, it was just like I had told her I felt the moment I met Clarence. She said Harry didn't give a hoot how much money her family had; what he had was hers now because she had his heart the moment he saw her.

She said, "It's funny how things like that happen, and you just know it will be forever. Only I didn't get to have my Harry forever. We weren't able to get pregnant, which made both of us unhappy, but we loved each other so much that we were all we needed. We had twenty-eight years of nothing but pure happiness. Then one day I got a call from his office that he had been taken to the hospital. My heart stopped that moment. I got to the hospital just in time to kiss him, and he told me I would never need for anything. I told him all I needed was him. Just a few seconds later, he smiled at me and took his last breath. So you see, my dear, how much pleasure you have given me by letting me do this for you. You and your Clarence won't have the money we did, and now you will get married and have some beautiful things to show off to him. Tell him I did this for you, for him, and for me."

By this time I was crying my eyes out. We hugged, and she told me not to give up, because she had talked with Joe, and he told her he had something in the works' he also had faith we would find Clarence. I told her it had been weeks, and she said a few weeks would seem like nothing, as we would have the rest of our lives together once Clarence was found. I told her I prayed she was right. She hugged me and said, "Don't worry, honey; it will all work out." I would see.

The next Saturday the house was so full of people buzzing around doing this and that, I just didn't know what to do. Mrs. Peterson said we were just in the way, so we should both go up to our rooms and take a long nap because it would be a late night. She said, "Pick out your favorite new dress and the shoes and all the things that go with it. And don't forget the jewelry that matches. Then take a long bath. I'll send up my hair stylist to help you fix your hair up real fancy." She said she couldn't wait to see her beautiful princess look just the way she should. Again I blushed. She said, "Go do as you're told," and then she winked at me. I loved this woman already. She was so generous and yet so down-to-earth.

By seven that night, I didn't even recognize myself. My new dress was a pretty pink and fit like my gloves did, and my jewelry had pink stones and diamonds, which I knew weren't really diamonds, but they were awfully expensive anyway, which was why they looked so real. My hair was all done up in curls, with a few strands hanging gently down the back. I couldn't believe my own eyes. I felt like something out of a fairy tale I'd read.

In just a little bit, Mrs. Peterson knocked on my door and said quickly, "Don't open it; I just wanted to tell you to come down the stairs in about twenty minutes. Some of my guests will be here by then, and we will be in the main entry; I want to see you coming down the staircase looking like the princess I know you'll look like, and I want to see their faces as they see you for the first time."

I felt a bit self-conscious, but I had learned already to do as I was told. When it had been twenty minutes, I left my room and very slowly and carefully walked to the stairs; I stopped for just a minute to see all the people. My eyes met Mrs. Peterson's, and she was beaming. I slowly walked down the stairs, making sure to make each step. I would die if I fell.

Everyone was looking at me, and I could tell they felt just like she had told me they would. For the first time since seeing Clarence, I felt truly beautiful. He always told me I was, but that was because of love. I thought he was the most handsome man I had ever seen. He was just gorgeous to me, so I figured that was why he thought I was beautiful. I thought maybe I really was after seeing all the faces as I walked down this beautiful curved staircase.

I was introduced to this person and that person, and I thought, oh my, I will never remember all their names. I whispered this to Mrs. Peterson, and she said not to worry. "After a couple of drinks, they won't even remember their own names." She knew I had never had anything to drink, so she made sure that the waiters all knew which glass to hand her. I felt so safe under Mrs. Peterson's wing, like nothing could possibly go wrong. Mrs. Peterson did not drink much either, so she also would be handed the same glasses as I received.

The evening was all so foreign to me since I had never been to a party in my life; I had no idea what to expect. Everyone was so nice to me. They all came up and talked with me, but thankfully no one started asking me lots of questions like the ladies that first day of rolling bandages. I think they must have thought I was a niece or some relative of Mrs. Peterson.

After a short while, several waiters all dressed in uniforms came around with trays they were full of drinks. I think they said it was champagne. It was all bubbly-looking. One of the waiters handed me a glass and winked at me, so I supposed that was what I was expected to drink. I got a nod when I looked over at Mrs. Peterson, so I thought all was well. After a few minutes, more waiters started circling the crowd, which was growing quickly. They held huge trays with only one hand underneath, and I thought for sure one would be dropped shortly; but no, they just went to each person one by one and offered what they called appetizers. I took one and had no idea what it was, but I ate it and I'm not sure if I liked it or not. It was different from any taste I had ever had. They kept coming around every few minutes offering things, and I just declined after that.

About ten minutes or so had passed, and the doorbell rang again. A man dressed like a butler I had seen in a picture book answered the door. A very handsome man, his beautiful wife, and their son came in. Mrs. Peterson rushed to greet them. She brought them over to me and introduced me to them. It was the mayor, Mrs. Stevens, and their son, David. What a lovely family they were, all dressed so beautifully.

David was about my age—well, the age that I had told them I was anyway. He immediately stated chatting with me and asking me questions about where I had come from, as I looked like something out of a vision. We heard music, and he asked me if I'd like to dance. The large double doors had been opened, and the room was so huge I couldn't believe my eyes. I just kept being amazed at rooms I hadn't seen yet. This house just seemed to grow every day.

Anyway, I told David I hadn't ever danced before. Maxine and I had goofed around when someone played some music in some of the camps we had been in, and a few of the people would just be dancing around with each other. If Daddy had been there, we would never have even come out of our tent, but we did when he wasn't home, and we just tried to copy what they were doing. It was fun, but the people in this room were moving around so gracefully, and I had no idea how to dance like that.

David said, "Oh, come on; I'll lead, and you just follow my feet with yours." I felt so afraid, but I didn't want to seem like I was the hick that I really was, so I said, "Okay; I will try." We danced very slowly, and he held one of his hands at my waist in back; we held our hands together, and he told me to put my other arm up around his shoulder. He made it seem so simple, and with his hand at my back, he just gently moved me and made it so easy to follow him. I felt so excited to be doing this and looking like I knew what I was doing.

In a while the music stopped, and we walked over to the side and sat down on fancy little chairs that were all around the sides of the room, except where the people were playing the music. He called them the orchestra. Whatever they were, they sure made the music sound perfect and beautiful. David asked if I would like something to drink, and not thinking, I said, "Yes, please." He quickly left and came back with two glasses of the champagne. Not wanting to look stupid, I took a few sips because I was very thirsty. The bubbles made my nose tickle, and David laughed. He said, "Is this your first taste of champagne?" I told him, yes it was, and I thought it wasn't too bad. We both laughed and kept sipping from our glasses.

Before I knew it, he asked if I'd like to learn a different dance. The music was playing a little faster, and I said I wasn't sure about this one. He again talked me into it, but as I stood, I felt a little dizzy. He said we had better get me something to eat. I admitted to him I hadn't liked what I took from one of the trays. He said, "Oh, that must have been the caviar. I don't like that either." He said there was lots of food on the other side of the ballroom. I took his hand because I sure didn't want to fall.

We went into the large room with long tables with silk-looking tablecloths on them, and they were filled with every kind of food I could imagine. He picked up two plates, handed me one of them, and then started putting different things on both our plates. When he finished, I thought I would never be able to eat all of this. I told him so, and he said, "Just eat what you want, and the waiter will take your plate away." He added, "Let's go outside to the tables there and enjoy the ocean." He said he loved the view from there. I guessed by that he had been to parties there before. We sat and ate and talked.

David asked how old I was, and I said nineteen. He told me he was twenty-three, a perfect age difference, and he would love to take me out to places and maybe we could go see a movie at the theater. I thanked him for asking, but told him I was engaged to be married. He asked if my fiancé was in the service. I told him no, that he worked construction. David said the reason he had not been drafted was because he was in his last year of college, and besides that, he had a slight heart murmur. I said how sorry I was, and he assured me it was no big deal, but the armed services just would not accept anyone with anything wrong with their hearts. He had wanted to enlist as an officer when he finished college last month, but he didn't pass the physical. So now he was going to go back to college in the fall and get his masters degree in medicine. He would go on from there and become a doctor after finishing his residency. I asked what kind of doctor he wanted to be, and he said he wanted to be a heart surgeon because he wanted to learn everything he could about the heart.

I was very impressed with him, and he was also very handsome—but not as handsome as my Clarence. Nothing could lure my heart in another direction. Just sitting there having dinner with him felt okay since there were at least a hundred other people all around us. I explained that Clarence was older, and that was why he had not been drafted. I didn't offer any more information, and he didn't ask—thank the Lord!

The party seemed to be a huge success. At one point I thought no one was ever going to go home, especially if the caterers kept filling all the tables with delicious food and amazing fancy little desserts. But even though they looked fancy, they still weren't as good as the cook's pastries.

Finally, at about two o'clock in the morning, a few people started saying their good nights, and thank-yous were said to all by Mrs. Peterson for all their generous donations. By three o'clock the house was cleared out except for a few of the caterers cleaning the last of the dishes. Now it was hard to imagine just how many people were there not long ago. I commented, "These guys really know how to clean up quickly, don't they? Mrs. Peterson said, "Oh, they are so used to it; they have it down to a science."

Before David left with his parents at about two thirty, he took me aside and said if for some reason it didn't work out with Clarence and me, that Mrs. Peterson would always know where to find him. I thanked him very much for the huge compliment, but assured him my heart belonged to only one man for the rest of my life. Of that I was sure! He said, "If only I had met you first." I told him I doubted he would ever have found me where I had been and left it at that. I didn't want to hurt his feelings, but I had to be honest about mine.

Mrs. Peterson told me I had been the talk of the whole party. I asked her why ever that would be. She said everyone talked about my beauty and said I should be royalty with my grace. I told her I felt so grateful that I hadn't done anything to embarrass her, since I really was just a young girl from nowhere important and was raised so poorly and had worked so hard all my life that all my grace was just all her for making me feel so welcome and teaching me so many manners without my even knowing it. Just watching her moves and table manners, I tried hard to follow her lead. She said that I had certainly succeeded. No one would ever think I'd been anything but a wealthy young lady. Hearing this made me so happy and so proud of myself that I had pulled off a miracle.

Sunday we didn't do anything but lie around and eat leftovers from the party and talk about the evening. She was so happy at the huge contributions from everyone who attended. She said it was her Harry who had taught her how to do things like this and have charity affairs and make so much for whatever charity was needed at the time. I thanked her so much for passing all this on to me in such a short time. She said, "No, Stella, you just learned how to be a lady on your own because it came natural to you." I hoped Clarence would be happy with the new me, instead of the frumpy girl he had met in a tent next door. But I knew nothing could change my love for him, and I felt he would feel the same.

We all went to bed very early because the next day was Monday and another day of work. I really did enjoy helping all the needy people, probably because I could still remember the Salvation Army taking us in when Daddy had been thrown in jail that time in Arizona. How wonderful it was those days having a warm bed up off the floor and all the food we could eat. Days like that were so rare for all of us; my brothers and sisters and I had all suffered things no child of any age should have to go through. So handing out sandwiches and fruits and cakes to the soldiers who were going to keep our country safe just felt so right and so good. And also, seeing the faces of the sweet little children when we dropped off baskets of food almost made me cry, wondering if my younger sisters and brothers were getting enough to eat and if Daddy was mistreating them and Mama. My wonderful sweet Mama. I thought of what I had gone through with Daddy, and then I would think, Oh Lord, my poor Mama had been going through it so much longer than any of us. I couldn't wait until Clarence and I were married and I could let her know where I was and that I was fine. Someday I hoped to get a chance to tell her all about Mrs. Peterson's help to me.

Monday morning came, and off to work we went after breakfast. One day turned into another, and with each passing day, I was getting more afraid that I would never find Clarence. I thought for sure by now that Lola would have written back to him and told him I was in Carmel, but I had heard the mail was getting slower and slower because so many were writing to their husbands overseas already or to wherever they had been sent. And husbands writing back to their wives were worried to death how their families were making it without them being home to bring home a decent paycheck. We were doing our part to help all we knew who needed help. And even if Clarence and Lola had gotten the news to each other, neither one of them would have any idea where to find me. I thought maybe I should be reading the paper each day to see if they ran an ad looking for me. I would start doing just that tomorrow.

CHAPTER 8

The Wedding

The next Thursday evening after dinner, Mrs. Peterson and I were sitting out on the back patio, and the doorbell rang. She said, "Who in the world would be coming by so late?" She jumped up to go answer the door, and then called for me to come talk to Joe. I thought he must be giving me an update on his search for Clarence.

I hurried to the door, and Officer Joe greeted me. Then he moved aside a bit and said, "Do you know this man?"

There in front of me stood my handsome, tall Clarence. I ran to him and wrapped my arms around his neck, and we kissed for what felt like an hour, then he picked my feet up off the ground and swung me around several times, and both of us had tears rolling down our faces. When we came back down to earth, we remembered two people standing there watching us. They both also had tears in their eyes.

I started asking Officer Joe how he found Clarence, and before he could answer, I grabbed him around the neck, kissed his cheek, and thanked him more than words could ever say. Finally, I gave him a chance to talk, and he told me that he had called everyone he knew in every nearby town and gotten the names of every single construction company that had pulled a permit in the last year. He said he mailed out a penny postcard to every single one of them asking if they employed a Clarence Rader. He assured them all that Clarence was not in any trouble of any kind, but he needed to contact the Carmel Police Department and ask for Officer Joe as soon as possible on a very personal family matter. Clarence and I finally got our heads to thinking straight, and I introduced him to Mrs. Peterson and told him that she had saved my life and we would talk about that later.

Mrs. Peterson said, "Let's all go in instead of standing out here on the front porch." We all laughed and thanked her. She asked Annie if she would see if the cook was still up to make some coffee and tea, whichever these gentlemen would prefer. Clarence and Joe both said coffee sounded great if it wasn't too much trouble.

Annie came right back and said the cook would be delighted to make a pot of each, and she would also send in a tray of sandwiches and some of this morning's danish that were left. She told Annie to be sure and tell them that she would warm them first. I thought, wow, that was a quick conversation for the few minutes Annie had been gone. I suspected the cook had been listening. We had become good friends, as I loved going into the kitchen and talking with her while she was doing her chores. She was such a sweet little lady, and it amazed me all the work she got done. She told me one time in private that Mrs. Peterson had tried to get her a couple of helpers, but she wouldn't hear of it; she had her way of doing things, and someone else would just be in her way, and Mrs. Peterson paid her way more than was necessary. I said I doubted that because no other person could do all she did in a day.

Annie rushed back into the kitchen. I know they were both so very excited for me. But no one could be more excited than I.

We all went into the front parlor, which was so fancy. I could see Clarence's eyes taking in this beautiful house. He looked at me and said, "Honey, I don't think I'll be able to get you a house like this for some time." I looked into his handsome face and said, "You are here with me, and wherever we live will be paradise to me." He said he would have to go into work tomorrow because he had no way of telling his boss why he didn't show up, but he would ask to get off early enough for them to get to the courthouse to get a marriage license. Just the thought made me throw my arms around him again. I said, "How long will we have to wait after that?" He said three days, so it would be next Monday or Tuesday before they could get married at the courthouse.

Mrs. Peterson said, "I hate to break into your conversation, but I just won't have you two kids getting married in the courthouse, even though I am a good friend of the judge." She said that she would throw us a wedding, and we could invite anyone Clarence knew, and she would make sure everyone I knew would get an invitation. She said, "I am very quick at doing these things when I have to. I know how much you both want to get married, but I've become so very fond of Stella, so please let me do this for you two. We can have a small reception here in the ballroom."

I told her that was way too much; just the wedding would be wonderful. But she would not hear of a wedding without a reception. I told Clarence there was no sense in trying to change this wonderful woman's mind; I knew from experience.

She went, grabbed a calendar, and said, "The Saturday after next is July 17—would that be too long to wait?" Clarence and I looked at each other, both thinking the same thing, but we just couldn't let this wonderful lady down. She could see our looks and told Clarence he could come over every night after work and spend the evenings with me, so that made things a bit more bearable. Annie came in carrying a huge tray filled with so many different things to eat, you would think it was a large party.

Officer Joe, who had been quiet, said he had better get home. Mrs. Peterson said, "Oh, Joe, can't you just eat a quick bite first?" He said he was afraid his wife would worry. She said, "I'll be glad when you get one of these phones. They are so handy." But she told Annie to run get a basket and lots of napkins and containers and she would fill it for Joe's family. He hugged her, told her she was always his favorite person, and he was so happy that it had worked out with her keeping me all this time. She assured him it was her pleasure, and Stella had more than earned her keep helping her with all sorts of things.

While she was quickly filling a basket, Clarence and Joe drank their coffee and had a warm danish apiece. They both said they looked too good to wait till after all the other foods. I laughed and told them how many I had eaten my first morning there and I was surprised I was not twice the size I'd been. Mrs. Peterson said, "Oh, you work it off; you take long walks on the beach almost every afternoon before dinner."

As Mrs. Peterson got up to walk Officer Joe to the door, Clarence and I held each other so tight and kissed long slow kisses. Oh, how I loved this man! I said, "How can we wait ten days to get married?" He agreed, but said, "Look how long we have been apart. Ten days will go by fast with so much to do getting ready and all." He said he had all the money that Lola had sent to the post office box, and she had returned a couple of letters he had sent to me with money in them. He told me Lola had not opened anything, as she explained to me in a letter; she figured they were personal and for me only. I laughed and told him how I had only read her a line or two and then gone in my room to finish his beautiful words to me. I also told him he had the most beautiful handwriting I'd ever seen. He ate a little more and finished his coffee, then managed to get down another danish or two.

We decided to take a walk on the beach if Mrs. Peterson didn't mind. She had just come back in the room and said, "You two just get out of here, and when you get back, you can eat some more, Clarence. You're a hardworking man and need more than that for your dinner." He looked at me and said, "Now I have all I need. She said she was so excited to get started on the wedding plans. Then she said quickly, "Before you leave, is it okay if I make arrangements at the Quaint Little Chapel a few blocks away?" We both nodded and said fine. "Oh, I can hardly wait to see what a beautiful bride you are going to be. My Harry and I were married there, so it will be so extraspecial."

As we walked along the beach, we couldn't go more than a step or two without stopping to hug and kiss for several minutes each time. We both had so much to tell each other. Lola had told him how I'd had to leave with just my clothes and the few dollars she had in her purse and then I fled out the back door and jumped quickly over the fence before Daddy could see me.

Then I told him all about my hiding for a couple of hours in the bus station for fear of Daddy driving around and finding me. I told all about me spending most of the rest of my money on an awful sandwich and a mushy apple, but all I cared was I was on my way to see him. Then I told him all about wonderful sweet Hazel, who had probably been the only reason I made it to Carmel. I hated to think of sitting on that hot bus without anything to eat or drink all the days it took to get there. I really believed she saved my life. Maybe not literally, but I probably would have passed out, and they would have put me off the bus in who knows what town, and maybe had me in a state hospital of some kind. My imagination was running away, just thinking of all that could have happened without Hazel. I wish that I would have thought to get her address so I could properly thank her again.

He hugged me again and promised I would never be hungry or thirsty again as long as we lived, and I believed him completely. He told me all about how he and Lola wrote back and forth to each other; both were worried sick because they had no idea where to look for me.

I told him it was just such a last-minute thing, me having to leave like that and not having remember to have either his post office box or Lola's address so I could get news to both of them. It was so stupid of me not to have memorized both of them, but who was to know that our plans for me to leave with plenty of money and a list of all of that information would not happen?

I grabbed him around the neck and just cried and cried about how sorry I was that I had worried him and Lola so much. I asked him if he had Lola's phone number so I could let her know what had happened. I was sure Mrs. Peterson would let me use her phone for just a minute to let her know that I was okay and we were together finally. I would quickly tell her that I would write her tomorrow and tell her all the details of my past month and a half or more. I'd lost track of the days. They just all seemed to run together. Thank the Lord also for Mrs. Peterson and her kindness.

Clarence said he could tell immediately that she was a great woman, and we both owed her so much. What a wonderful thing she was doing for us—being able to have a church wedding and all of those things that he was so sure meant a lot to me, whether I knew it now or not.

We had been sitting by a little cove for probably hours. As much as we enjoyed lying there and talking and kissing, we both jumped up and said we'd better get back before Mrs. Peterson called the cops. We both had a big laugh at that. But seriously, she was no doubt worried after all this time, even if she did know how happy we were to be together finally.

As I got up, I looked back into the cove a little and went over to pick up what I thought was a balloon, There were several all around there. Clarence yelled, "Don't pick that up, please, Stella." I asked him why, weren't they just some balloons? He said no, that's not what they were. When I tried to ask what was so wrong, he just said he would explain about them after we were married; it was just not important now. I took his word for it and dropped the subject.

When we arrived back at the beautiful house that I had been telling him all about, Mrs. Peterson was just sitting and reading. She said she was not surprised at all that it took us a while to catch up and she had not been worried at all. She was just reading a good book, and the time flew by.

Mrs. Peterson said before Clarence left, we needed to sit and talk for a few minutes to get a few details of the wedding decided. She said she really doubted that we could have invitations printed up this fast. She then asked me if I would be able to help handwrite some of them with her.

I looked at Clarence with a pleading eye, as he knew how bad my handwriting was. I had hardly any practice since I had gone to school so little. He immediately spoke up and said he had done a lot of writing for himself and other friends in college, and if I just gave him the names and addresses, he would be more than happy to do that. He told Mrs. Peterson there was so little he could do, he at least felt he would be helping out in some way if that was okay with her.

She said I had mentioned a while back how beautiful and perfect his handwriting was, so as far as she was concerned, that job would be his. She told him if he could get the addresses of any of his friends or family, she would have the rest together by tomorrow, and he could come for dinner, of course, and afterward he could go to her office and sit in her comfortable office chair at her desk; that would make it much easier for him.

He said he did have a few close buddies that he would love to invite, but unfortunately, all his family were back in Oklahoma, and there was no way they'd be able to get here on such short notice. He said he could hardly wait until his mom and dad and all his brothers and sisters could meet me. He knew they would all love me almost as much as he did. He looked at me and winked. So that part was settled.

Now she wanted to know if we had thought about what flavor cake we wanted. We both looked at each other and said it didn't matter; we would let her decide. She said her cake lady made the most beautiful cakes, and they were always delicious. So one more decision was made.

Then, she turned to both of us and asked if we had a kind of minister that we both agreed on. We had never talked about this at all, but at the same second, we both said, "I am just a Christian; it's all I know." She asked if a Baptist minister would be all right, and we both nodded our heads and said that would be fine.

We got closer together, took each other's hands, and just shivered at the excitement of all this really happening. He leaned down and kissed me quickly.

Mrs. Peterson said, "Okay, you two, we have lots to do, and you have the rest of your lives for all that stuff"—but she winked at me to let me know she was kidding. We both giggled like a couple of young girls the same age. We had become so close the past six weeks or so—however long it had been, I wasn't sure to be exact. We stayed so busy that the days just flew by.

Then all of a sudden a thought came to her. "Oh my, I hadn't even asked you two if you minded me inviting a few of my friends that Stella has met." We both said of course not. Clarence spoke up and said, "Are you kidding? You're asking us a favor after all you're doing for us? You just do anything that you know will be okay with Stella. If she knows them and likes them, then I will too. I can hardly wait for my buddies to meet Stella; I've told them for months now how beautiful she is. I think they were beginning to doubt she existed."

We all laughed and decided it was time to call it a night for now. Mrs. Peterson said she was going on upstairs to her room and let us two lovebirds have some privacy to say good night.

Clarence and I walked out on the front porch and sat on the really nice swing, which I had never even noticed before now. It's funny how you can just walk by something so many times and never see it. Oh well, I saw it now, and we sat there just holding each other and kissing over and over. We just couldn't stop touching and exploring just a little of each other's body.

Clarence and I had talked about it before he left Texas, and we both decided we wanted to wait until we were really married to have intercourse, so it would be so much more special. Even I was having a hard time sticking to that now. I had never been with any man before Clarence and so knew nothing about sex except what my body was now telling me. I asked Clarence if it was still okay to wait since it was going to be nine more days.

He said he would wait for as long as I wanted to. I told him I was very nervous about it because I was a virgin, and he said, "Stella, look at me. Really look in my eyes when I tell you how much I love you; I want our wedding night to be perfect for both of us, so I don't mind waiting at all. You are the most important thing in this whole world to me, and when I went so long worrying what had happened to you and wondering if we would ever find each other, I thought I was going to die. But really in my heart, I knew somehow we would find each other, and now that we have, nine more days of waiting is nothing compared to not seeing you these past few months. Lola and I both were worried. I will be so happy for her when you can call her tomorrow. She was blaming herself so much for sending you off with so little money. But she said she thought just like you did, that you would get to Carmel and find the construction site. How were you both to know? There was just no way, but you're here now, and I am the happiest man in the world. I only wish I didn't have to go to work tomorrow and next week, but work is pretty hard to come by, and I have a good-paying job and don't want to lose it. We are going to be married, and I will have a wife to support now. I thank God that he brought us together finally.

"It is really late, and I do need to get a few hours sleep before I have to get up at six thirty in the morning. I feel like I'll be walking on clouds waiting for four o'clock to get off tomorrow. I'll be here by four forty at the latest, and we will work together every night doing whatever Mrs. Peterson says she needs us to do. I love you, my darling Stella, so very much, and I also thank God for Officer Joe and for Mrs. Peterson for taking such good care of you. Whatever would have happened to you in this town with you having no money or a place to stay makes me sick to even think about it. One more kiss, and I'm off, feeling like I'm on wings driving back to my room, which, by the way, I will have as clean as can be for our wedding night. Good night is so hard, but I must go now. I love you, my darling, precious Stella."

I stood there watching Clarence drive away, feeling like tomorrow would take forever to get here. We both threw kisses as he drove away. I had to get to bed and sleep myself so tomorrow would be here. I quietly locked the door and crept upstairs so as not to wake Mrs. Peterson. When I was in my beautiful room, I took a quick bath and fell asleep before my head hit the pillow. I just wanted it to be tomorrow.

As soon as I came downstairs the next morning, I asked Mrs. Peterson if I could ask one more huge favor from her.

She said, "What is it, Stella? You look so worried."

I told her I wanted to use her phone to make a long distance call to my sister Lola. I told her about Lola and Clarence writing back and forth these past weeks since my leaving her home that hurried night in Texas, and how worried they had both been about me, not knowing how well I had been taken care of. I told her Clarence would pay whatever the call cost. He had given me Lola's number that she had mailed to him so he could let her know as soon as he found me.

Mrs. Peterson said, "Of course, you go call her right now before breakfast."

I told her how thankful I was for her and for my mother's always telling me God would take care of things. She had instilled that faith in me from the time I was old enough to listen to her read the Bible to us all when my daddy wasn't home yet. He would tell her that was all nonsense, but we all knew better than to listen to a mean old drunk man whom we all hated.

Mrs. Peterson said, "Get yourself in my office and make your call, sweet girl."

When I dialed all the numbers Clarence had written down for me, I held my breath that I had done it right and that Lola would be home. She answered on the third ring, and I started crying as soon as she said hello.

"Oh my dear Stella, what has happened to you, and are you all right?"

I told her very briefly about going to the police station when I was so frightened and didn't know anything else to do.

She said, "What a smart little sister I have."

Then I quickly told her about being taken to this beautiful house to help out with Red Cross work and how Mrs. Peterson had said I could stay here while the police looked for Clarence, and just last night, they brought him here. I was talking and crying at the same time, but I told her when we were getting married and about Mrs. Peterson making all the arrangements for us and we were to be married by a Baptist minister in a beautiful little chapel.

Lola was so happy for me. I said I would write her a long letter and give her every detail about the last couple of months, but I needed to hang up so we didn't have to pay such a big long distance phone bill. We said good night and how much we loved each other.

I went in to breakfast and asked if she would be able to find out today how much the bill was, so I could tell Clarence tomorrow.

She said, "Listen to me, child. I have plenty of money, and don't you worry about one little call; it was nothing. Now let's eat and get to work so the day will go by faster. I know how hard it will be for you to keep your mind on things today, so if you can't or don't want to, you are more than welcome to go take a walk or whatever you want."

I told her no, of course I wanted to work and be all the help I could possibly be. So that is what we did; we just went about the day as usual.

About four o'clock I started getting anxious, and Mrs. Peterson could tell.

She said, "Stella, you go up and take a good smelling bath and put on a pretty dress for Clarence. He will be here very soon, and I know you are looking so forward to that."

I agreed and went upstairs, feeling like I was floating rather than walking. Just forty minutes more, and Clarence would be here.

Clarence rang the doorbell just a minute after I had come back downstairs.

Mrs. Peterson answered and told him to come right in and greet his beautiful fiancée. He leaned down, kissed her cheek, and immediately said, "Oh, I hope that wasn't too bold of me. I am just so thankful for all you're doing for Stella and me, and even more thankful for your taking care of my bride-to-be so well." She said that was the sweetest kiss she had had from a handsome man in a good while and not to give it another thought. He asked how much he owed her for the call to Lola. Again she said, "Don't worry about that; it was nothing."

She escorted him into the parlor, where I stood waiting. He took me in his arms and said he had never seen such a beautiful sight. I kissed him quickly and said, "Thank you, my handsome husband-to-be." We tried not to overdo the kissing and hugging in front of Mrs. Peterson because it just wasn't the right thing to do. But it was sure hard being close together and not touching.

She said, "Clarence, did you get the addresses of your friends you want to invite?" Clarence told her he had gotten his boss's address and those of eight of his best buddies. Some of them were married, so as close as he figured, there would be thirteen or fourteen guests. "Would that be okay?" he asked. She said, "Certainly. It is your wedding, you know." She said she had about thirty on her list, and she had all their names and addresses all ready for him. She had written out a sample invitation for him and told him to have a seat in her office and see how it went.

Within twenty minutes he had finished all of his list and started on hers. She picked up the first one he had finished and addressed and said, "Look at this, Stella. You are marrying a man with the best and fanciest writing I've ever seen, and he did all these so fast. I am very impressed." I said, "I told you he was perfect," and we laughed.

By six o'clock when the cook said dinner would be ready in just a few minutes, Clarence had finished all the invitations.

"Wow, I'm amazed, Clarence. You could probably make a fortune just writing for people," said Mrs. Peterson.

He thanked her and said he had a job for now, but maybe if ever needed it, he would look into the possibility of something like that.

We sat down to dinner, and the cook had outdone herself. She made a huge beef roast, cooked with carrots, potatoes, and onions. She served us soup and then a delicious salad. I could tell she really wanted dinner to be perfect; it was so delicious, and I think Clarence agreed it couldn't be better. She told Annie she could serve tea, coffee, and dessert on the back veranda. The cook had made a huge chocolate cake— Clarence's favorite; I guess she remembered me saying one time how much Clarence would love this cake. Such a good memory! Just like I thought he would, Clarence took a second piece when offered. He said he never remembered having such an excellent meal and to please give his best regards to the cook.

After dinner and dessert, we were so full, we decided taking a walk would be a good thing.

Mrs. Peterson said, "You're not fooling me; I know you just want to be alone, and I don't blame you a bit. Go have fun!"

We assured her that we would be back in just a short while this time so we could talk about anything else that we might be able to help with for our wedding plans.

She said all was taken care of, and she would have the invitations delivered first thing in the morning, so we could go for a drive or whatever we wanted to do and not worry about keeping her up, because she was going to her room right now to take a long bath and finish the great book she was reading.

So Clarence said he would drive me all over Carmel and show me the sights and great places he had found while driving around every day when he got off work as he looked for and hoped to find me. We drove up on a cliff where you could see gorgeous rocks and the ocean crashing on them every few minutes. It was just a breathtaking view, and we sat there holding each other and enjoying this beautiful view. I loved this man more every minute that passed. Now there were only eight days to go. We were both so excited. I asked him to take me to see our room where we would be living. He said no, mainly because he didn't know if he could trust himself alone with me in the place that would be our first home. But also it was a mess as it was so late when he got in last night, he didn't have time to clean up; he wanted it to look perfect when I saw it for the first time on our wedding night. We had a quiet beautiful evening just enjoying our precious time together.

Every day was bringing me closer to being Mrs. Clarence Rader. The thought brought chills to my whole body. I loved the fact that every minute together now was ours, with no worries about someone coming in the fields, where we used to park and hold each other like tomorrow would never come, but always with the fear of being caught, like the time W. K. had come upon us and laughed and said, "I'm telling Mama that Clarence is touching your titties." I was horrified that Daddy might come in as he was telling the story. But thank the Lord, he hadn't. W. K. told me Mama paddled his butt, but she never said a thing to me. I thought then that Mama knew Clarence to be a wonderful man and that he respected not only me, but all women.

Mama was a smart woman and wanted the best for all her children. She just didn't know how to fight Daddy. She had been afraid of him for as long as I was old enough to notice what a horrible drunk he was. I asked her once, "Mama, why don't you leave Daddy? All he does is beat you and all of us kids." She said she was raised to believe when you married someone, you were his wife for better or worse. I said, "Well, you sure got the worst ever." She just patted my head and said, "Make sure, Stella, that you find a good loving man." And I certainly did. I couldn't wait until I could write to Mama and tell her everything. Lola told me this morning she would get news to Mama that I was finally with Clarence and all was well now. I knew how happy that news would make Mama, and the thought of her having just a few happy thoughts made me smile.

"Hey, Stella, where did you go, and what are you smiling about?" Clarence asked.

I told him what I'd been thinking, and he said he sure wished that mean old bastard would get thrown in jail forever like he deserved. "It breaks my heart," he said, "that we can't do something for her."

I said, "Even if we had extra money to send her, Daddy would find it and go on a huge bender. Poor Mama never had a new dress for as long as I can remember. When we get married and have enough money, you wouldn't mind if I sent Mama a pretty new dress with bright colors and flowers, would you?"

Clarence said, "You know better than to even ask that. I will do anything I can to help your sweet mama. She was always so polite to me any time she could be; I knew she didn't dare speak to me if he was around. She thanked me several times for buying treats for the kids that she would never have been allowed to waste money on, as her old man said. I patted her shoulder and said, 'I wish I could do more for all of you.' She looked me in the eye and said, 'Just take care of Stella. She is a special, smart girl, and I'll be so proud to have you in the family.' She smiled and winked at me, letting me know that she knew we loved each other. I told her I would never harm a hair on your beautiful head."

I hugged Clarence tight and said how much I loved him as if I'd never said it before. He said he would never tire of hearing it. I said, "We had better get back now so you can get a good night's sleep tonight. I want you to be well rested for our wedding and reception." Then all of a sudden I had a thought. "Clarence, you do have a nice suit for the wedding, don't you?" He looked at me and said, "You mean I have to have a suit?" I told him yes, he had to, "so take all the money of mine that Lola sent you and buy a really nice suit and some new shoes and a white shirt and tie." He laughed and said he was only kidding me. He had bought all that when he knew I was on my way to Carmel, not realizing it would be so long before he found me. I pushed him back and said, "You are terrible for scaring me like that." We both laughed and kissed for a while, and then he started the car and took me back.

I told him not to forget that Mrs. Peterson said he was invited every night for dinner except the night before the wedding. She was giving the cook that night off so the caterers could get into the kitchen and start preparing a feast for the reception. I told him, "She said right after you get off work on Friday, we both have to be at the church just to meet the minister and go over the wedding plans. Then we will all go out to dinner at her very favorite restaurant, and then we have to get to bed early so we have a beautiful, perfect wedding."

Clarence walked me up to the door and reminded me he had to work on Saturday because they were busy and also he got paid time and a half for any weekend work. He said he might even get to work on Sunday if I didn't mind. I told him I didn't care as long as he got enough rest so he wasn't overtired before the wedding. He promised to go back to his room and clean up a little each night. He also said, "I forgot to mention my boss told me he was giving me three days off the week after the wedding with full pay." I was so excited I jumped up and down like a little kid. He laughed, picked me up in his arms, and gave me one last kiss before he left.

Saturday morning when I went down to breakfast, Mrs. Peterson said, "I have a surprise for you, dear."

I said, "Oh what more could you possibly do?"

She said I would see after we finished eating our breakfast, which was delicious, as always.

I asked her if Kathleen and Annie were going to be able to come to the wedding, and she said, "Well of course; I know how much you love them both, and they adore you also." I really thought that was my surprise, but no, when the table had been cleared, she said, "Okay, ladies, let's go." At that moment, the cook and Annie both came out. We all went outside, and her driver was standing there holding the door open for us. They had already been told where we were going, but I was still in the dark.

The cook spoke up and said, "Stella, honey, I think it's about time you call me Kathleen."

I said I would love to; I just hadn't wanted to not show her respect.

We laughed and chattered away while driving into town.

Mrs. Peterson finally said we were all going to get new clothes for the wedding. I told her she had already bought me so many beautiful fancy dresses. She said, "Don't argue with me, girlie; it's your wedding, and everything must be new and beautiful." She asked if I wanted a white wedding gown, and I told her that even though I was a virgin—I blushed saying it—I thought a nice suit or dress would be

87

fine, as I didn't think a formal gown would be appropriate for a small wedding. She said it was my wedding and I was to pick whatever I wanted.

We went into a couple of the same shops as before, and Kathleen and Annie had already picked out beautiful summer dresses. We then went into a new shop, and the saleslady brought out a rack of gorgeous dresses; I spotted a pretty soft pink suit that looked so perfect. I tried it on, and it fit like it was custom made for me. It was more like a beautiful dress, with a short matching jacket. They all said it fit my many curves in all the right places. I laughed and said, "So does everyone agree—this is perfect?"

Everyone's head nodded, and Mrs. Peterson said, "Sold. Now we are off to shoe stores to get us all matching shoes for each of our dresses."

She bought us all new fancy silk underwear and new gloves and hose in fine silk. We all felt like a million dollars, and I also felt like she probably had spent that much.

After our shopping spree was over, the driver took us to a restaurant and stopped and opened the car doors.

A hostess opened the restaurant door and said, "So happy to see you after such a long time, Mrs. Peterson. Welcome to all your guests."

We were taken to a large table with a view of the ocean. It was another breathtaking view. We were brought very fancy-looking menus, and inside were so many delicious sounding meals that making a choice was impossible. Mrs. Peterson said, "Let me order for us all; is that okay?" We all agreed that sounded great. I really had never been in a restaurant before, except the little diner inside that first bus stop. This was just too much.

Mrs. Peterson asked if any of us wanted a cocktail, but we all declined. So she ordered several different appetizers and the lobster bisque soup to start. Then we had a fruit salad, which was amazing. It had a sweet creamy sauce covering it, and it was just so good. Finally, they came out carrying a huge tray with our plates of large lobster tails. There were little bowls of butter with a small candle under each to keep the butter hot. Mrs. Peterson could see the look on my face, and she said, "You will love it, dear. Just cut off small bites and dip them in your butter. It will melt in your mouth." And it did. Even the fresh vegetables were delicious, a combination of several different types.

Kathleen said, "After coming here, Mrs. Peterson, how could you like my simple cooking?"

We all looked at her and said as one, "You have got to be kidding. Your meals are just as delicious, and no one could make danish like you do."

She smiled and said, "Thank you, ladies. I appreciate your saying this, even if it's not true."

Mrs. Peterson said, "Look, Kathleen, think about it. Do you think for a minute that Mr. Peterson and I would have kept you all these years if we weren't very pleased?"

She said, "Okay, I'll hush!"

"Good idea," we all agreed.

After dinner, a dessert tray was brought around with at least eight different items, and each looked better than the rest. We each made a different decision, and everyone tasted each other's. We were all so full, and still every single dessert tasted just amazing.

Finally we left, and the driver took us to a jewelry store to get things to match our outfits. We all agreed that this was just too much, but as usual, Mrs. Peterson got her way. She bought Kathleen and Annie both things that matched their dresses, and then she said, "Okay, Stella, it's your turn." She said a simple strand of pearls would look beautiful with my pretty pink suit, so we found one that hung to just the right length. And then she said for me to pick out a pretty wedding band for Clarence. She said, "He told me he had bought your wedding ring in Texas, but he had been keeping it because of what would happen if your Daddy had ever found it." I told her I would find a job and pay her back. She patted my shoulder again and said not to worry—it wasn't much to her, and she wouldn't hear of me paying her back a penny.

Then we got in the car and were driven home. It took the driver and all of us two trips each to get everything carried in. What a day!

All of a sudden I realized it was time for Clarence to be here. My heart jumped a beat as I watched out the window and saw his car pull up. Then I thought how stuffed we all were and Clarence was expecting dinner. I told Mrs. Peterson I would go somewhere with him so he could eat.

She said, "I knew you weren't paying attention when they carried a large box of food out to the driver; it is in the oven being kept warm for him."

I hugged her tight and told her she was the best thing that ever happened to me—except for Clarence, of course, and my precious mama, who always did the best she could with what she had. As Annie let Clarence in, I all of a sudden thought, Oh dear, I haven't anyone for my maid of honor. I looked at Mrs. Peterson and said, "Would you be my maid of honor?" She said she would be thrilled and honored. Each day all things were coming together, and I felt like the queen of England.

Clarence came in, hugged me, kissed Mrs. Peterson on the cheek again, and winked at her. He got down on one knee and opened the black velvet box. Then he asked, "Stella Mae Attebery, will you marry me?" I laughed and said, "Well, I guess it's the right thing to do since we've made all these arrangements." He put the engagement ring on my finger, and I said, "You have lovely taste, my darling."

Then Clarence and I stepped back out on the porch and kissed until we neither one had any breath left. I told him as I did every chance I got how much I loved him. He said he knew he would love me until the day he died.

We went back inside, and Kathleen said, "Mr. Clarence, your dinner is waiting for you in the dining room." We walked in, and he was served each course one by one just as we had been in the restaurant. He said, "How in the world did you get all this cooked after shopping all day?" She winked at me and said, "It's just my talent."

After he finished his meal, we decided a long walk would be just what we needed. We didn't go far without stopping and gazing out at the beautiful ocean. I said it was actually getting chilly tonight. He put his huge arms around me and said, "I'll keep you warm and always happy, my precious darling." I told him I had no doubt about that. I couldn't imagine being happier than I was at this moment.

After walking a mile or so, we turned around and went back. Clarence said he needed to leave early because he had stopped and bought a gallon of paint; he wanted to give our room a fresh coat of paint on the walls before he went to sleep. I hugged him and said I thought he had to be the sweetest man in the world.

The next few days just seemed to fly by; we worked the biggest part of the day with our Red Cross work, and best of all, I looked forward to Clarence being there for dinner every night and our drives or walks on the beach and holding each other like there was no tomorrow. And best of all, kissing and touching until we would almost get to the point of no return. But Clarence always stopped before things got too far. I think he had more willpower than I did, which was surprising, being that he had been married for years and had sex on a regular basis. He told me to stop thinking about those days. They were over years before, and he had not been with a woman since his divorce. So in his eyes, he said our wedding night would be the first time for us both. I told him I couldn't believe that in less than a week, we would be lying in each other's arms making love as a newly married couple. Honestly and truly married. It was so exciting for me to think about. It seemed to me that we loved each other more with each passing day, and I couldn't see how anything could be better than how we felt now.

One morning I woke up to Mrs. Peterson screaming and laughing with delight and calling for me to hurry down right now. I threw on a robe and ran downstairs to see her holding the newspaper and jumping around like a teenager. I asked what was so great in the newspaper; we usually didn't talk about it because it was so depressing and all about this horrible man named Hitler and the war, which seemed to get worse every day. She said, "Stella, sit down, and I'll show you."

I sat down, and Mrs. Peterson laid the newspaper in front of me, opened up to the Society page. I looked down, and my eyes scanned the page quickly; then they fell on what caused her excitement. Before my eyes I saw a large heading saying words I could hardly believe I was reading: "Penny Postcard Finds Love." I knew immediately that the article was about Clarence and me. As I started reading, my heart was beating so fast I thought I would have a heart attack.

The article was all about how I went to the police station without a dollar to my name and how Officer Joe mailed out hundreds of penny postcards using his own time and money, because this beautiful young girl touched his heart and he just knew that God meant for him to help her. It went on to say what I had been doing to help the Red Cross, and also it told about me being at a very high-society party, meeting the mayor and a couple of judges, and all were taken with my grace and beauty. I was just so excited. I wanted Officer Joe there right now so I could hug his sweet neck for putting this article in the paper. I was sure it had to be him.

I turned to Mrs. Peterson, and she had a sly look on her face. I asked her, "Did you have something to do with this?" She smiled and said, "Well, I may have put a little bit of information in the editor's ear, and I guess he decided it was newsworthy." I hugged her and told her how very much I had come to love her. She assured me the feeling was mutual. The article even had where we were getting married and the date. She said she figured with people hearing of Clarence's and my difficult story, we might even get a few wedding presents from people who had met me at the party. I knew she'd had her driver deliver invitations to the mayor and a few other important people that she knew had admired me.

I told her she was going way above anything I had hoped for. She had bought me so many clothes and now a complete wedding outfit, along with surprising me with the most gorgeous white pure silk nightgown for our wedding night. I told her Lola had given me a really beautiful one also, but as much as I loved Lola, I had to admit it didn't compare to this. I had held it up to my face, and the feeling of it was pure heaven. She said while I had been busy looking for what I wanted to wear, she picked it out and had it delivered to the house so I wouldn't see the extra box. There were so many that I probably would not have noticed it anyway. She said at least I had a white gown to walk over to Clarence in on our wedding night.

I laughed what I feel sure sounded like a nervous laugh, and Mrs. Peterson came over and put her arms around me tight and said, "Stella, you will be just fine on your wedding night. I have come to know Clarence enough in the past week or so to know beyond a shadow of a doubt that he will be very gentle with you and not rush you in any way. He loves you so much; it shows on his face every time he looks at you, and that is for certain."

I confided to her that Clarence had already told me pretty much the exact same thing. He said nothing would happen until I felt safe and all right about it. I added, "I know that I am ready, though, not only because I love him so much, but also because it is getting harder and harder to stop when we are alone. Clarence even told me I was getting in too deep one night this last week. He said, 'We've waited this long,' and he wanted our wedding night to be something very special for us both." I giggled and told her what he'd said about it being so long for him that he felt like a virgin too. We both laughed and then changed the subject.

When Clarence arrived that evening, I could hardly wait to show him the newspaper article all about us. He was just as excited as I had been and thanked Mrs. Peterson again for all she was doing for us. I told him he didn't know half of it, and Mrs. Peterson winked at me, knowing I was thinking of my beautiful white gown and our wedding night. After dinner and a quick walk, Clarence said he still had some things he wanted to get done to our room before Saturday, so he was sadly going to leave me early tonight. We kissed a while longer, and then he said good night to Mrs. Peterson and Annie, who happened to be talking to her when we came in.

On Thursday morning, I woke up thinking I would only be waking up in this beautiful room two more mornings. I was not sad at all about that, but I just knew I was going to miss everyone here so much. I had already told Mrs. Peterson that when Clarence taught me how to drive, I could take him to work and come over and still help with Red Cross projects. She said not to worry my pretty little head about that. She said gas was getting so high that it would take a lot of money that we didn't have going back and forth since Clarence worked quite a ways out of town. And I needed to learn to be a wife and be at home when my husband got there. I said that sounded so great—my husband. I could hardly wait.

I dressed quickly and ran down to be on time for breakfast. As usual, everything was delicious, and we ate and chatted about what we were going to be doing today. She said there were only a couple of ladies coming today, because they wanted to go shopping and get new outfits for my wedding and also look for a wedding present. Now I was really getting excited.

It was hard to keep my mind on rolling the bandages, and I ended up making the rolls bigger and bigger. Mrs. Peterson looked over and laughed so hard, and I still didn't realize why. She looked on my lap, and I looked down and saw how big this roll was. I said, "I am so sorry; I will pay closer attention, I promise." She said, "It's fine, Stella. You have more important things to think about. You go on up to your room and take a long nap before Clarence arrives and dinner is served."

I agreed only because I couldn't keep my mind on my work anyway. I said good-bye to the ladies there helping today, and they all said how excited they were about being invited to my wedding. I told them I was thrilled they were coming, but all the thanks had to go to Mrs. Peterson since she had literally done everything and made all the plans.

I went to my room and filled the tub with hot water and lots of the great-smelling bath salts. I sat in the tub and soaked for at least an hour. My hair was shiny and clean as I pulled the comb through it, and I sat there combing it until it was almost dry, then I tried rolling it on the rag rollers that had been used by the lady who had done my hair for Mrs. Peterson's fund-raising party. I had watched her carefully when she was doing it so I could do my own hair next time something special came up. And nothing was more special than looking beautiful for Clarence.

After I finished doing my hair, I climbed into the big bed, and just before falling asleep, I thought I'd better set my alarm so as not to sleep too long. I had about three hours to sleep and still get ready and be downstairs before it was time for Clarence to arrive. Almost immediately I fell asleep and had beautiful dreams of my life with my special wonderful man. He could not be any more perfect if I had just dreamed him up.

When I woke up just a little before the alarm went off, I reached over and shut it off, then went to my dressing table and took out the rag rollers. I had to laugh because my hair looked so curly I didn't know what to do with it. I brushed and brushed until it finally calmed down a bit and looked pretty nice I thought. I picked out a dress to wear, and then I sat and put on just a bit of face powder and a little rouge. I didn't need much because the Lord had blessed me with a very nice complexion. I put on a little light pink lipstick, then brushed my hair high up on top of my head, twisted it around, and held it there with a pretty pearl comb set that Mrs. Peterson had bought me a few weeks ago. With a comb on each side of my hair, the back hung really beautifully in back. I hoped Clarence would like it.

It was a little after four, so I decided to go down and see if Mrs. Peterson was down yet. She always napped a bit before dinner, but I decided to go down anyway. I was in luck that she had come down early also. She took one look at me and said, "Hey, I thought the wedding was Saturday." I didn't catch her meaning until she said, "Turn around and let me see the back of your hair." I did so, and she said it looked so beautiful—like I'd just come from a fancy salon. I felt so excited that she thought I looked that nice. I wore a pale yellow dress that was the softest cotton I'd ever felt, and it had tiny little dots all over it. I twirled around because I loved the way the dress moved with me. She told me when she bought that dress, she just knew I would look amazing in it, and I sure did. I hugged her and told her if I lived to be a hundred, I could never repay her for all she had done for me and was now doing for Clarence and me both.

She said my almost black hair looked like it had stars in it because it was so shiny. I told her about how funny it looked when I had first taken it out of the rags. Then we laughed because it sounded so funny having my hair in rags, but it definitely curled it, that's for sure. I was glad I woke up early and had plenty of time to brush it out some. She said with my pretty veil, it would look beautiful pulled up like it had been at the party. I told her I wasn't sure I could do that yet; I hadn't watched closely enough to know how. She said, "No worries, my dear. The same lady is coming to do your hair before the wedding. And also, another surprise I have for you—I hope you're happy about it."

I said, "What? What?" I couldn't stand the suspense.

"Well, Officer Joe called me this morning and asked if you had anyone to walk you down the aisle. I told him that was one thing we had overlooked. He said he hoped I would say that, because he would be honored to do it if I thought it was okay with you."

I said, "Are you kidding? I am the one who is honored that he would even think of me. You did tell him yes, didn't you?"

She said of course she did; she knew how I felt about him and his taking all that time to write over a hundred postcards. Without him, there probably would not be a wedding, at least not this soon.

I was about to spin myself around again when the doorbell rang. I knew it would be Clarence. Mrs. Peterson always answered the door. She said, "Run to the parlor. I want to see the look on Clarence's face when he sees how beautiful you look tonight."

I heard them exchange hellos and how was your day at work. He said it was pretty slow today, and the foreman had sent a couple of the newer guys home a few hours early. He was glad it wasn't him because he wanted to make all the money he could so he could support me in this style. They laughed, and he said, "Well, maybe in another life," but all he wanted to do was make me happy. She told him that she had no doubt he would.

He asked if I had come down yet, and she said, "Oh yes, she is waiting in the parlor for you." She came in first, and he followed.

As he caught a glimpse of me, he said, "Wow, is this my little cotton picker that I found out by my tent one day?"

I laughed, ran to him, and said I was the one for sure, and there had better not be another.

He assured me I was his one and only for the rest of our lives. He said he couldn't believe that in less than two days, I would be Mrs. Clarence Carl Rader.

I said, "I know. It seemed so far away when Mrs. Peterson first said ten days, but they have flown by so fast with all we have been doing."

We all sat and talked until the cook called us for dinner. We all told Annie to tell the cook that everything was amazing as always. The cook yelled just loud enough for us all to hear, "Thank you very much." Dessert was served out on the veranda as usual.

Clarence said, "I hope you don't mind, Stella and Mrs. Peterson, but tomorrow night, I cannot come over." We both looked a bit surprised, and he said that a few of the guys had asked if they could throw him a bachelor's party tomorrow night. He went on, "It's kind of a thing that the guys do. I told them I would let them know later tonight, as a couple of them live in the same area that I do."

I told him that was fine since I had heard of these things before, but I said, "Are these nice men?"

He laughed as if he could read my mind and said yes, they were all very great guys, and most had wives of their own, so there would be no wild women or anything like that. "They just want to take me out for a last dinner as a single man and buy me a drink or two. And believe me, as little as I drink, two will definitely be my limit. I have to get my beauty sleep so I look good for my bride."

I told him we were all going out for dinner tomorrow night anyway, even Kathleen, because the caterers had to have the kitchen to get started on things for the reception. Then I realized this was the last time I would see him until I walked down the aisle. All of a sudden, I couldn't help myself; I just started to cry. He quickly got up and said he didn't have to have the guy party thing. I told him, of course he would go. I was just crying because I was so happy thinking we would be married shortly after I saw him next.

He hugged me tight and said he was also so happy he could cry and probably would when he was alone so as not to embarrass himself.

We all laughed, and then Clarence said good night to Mrs. Peterson, and he picked her up and hugged her too. He told her she had been so wonderful he didn't know what to say but thank you again and again.

She said, "Oh, stop that. I am getting just as much pleasure out of all this as you two are. I think you have made me feel twenty years younger just being around you two lovebirds. I can feel my Harry watching down on us, and he is very happy that I feel young again. You two go out on the porch now before you have me crying. Good night; I am going upstairs now."

Clarence held me up in the air, looked at me, and said, "How did I ever get so lucky as to stop in a little nowhere town in Texas and find the most perfect woman in the world and have her love me back, even me being an old man next to you?"

I told him I was the lucky one. "Look at how I lived, and now I will be living with you, and we will be husband and wife for the rest of our lives."

We kissed until we were both out of breath, and then he was off to see that the room was finished and perfect for me. I waved good-bye as he drove away, and all of a sudden, the day after tomorrow seemed a million years away. I knew it wasn't, but since we had found each other, we had spent every night together. To think of not seeing him tomorrow made me so sad. I shook it off and went upstairs to go to bed. I wanted to sleep until my wedding so I wouldn't feel lonely tomorrow. Then I got upstairs and thought how silly I was being. Mrs. Peterson probably had a million things we needed to do tomorrow. As I dozed off, I thought of nothing but my wedding, which was only one more day away.

Mrs. Peterson surprised me the next morning by knocking on my door before I was even dressed. I went to the door expecting maybe Annie, but I was shocked when I saw who it was.

She said she was sorry if she frightened me, but she just wanted to tell me that she was sending Annie up with a huge breakfast for me, and she wanted me to stay in my room and take my time getting all my things ready to pack. "And, oh yes, I forgot …" she said, and she opened the door and brought in a beautiful set of luggage for me. She said, "This is my present to you and Clarence. I know before long you're going to be wanting to go visit your mama and brothers and sisters, so I thought just a bag wouldn't do. Here is a full set of everything you should both need."

I sat down on the bed and cried; I was just so overwhelmed that I didn't know what to say. Approximately two months ago, this wonderful woman didn't even know me, and now she was giving me the world.

She sat down next to me and said, "I know you're probably thinking, why is she doing all this for me? Well, I'll tell you a secret. I'm doing it for me. You have given me so much happiness in the months you've been here, and there has not been so much happiness in this house since my Harry went to heaven. I feel alive for the first time in all these years.

"And I know you're also wondering, what about Kathleen and Annie? They are like my family, and I love them both dearly, and believe me, they get plenty of their share of gifts from me. They just don't feel right bragging about it. And they are both in my will. Kathleen has no one in this country, and Annie is an orphan and came here looking for a job when she was only fourteen years old. She lied and said she was eighteen, but she was such a sweet little thing that acted like I believed her even though I knew she wasn't even close to eighteen. I gave her little chores to do and told her she was earning her room and board. Kathleen and I both took her under our wings and kept her safe from whatever she had run away from. She's never told me, but I guessed she'd been in a terrible orphanage and ran away. A year or so passed, and she finally felt comfortable enough to tell me she had just turned sixteen. Kathleen and I planned a party for her and just had a couple of people over whom I trusted.

She's been here ever since then, and I never adopted her, because it could have caused a lot of trouble for her and for me, knowing I was harboring a runaway.

"So the years have passed, and she feels better doing something, rather than just living here. She has a beautiful room on the third floor that is twice this size, and it is decorated just the way she wanted it. She loves purples, so it is done in all different shades of purple, with beautiful Austrian shades on her windows, of which there are many. Sometime today, I want you to ask her where her room is; I know she will be so proud to show it to you. Not many people even close to her age come around, so no one has seen her room but Kathleen and I.

"Kathleen just can't take walking up all these stairs anymore. Her room is off the kitchen and is also very beautiful. I am only telling you all this because I want you to know that I have treasured them all these years. You have just brought so much happiness to all three of us. We all love you and feel the same. You've brought fresh life to us, and you finding Clarence has just brought a world of joy to us. And by the way, I know you're not nineteen either. I'm pretty good at telling ages, and I'd say you're not a day over sixteen."

I was so surprised, and it showed.

"Am I right?" she asked.

I said, "You're exactly right, but I thought in the beginning if anyone knew my age, they might send me back to Texas, and my daddy would have made my life unbearable until I could find a way to run away again." I told her that was the only lie I had told her. Lola really helped me, and I did have to leave quickly because my daddy was after me and he was mad. He couldn't touch Lola because she was married and had two daughters, and Daddy also knew Lola's husband would kill him if he ever tried to go in their house without being asked to, which would never happen. I told her some more things my daddy had done to my older brothers and how they had all run away as soon as they got the chance. I was the number six child and loved to read anything I could get my hands on, so I taught myself things, like not letting Daddy get away with hitting Mama even though he just took it out on me then. I told her about the time he'd been beating me and Mama hit him in the head with a hammer because she knew he would probably not have stopped before killing me, and as frightened of him as she was, she just wasn't going to let that happen. Her thoughts were only of saving me.

Someday Clarence hoped to be able to help her out somehow. Clarence just loved my sweet mama, and he saw what a horrible worthless drunk my daddy was. "So that was why we planned my running away, but as I told you when I got here, I had to leave in the middle of the night with just my bag of clothes and what money Lola could get from her purse quickly. So now that you know pretty much my whole story, are you sorry for all you have done for me and for Clarence and me? Our wedding and all that?"

She hugged me tight and said she didn't regret a single thing except she wished she could have gotten my mama and family here for my wedding, except of course my daddy.

"Maybe if there had been more time, we could have figured out something, but we can't dwell on the past. Now, sweet girl, you get up and start packing your things and all the things in the bathroom too. The soaps, the bath oils, and everything. It is yours. I can get more anytime I need it. I want you to start off your married life with all I can give you. Clarence says your room is small, but he hopes to save enough to move to a little larger place. I would never hurt his pride by telling him I could help. I can tell he wants to take care of you himself. And I respect that in him so much. You're right about one thing though: I would not have guessed his age. He does look about twenty-five or not much more. He is such a handsome man."

I smiled and said, "I know, and thank you for thinking so too."

"I'll be seeing you a little later this afternoon after you're all finished with packing everything—except all your wedding things, of course. You do have to get ready here." I giggled and hugged her.

When she left, I sat there running my hands over the beautiful luggage; the leather was so soft it almost felt like butter. It was just so amazing, I couldn't believe it was Clarence's and my. He would love it also, I knew. I carefully took all my clothes out of the drawers and my dresses out of the large closet. Then I started folding them very carefully—or so I thought.

About that time, there was another knock on the door. I knew this time it was Annie. I opened the door, and she pushed in a cart filled with all my favorite things for breakfast. There was plenty of food for three people, so I asked her if she couldn't stay a while and have breakfast with me.

She laughed and said, "Oh, I had hoped you would ask me. I am going to miss you so much."

We hugged, and I told her how much I would miss all of them. "This has been such a wonderful treat for me. I have been spoiled beyond my wildest dreams. This room is just so beautiful, and I know my room with Clarence won't be anything nearly this fancy, but I'd be happy in a shoe box when Clarence and I are married tomorrow." I held my breath a second and said it again, "Tomorrow! I just can't believe in one day I'll be married. I am so happy." But again, I said how much I would miss her and Kathleen and Mrs. Peterson. I would come and visit when I could. "After we have had a few weeks together, one Saturday we will come and visit, I promise!" Then I asked her if she didn't ever want to get married and have children.

She said she would love to, but she just didn't get out much to meet someone.

I told her once I had met all of Clarence's friends that he worked with, maybe one of them would be around her age, and we could fix them up by asking her to go out to dinner with us, and he would just happen to be at the same restaurant.

She giggled like a schoolgirl and said that sounded like so much fun. She told me about running away from a terrible home for children that no one had adopted and how awful they treated all the kids, especially the ones who got older and were expected to do all the work. She said if it wasn't done as soon as they thought it should be, they had a strap taken to their naked backs. They made her pull down her dress in front of all the boys and let them watch. "It was so terrible, because I had developed breasts so early, and they never bought me a bra, so all I could do was put my arms across my chest. I never told Mrs. Peterson any of this, because at first I didn't want her to know how young I was—only fourteen, but I had told her eighteen. I knew she didn't believe me, but it didn't matter to her. She could just tell I needed help. I guess I looked pretty pitiful. I had been running and walking for over a day because I had to get faraway from that place for fear they would find me."

I told her how very much alike we were, except in my case, it was my own daddy who was a mean terrible drunk and beat my mama and all of us kids as soon as we were old enough to work and make money for him to drink on. We hardly ever had enough to eat, and my poor mama did the very best she could with what little money he let her buy food with, usually potatoes and beans and sometimes cornbread. He had to make sure we were strong enough to work hard in the cotton fields or picking fruit or whatever jobs he could find us. I told her how guilty I felt leaving Maxine and W. K. and Velma; they would be the ones who had to work so hard now. "Someday, in some way, I will find a way to help them get away from him too—and my mama too. She was so afraid of him, but with all us kids, she just was stuck. Life can sure be unfair sometimes, can't it?"

We both decided our pity party was over and we'd better eat all this delicious food. After we finished eating, I said I'd better get back to packing.

She saw the way I was folding my dresses and asked if she could show me a better way. I told her sure, so she laid them down one by one, smoothed them out, and carefully folded each side in and then brought the bottom smoothly up about a third of the way and then the top down over, and it looked like it had just come from the store out of a box. I asked her where she'd learned to do that, and she said Mrs. Peterson had shown her when she was packing to go away for a weekend with a few of her friends for some meetings about something. She said she didn't know any details because "I try never to pry."

We both agreed that Mrs. Peterson was the most special lady ever put on this earth. I told her how wonderful my mama was when Daddy wasn't around and she could hug and kiss us and tell us how much she loved us. She always read the Bible to us every night Daddy was out on a drinking binge, which was more often than not, but we always knew how bad it would be if he ever caught us just sitting around and not working. He thought if we were awake, we should find something to do.

By the time I finished yacking all about my mama and brothers and sisters, I looked over, and she had all my dresses folded perfectly and was starting on my other things. I told her I just wanted her to have breakfast with me, not pack up all my clothes. She said she enjoyed doing it while she listened to me tell my stories. I then took the opportunity to ask her where her room was. I said, "I don't know why I never thought to ask before now. I guess I was always trying my best to get downstairs and help all I could to earn my keep here."

She looked excited and said she had the whole third floor to herself, and it was like a paradise. Then she asked if I would like to see it. I said yes, I would love to. "Do you have the time?"

Annie jumped up and said, "Let's run up there now, before I need to go down and take lunch to the ladies helping with Red Cross today." So off we went to the other side of the second floor, opened up a door, and there was a nice beautiful set of stairs.

Annie said, "It's been quite a while since anyone except me has been up here, so I am so excited to show you." When she opened her door at the top of the third landing, I gasped at the beauty. It really did look like a paradise. She showed me all her closets and fancy dressers and dressing tables to match in a beautiful ivory-colored wood, and the bedspread was the most gorgeous thing I'd ever seen. She said, "Mrs. Peterson asked my favorite color and I told her purple, and before I knew it, I had all these custom-made bedspreads and these fancy curtains that open so easily."

I pulled a few strings here and there, and the view was just beautiful. You could see the ocean, and around the side windows, you could see toward the front of the house. I said, "I think I could live in this room forever—but not without Clarence."

Annie said, "I love you a lot, but no way am I going to give up my room to anyone."

I laughed and told her I was only kidding, but to be honest, my favorite color was also purple; I told her someday I would have a purple room in my house somewhere. I enjoyed her room and admired everything she showed me, and I could tell she was thrilled.

She looked at her clock and said, "I better get myself downstairs, or I'm going to be fired."

We both laughed a lot at that joke. But down we went, and I went back to my room to finish what little I had left to do. I thanked Annie so much for having breakfast with me and then doing most of my work and especially thanked her for showing me her mansion on top of the world. It truly was a paradise.

It didn't take long for me to finish my packing and get most of the things in the bathroom packed except what I would need for my bath before the wedding, and then it hit me again: tomorrow I was going to really be Clarence's wife. How thrilled that made me. I got all my wedding things laid out over on the settee at the foot of the bed. My pearls and combs for my hair were all laid out in the bathroom. It was very strange, I know, but I felt so thrilled that this would be my last night here. For the rest of my life, I would be with Clarence.

I went downstairs just as Annie was serving lunch to seven ladies working on getting food together in large baskets to take to the train station this afternoon. I said, "I could help do that," and Mrs. Peterson said very quickly, "Oh no, you won't, missy. You're getting married tomorrow, and you will do nothing but rest and eat; then we all need to go to bed early, because it will be a very busy morning tomorrow getting ready for the wedding at two o'clock. The lady is coming to do your hair at ten thirty, and then it will be time for us to get you dressed and looking like the most beautiful bride ever to walk down an aisle." I was going to be pampered like a princess again, and this time I felt so excited because I would be walking down that aisle with Officer Joe to be given to the love of my life.

I just wandered around all afternoon doing nothing in particular but enjoying every minute. I went out and walked on the beach for a little while and remembered finding the balloons on the beach that night and how upset Clarence had been when I started to pick up one. He said he would explain after we were married. Funny how I hadn't thought of that again since that night. I guess there were just too many things going on and we were always busy every night doing something. This past ten days had flown by, and I was so glad about that.

I walked back to the house, and all the workers that I had met doing Red Cross projects were all there and yelled, "Surprise." I was shocked, and they said, "What would a wedding be without a surprise shower and a girls' night for the bride's last single night?" I laughed and said, "Thank you."

I had so many gifts to open. Some were kitchen items that would be very much needed, and then several ladies brought very sexy short nighties with fancy matching panties They said they were guaranteed to please Clarence very much. I felt my face turn about ten shades of red. I don't think my face had ever felt this way before. The next present was another nightie, even sexier than the one before. It was bright red and so lacy and really quite pretty, but I just could not imagine putting it on in front of Clarence, I told them. They said, "No, you go in the bathroom and get all dolled up, and when you come out, the night will sizzle." Again I blushed all shades of red. They laughed and said that they guaranteed that in a few nights, I would get the hang of it and love the teasing. I had no idea what they were talking about. But I laughed and thanked them all so much for this fun evening.

In just a little while, Annie and Kathleen came out with big trays of delicious kinds of food as usual, and this time they brought a large tray of wineglasses and a few bottles of wine. They poured us all a glass, and it tasted okay, but it went right to my head and I said, "That's enough of that for me. I don't want to look like a puffy-eyed bride." So they all drank and laughed, and some told a few jokes that I didn't get. They said, "You'll get them in a few days," and laughed again. About that time Mrs. Peterson said, "Okay, girls, the party is getting a bit rough, so I think we'd better call it a night. You girls divide up all this food and take it home to your husbands." So it was time for us to go to bed.

I woke up earlier than usual and thought in just a few hours, I would be married. I just shook all over with excitement. I took a long delicious-smelling bath, and I felt like I was going to bust. My insides were full of butterflies. I could feel them flying all over inside me. I was just too excited to think what to do next. I got out all my wedding outfit. Everything just looked so perfect, I started crying.

At that moment someone was knocking on my door, and I just stood there. Another knock, and I went over and answered it. I said, "Oh, thank you, Lord; it's just Annie."

She looked at me very strangely and said, "What in the world has gotten in to you, girl?"

I said, "I just think I am having a panic attack."

Annie said, "Stella, last night all you could think about was today getting here so you marry Clarence, and now you're in a panic. I don't get it."

I got up, hugged her tight, and said, "Thank you, Annie."

She said, "What did I do?"

I told her just hearing Clarence's name made me remember what I was doing.

She shrugged her shoulders and said, "Well, I'm glad I helped; now sit down here and eat every bit of this delicious breakfast while it is hot. That is orders from the cook."

I uncovered the tray, and there was a large plate of eggs, potatoes, ham, and toast—and best of all, a saucer piled high with danish. Okay, now I know I'm fine because I think I can eat every bite of this. And drink this nice cold milk, and probably down the pot of tea. I started eating my eggs and ham, with the perfectly browned toast smothered in butter. Oh, how the cook had come to know me. I ate most of that and left the potatoes. Then I buttered a few danish, and down they went, followed by half of my milk. Then I ate the rest of the danish and finished my milk.

Annie sat there in the chair across from me. She laughed and said, "Do you think Clarence won't be able to feed you?"

I said, "No, that's not it at all; it's just that I am so nervous, and eating all this delicious food is calming me. I didn't eat hardly anything last night, and all this food just looked so good all of a sudden. I sure don't want my stomach to be growling during the ceremony."

We had talked with the minister one night last week, and he said we would be exchanging vows for about ten minutes—or we could say anything we wanted to each other if we wanted to write our own vows. We both said we thought he would do a fine job. So he then went over basically everything else that would happen and in what order. Clarence and I had laughed later that night because he asked me if I remembered what the minister had said, and

I said, "No. Do you?" He shook his head, and we laughed and said, "We are a great pair." I think we were both just too happy and too excited for any of it to sink in. But we felt quite sure we could get through it fine.

As I finished a cup of the hot tea, all of a sudden I said I felt stuffed.

Annie said, "Gee, I sure don't know why. There are still potatoes on your plate, and then there's always the silverware."

I punched at her and laughed. "I meant it last night when I said how much I am going to miss all three of you."

She said, "Probably not nearly as much as we will miss you."

Just as Annie picked up the tray, I panicked again and said, "Sit for a moment."

She said, "What could possibly be the matter now?"

I told her I was just thinking of what she had said a little while ago about Clarence not being able to feed me.

She said, "Why has that got you in a panic again?"

I told her that all of a sudden I realized that I had never cooked one single thing, ever!

She looked a bit confused and said, "You are kidding, aren't you?"

I shook my head and said that Mama was always doing the cooking, and we were usually working outside or doing whatever work Daddy told us to do. "Mama was just too busy feeding babies and cooking for all the rest of us. There was just never a time for her to show us anything, and it probably never entered her head. I think she was just so afraid of Daddy that she just made sure his meal was ready when he came in, and we were all fed later, except the baby, who poor Mama was nursing while she worked. There was hardly ever time for her to sit and play with the baby or rock and nurse like mothers I had read about in books always do. She would no sooner have the baby weaned, and she was pregnant again. All of us kids were two years apart, and she probably would have had ten more kids than she did if it weren't for nursing. At least I had read that in a book once— that when you are nursing a baby, you probably won't make the eggs or something like that." Annie said she remembered reading something like that also. "But anyway, back to the problem at hand. Do you think Kathleen could teach me to cook some this morning?"

Annie fell back on my bed and laughed so hard.

I told her, "There is nothing funny about this. How am I going to feed my husband?"

She said, "Quit worrying. Clarence has been a bachelor for long enough to know how to cook, and it won't take you long to get the hang of it. He met you in your circumstances where you were living, and I feel quite sure he knows you haven't done any cooking."

I said, "He might think that the cook taught me how to cook all those delicious meals she has been feeding him the past week and a half."

She said, "Stella, think about it. He knows you were helping out every day with all the Red Cross work. I heard Mrs. Peterson tell him how much you did every day and what a great help you had been, so he knows—trust me. Now I need to get this tray back to the kitchen. You know the rest of us all have to bathe and get ready for some wedding this afternoon, if I'm not mistaken."

I said, "No, there is definitely a wedding we are all going to be at this afternoon."

As Annie went out the door, my hair lady came in, and then I knew this was so real. I sat there as she worked magic with my hair and my face. I didn't dare cry now, or I would mess up the hair and makeup that this woman had worked on to actually make me feel beautiful.

In about a half hour, Annie, Kathleen, and Mrs. Peterson came in and started helping me dress. I told them I felt like a queen. Mrs. Peterson said, "My dear, today you are the queen." They all looked so beautiful too. I felt so happy. Then I was all dressed except for my veil and shoes.

Mrs. Peterson said, "Now it's time for the rest of the things you have to have."

I looked surprised and said, "What could that be?"

She said, "You must have something new and something old and something borrowed and something blue."

I told her everything on my body was new.

She laughed and said, "Yes, we have that one covered."

Then Kathleen stepped up to me and handed me a most fancy little lace handkerchief. She told me it was her mother's, and she had given it to Kathleen when she left Denmark.

I said, "I can't take this."

She looked at me sternly and said, "My dear, it is a gift from me to you, and it is very old."

I thanked her and hugged her carefully so as not to mess either one of us up.

Then Mrs. Peterson stepped up to me and said, "I'm not going to be able to say too much, or I'll cry and mess up all our faces. Anyway, my dear, this is your something borrowed. I know we bought you pearls to wear, but you can wear them at the reception when I take back my diamond necklace that my Harry bought me and gave to me for a wedding present. This is my most prized possession. I want you to wear it at your wedding so you and Clarence will be as happy as my Harry and I were." She fastened a gorgeous diamond necklace around my neck, and we all gasped. The diamonds sparkled so beautifully, and now I knew I was a queen for today anyway. I hugged her and just quietly said,

"I love you so much." She patted my hand and smiled such a happy smile.

Then Annie stepped forward and handed me the prettiest blue ribbons. She said I could tie them around my flowers. I told her they were beautiful and would make my bouquet look much prettier.

Mrs. Peterson opened a fairly large box and handed me a bouquet made of pink roses, yellow daisies, and pretty blue primroses. In the middle was a white orchid. I said, "I've never seen such a beautiful arrangement of flowers." She took out three white orchids, and Mrs. Peterson, Annie, and Kathleen pinned them on one another. Left in the box were two smaller orchids for Clarence's and Officer Joe's lapels.

"Okay, ladies, our driver awaits us. It is one fifteen, and this wedding is going to start on time at two o'clock," Mrs. Peterson said.

So down the stairs we went. Annie was holding on to Kathleen so she didn't fall—heaven forbid. I felt so honored that she had walked up the stairs just to help me dress and give me her mother's hanky.

"Oh," Mrs. Peterson said, "Annie, will you run get the other two small orchids out of the kitchen for Clarence's best man and for the minister? Officer Joe will meet us at the car and take them to the back room of the church, where Clarence, his best man, and the minister will be, and then come right back to walk each of us down the aisle. Remember, Stella, you stay over to the side until Officer Joe comes back for you and the "Wedding March" starts playing. Don't forget to take a deep breath and walk slowly. Joe will hold on to you."

My suit skirt hung just above my shoes, and they matched it perfectly. Officer Joe walked Mrs. Peterson down the aisle to the front row. She was wearing a very beautiful suit that was a very dark pink. While they walked, Annie fixed my veil over my face and fixed the back so it hung perfectly halfway down my back. Then Officer Joe came for Kathleen, who looked beautiful in a pale yellow silk dress and a fancy little hat to match it. Next he came back for Annie, who wore a beautiful—guess—purple dress that had matching shoes. She looked like an angel. Oh, at that moment I hoped some of Clarence's single friends were here. I knew he had invited quite a few of his coworkers.

Now Officer Joe was back. He smiled down at me and said I was the most beautiful bride he had ever seen. Then he confided, "Don't tell my wife I said that." He always knew how to make me laugh. The music started, and he said, "It's showtime!"

I took a deep breath, and we started walking until we got to the door; then we stopped for effect, I guess. They played the "Wedding March," and we walked slowly down the aisle. I couldn't take my eyes off Clarence. He looked so handsome in his dark blue suit, and that white orchid looked so beautiful with his white shirt and beautiful blue-and-white-striped tie. All he was doing was looking at me like I was the most important person in the world. When I was just about to the steps of the altar, Clarence and his best man stepped down, and Mrs. Peterson got up and walked over beside me. I took another very deep breath to keep from crying.

As the minister told us to turn and face each other, Clarence and I were both doing everything we could to keep ourselves from crying, not for any reason except happiness. The minister asked if anyone had any reason why these two should not be married. There was silence for a moment. Then he asked, "Who gives this woman to be married?"

Officer Joe, in his full uniform, stood up and said, "I do." He then took my right hand and placed it in Clarence's left hand.

The minister then said, "Dearly beloved, we are gathered here together in the sight of God and in the presence of family and friends to join together this man and this woman in holy matrimony, which is instituted of God and therefore is not to be entered into unadvisedly or carelessly, but reverently, joyfully, and in the love of God. Into this holy estate, these two persons present come now to be joined." He then asked Clarence, "Do you, Clarence, promise to love, honor, and cherish this woman in sickness and in health, for richer or poorer, for better or worse, until death do you part?"

Clarence said, "I do."

Then to me the minister said, "Do you, Stella, promise to love, honor, and cherish this man in sickness and in health, for richer or poorer, for better or for worse, until death do you part?"

I said, "I do."

Then the minister said, "If you wish to exchange rings, you may do so now."

Clarence took my left hand, put the wedding ring on my finger, and said, "I take you, Stella, to be my lawful wife."

I took Clarence's left hand, placed the ring on his finger, and said, "I take you, Clarence, to be my lawful husband."

The minister said, "For as much as Clarence and Stella have consented together in holy matrimony and have witnessed the same before God and those present, and have pledged their faithfulness, each to the other, and have declared their love by giving and receiving rings and joining hands, I now, by the authority committed unto me as a minister of the State of California, declare that Clarence and Stella are husband and wife according to the ordinance of God, in the name of the Father, the Son, and the Holy Spirit. Those whom God has joined together, let no man put asunder." He then said, "You may now kiss your bride."

Mrs. Peterson quickly took my veil and pulled it back, and Clarence leaned over and kissed me for it seemed like three minutes.

The minister then said, "I now for the first time introduce Mr. and Mrs. Clarence Carl Rader."

Everyone cheered as we walked holding hands back down the aisle. As they all gathered around us, Clarence started introducing his new wife to all his friends and then said, "I am so happy. I just don't know what else to say."

Mrs. Peterson said, "Clarence, you and Stella get in the back of my limo, and the three of us will get a ride with Officer Joe and his wife. And all of the rest of you follow us to the reception at my home. If you lose us, just go to the police station and ask where the reception of Clarence and Stella Rader is being held. They all know where I live."

Clarence and I sat in the back of her gorgeous car and just stared at each other as if we were both in disbelief. But after a minute, the window separating the front of this long car— limo, as Mrs. Peterson had called it—from the back rolled up like magic, and we were alone in the back. We kissed and hugged and told each other what a wonderful life we were going to have. It seemed we had just left the chapel when we were driving up in front of Mrs. Peterson's house. The driver came around and opened the door for us, and right behind us was Officer Joe and the rest of them. Car by car people arrived, and the driver told everyone where to park.

Before we knew it, we were all in the house, and it was like the party was starting just like that night of the benefit. Men in tuxedos were walking all around and asking each person if they wanted champagne or would prefer a cocktail or maybe a cold beer. Most of Clarence's friends said they would love a beer, and their wives took the champagne. Clarence and I both said we would love some sweet iced tea. They looked at us a little strangely, and we both laughed,

125

realizing that they weren't familiar with sweet tea since they weren't from the South, as we both were. Everyone in the South knew that sweet tea was just a staple. We both said, "Never mind; a glass of any soda you have will be fine." We had discussed on the ride here that we didn't want to be drinking and not feel well on our wedding night.

Clarence said he had told the guys last night that he knew they could handle a lot more beer than he could, but this was a really nice house, and he didn't want me embarrassed by them drinking too much. The married guys said, "Don't worry; our wives will see to that." And the few single guys said, "No problem, Clarence; we understand completely."

I looked around for Annie; she was sitting on one of the settees, and a very handsome young man was sitting with her. I asked Clarence who he was, and he said, "That is Mike; he is a really nice man from a nice family." They had him over for dinner a couple of times. I was relieved, as I didn't want Annie messing with a wild guy. Annie didn't waste any time, and I was worried she would be too shy to talk.

About that time the mayor, his wife, and their son David walked up. I introduced Clarence to the mayor, Mrs. Stevens, and David. The men shook hands and said how nice it was to meet the man who had stolen Stella's heart. Clarence said that we had stolen each other's hearts the moment we had met in Texas. And it would be that way for the rest of our lives. David said, before he knew about their engagement, he had tried to ask Stella out, but she made it very clear she was already taken and that would never change. "You are a very lucky man."

Clarence smiled at me and said, "Don't think for a minute I don't know that. She's all I have thought about since we met, and leaving her in Texas to come here was the hardest thing I have ever done, but I had to get a job and make enough money to support her. Things got a bit confused, and we were separated way too long, but it will never happen again. We are together for the rest of our lives."

Everyone seemed to be having a wonderful time, and surprisingly, all the construction guys and their wives got along great with the mayor, his wife, and the judges and their wives. It was as if they had all known each other their whole lives. Everyone enjoyed the delicious food, and the drinks were flowing.

All of a sudden, Mrs. Peterson said, "Hello, everyone. It's time for the bride and groom to cut the cake. So let's all surround them and watch."

Clarence and I had already been admiring how gorgeous this cake was and saying it seemed a shame to mess it up by cutting it, but, oh well, it had to be done. We were handed the beautiful silver knife, and we put both our hands around the handle and cut a small piece and laid it on one of the crystal plates. We then took a small piece each, and with our arms folded together, we fed each other a bite. Everyone clapped and cheered. We then crossed arms, and both of us took a sip of champagne. Again the cheers, and then one of the waiters took over and said he would remove the top of the cake for us to freeze and have on our first anniversary.

About that time, Mrs. Peterson started to cry. Clarence and I both ran over to her to see what ever could be wrong. She said, "I thought I was doing so well at planning everything, and I forgot a very important part." We asked what that could be, and she said she was so used to planning parties for different events, and this part was never needed so she completely forgot. She was really crying, and we couldn't get her to spit out what she had forgotten. Finally, she said she had forgotten all about hiring someone to take all the photos of the wedding and the cake, reception, and all. Now it was almost over, and we had no pictures to remember it all. We both hugged her and told her it could never be erased from our memories no matter how hard anyone tried. It was just etched there forever and ever. And we both knew it was all because of her, with a bit of help from Officer Joe. He bowed and said, "No problem. Nothing but the best for this beautiful bride." He had a few drinks in him, but was handling it very well. Clarence and I said, "It's about time we all get a piece of this amazing-looking cake."

By this time the waiter had plenty of large slices of cake being passed around on trays for everyone. I never counted exactly, but I would guess there were about fifty people there, and everyone was saying this was the best wedding they had ever attended. And definitely the best wedding cake. Mrs. Peterson finally calmed down and had a piece of cake herself. What a wonderfully perfect day it had been.

I looked over and saw Annie and Mike still sitting together enjoying a piece of cake and looking even more cozy than before. I looked around the room for Kathleen, and I saw her with a judge whom I remembered meeting at the party, so I immediately found Mrs. Peterson and asked who he was.

She said, "That's Judge Daniels; he is a wonderful man who lost his wife four years ago by a drunk driver. It was so sad, and he mourned her for so long that I never thought I'd see him talking alone to another single woman. And for that matter, I never thought I'd see Kathleen with a man. She's always been here since coming over from Denmark. It looks like they are having a good time. Why are you looking so concerned?"

I told her I was just worried that Kathleen might be with a married man. "I have already asked Clarence about Mike, the guy sitting with Annie. He's a very nice man from a good family, Clarence said, so I am worrying for no reason now. I wouldn't want either of them getting into trouble."

She told me I sounded like an old mother hen. We both laughed and said we hoped they were having a good time.

Clarence walked up about that time and said, "Is this a private joke?"

We said, "No, not at all." Then I quickly explained to him why I had been worried.

He laughed and said, "What would all these nice people think if they knew our age differences?"

I said it was none of their business; we were an old married couple. Now I felt like a fool for acting like I was their protector.

There were several couples still dancing and enjoying the evening as the music was being played so softly and beautifully. I asked Clarence if he knew how to dance, and he said, "Of course, and I am ashamed that I haven't asked my bride if she wants to dance." I said I would love to since it was our wedding. He took me in his arms and held me close as we moved along with the beat of the music. He leaned down and kissed me a long, slow kiss as if we were the only two in the room.

When we looked up, everyone else had gotten off the dance floor and were watching us. We were both embarrassed and I am sure it showed, but everyone clapped and said it was about time the bride and groom were having a dance. So we continued to move with the music and dance.

After the song was over, we bowed and said, "Okay, we are turning the floor over to the rest of you. We have other things to do."

As we started over to Mrs. Peterson, we saw Annie and Mike talking to her. We waited a minute until they were finished, then went to her and asked if she thought it would be rude for us to leave pretty soon. She said, "It looks like everyone is about to leave."

Several couples who were friends of Clarence came up and said what a beautiful wedding it had been and thanked us for inviting them. Then they turned to Mrs. Peterson and told her it was such a pleasure to meet her and thanked her for inviting them to her beautiful home. She said she had loved every minute of meeting all of Clarence's friends, some of whom had already said their good-byes while we were dancing.

The mayor and his family came over and said good night to everyone and what a wonderful wedding and reception it had been. They hadn't had such a lovely evening in they didn't know how long. "Thanks," Mrs. Peterson said with a wink in her eye. She was, of course, referring to her previous parties. They laughed and told her she always threw a great party, and this topped them all. Such a beautiful bride they had never seen. I thanked them, and so did Clarence.

Within a half hour the room was pretty much cleared, except for Kathleen and Judge Daniels, who were still talking. They looked up, saw us looking at them, and walked over to us.

The judge asked if Mrs. Peterson ever gave this lovely lady a night off.

She said, "Why do you ask?"

He said, "I thought it would be nice to take her out to dinner and the theater some night if you approve."

She said Kathleen was free to make a date for herself anytime she wanted to and that she had been held up in this old place for too many years.

Kathleen said, "You know I have never felt like that."

"I know; I was only kidding, but not about it being fine for you to have an evening out whenever you wish."

So it was left to them to decide when and where they would go out.

Finally, Mrs. Peterson said, "I think it's safe you leave since everyone else has said their good-byes." We both hugged her at the same time and told her we could never repay all she had done for both of us if we lived to be a thousand years old. I kept hugging her and crying; I told her how much I loved her and thanked her for all she had done for me and for letting me stay in her home for these past months. She assured me the pleasure had been hers.

I held her tight and then asked, "By the way, where did Annie go?"

"She asked permission to go out for a drive with Mike. I told her she was a big girl and also a free one, so to go have a good time. It looks like I might start having some evenings alone these days."

Clarence and I told her to get word to us when that happened, and we would take her to dinner.

She said, "Oh fiddle, you two get out of here and come back in a few nights after you are all settled and get all your wedding presents. Kathleen said there had been dozens of them delivered to the house, and they were all safe up in your room."

I said, "When did she do that?"

Mrs. Peterson said, "I had my driver carry them all up there as they came, and he put them in a large storage closet until you had left. Then he came back and put them in your room during the wedding. He is a sly fox. I just hope he didn't meet someone tonight."

I told her I hadn't seen any single women here. We laughed, hugged her tight again, and then Clarence and I were off to our home! That sounded so good.

CHAPTER 9

Our Night

When we arrived at our home, Clarence unlocked and opened the door. He then picked me up and carried me across the threshold. I looked around, and everything looked so fresh and clean. He had painted the room a very soft pale yellow, and it had curtains that were white, with tiny little yellow roses on them. I looked over at the bed, and it had a beautiful yellow bedspread of a soft chenille. I loved it, and it was all ours. A cute little dinette set was over by the small kitchen, and it was all white, with four pretty little chairs. He told me he had found that at an antique store a few weeks ago when he was trying to make the room look cozy. I told him it was perfect and I loved it all, but mostly I loved him.

He came over to me and kissed me a beautiful soft kiss that said, "Let's get ready for bed." He asked if I would like to take a bath or shower first. I told him to go first since I would probably take a bit longer. He said okay, went into the bathroom, showered, and was out within ten minutes.

It had been just enough time for me to explore our room. Then I took my small suitcase, went in, and took a bath, making sure I used my bubble bath. The bathroom was very small, and it had a little ledge where I could set things. After my bath, I dried and slipped on my white gown that Mrs. Peterson had given me.

I walked out, and Clarence looked at me like he was seeing me for the first time.

I asked if everything was okay.

He said, "Are you kidding? You look good enough to be a movie star, and you're all mine. I love you so much."

I walked over to him in nothing but my silk gown, and he took me in his arms and kissed me for several minutes.

Then he asked, "Is it okay if I carry you to our bed, Mrs. Rader?"

I said, "Certainly, Mr. Rader, I am all yours."

He turned down the bedspread, I walked over to him, and he picked me up and gently laid me on the bed. As he sat and started to lie down next to me, the bed slid out from under us.

Clarence said, "Those dirty dogs are gonna pay for this. I'll beat them all when I go back to work again in five days."

We both laughed, and I said, "Oh, honey, you know they meant no harm, and it's all fixable, I'm sure."

He said yes, he was sure the guys all did something like this on each other's wedding night. "I wish we could have gone to a fancy hotel for our wedding night, but I am trying so hard to save all the money I can to get a bigger place for us."

I told him I loved this place. It was our first home together and would always be special.

We both got up, picked up the mattress, and saw that they had removed all the strong slats that held up the box springs and mattress. We replaced all the slats and put each piece back together. It took all of ten minutes. I told him not to even mention it to the guys and wait to see who started coming clean with their dirty deeds.

He agreed and said, "Thank you, Stella, for keeping me so calm."

I wrapped my arms around his neck and gave him a long kiss that said, "Okay, I'm ready." As we lay there kissing and touching each other's bodies, I felt his hand slide up my gown and touch me gently in my private part, which had never been touched before, except by me, of course, when bathing. As soon as I felt his finger softly touch my insides, I felt like I had just exploded into a million pieces, and they were all good. I told Clarence that it felt so good, and I was sure I was ready.

He slipped out of his underwear, and then he slipped my gown carefully over my head and laid it on the chair by the bed. He started kissing me and went down my throat and then to my breasts, kissing each one so softly I was about to explode. He put each nipple in his mouth and kissed and sucked just gently. Then he knew I was ready, as I was about to come off the bed. He whispered in my ear that he thought we should probably use a little lubricant since it was my first time and he didn't want it to hurt too bad. He warned me that his penis was rather large, and when my hymen broke, it would probably bleed some, so he laid a soft blanket under me. I was so excited I couldn't see how anything could possibly feel anything but wonderful.

As Clarence raised himself up over me, I reached down and touched his penis. He jumped as he hadn't expected me to be so bold, but I told him I couldn't stand this teasing me. I just wanted to make love with my husband for the first time now.

As he gently entered me, I thought I heard bells and whistles; it felt so good, and there was no pain at all because he had put a little something on and it made him slide right in. My hips moved up to meet his, and we started moving together up and down. All of a sudden I felt an explosion, and Clarence did at the same time, and we just moved slowly to enjoy the moment.

As we lay there with him still inside me for several minutes, suddenly I felt his penis becoming very hard again. I didn't know all the correct terms for these things that were happening, but I felt I would quickly learn. I would ask him to explain to me at another time when I wasn't so excited.

As soon as Clarence started moving again, he asked if I would like to be on top. I said that sounded exciting, and he rolled me over on top of him. I started moving back and forth, and this was just like heaven (as Lola had said). Then he leaned up and kissed and touched each of my breasts, then took them into his mouth and gently nibbled on my nipples. I thought I would die with excitement. We both explored each other, and he took my breasts in his hands and gently massaged them. I thought, Oh, how could anything feel this good! After a little more exploration of each other's bodies, to continue to enjoy the sex, we kept up the moving back and forth; and minutes later, we both exploded again. That's the only way I knew how to explain my feelings at that moment. As we lay there, just kissing and doing a little more exploring of the bodies, both of us just held on to each other.

Clarence said to me, "Stella, you are what I have been waiting for my whole life. For the first time in my thirty-five years, I feel complete!"

I told him I had never thought anything could feel this wonderful; I told him exactly how I felt and asked him, "What happened when we both exploded?"

He explained that it was called a climax; we both had one at same moment twice, and it was amazing both times. He said he was so happy that I seemed to enjoy the sex. He said that we had just climaxed twice in a row, "and though it was your first experience, you seemed to have no pain. Am I correct, Stella?"

I told him all I felt was pure joy and so much love for him, more than I ever thought possible.

There was a little blood on the blanket. As we lay there for at least an hour just kissing and touching each other everywhere, every time he touched me somewhere, he asked if I liked it. I told him I loved everything he was doing and asked if there was something else he wanted me to touch or to do. He said I was doing everything perfectly and we had the rest of our lives to find out everything about each other. It would be just wonderful to explore each other's favorite things as they happened. He added, "The most important thing is to always talk to each other and say if we like something or if we don't." We agreed that would always be important, and we would always talk.

We got up and removed the blanket he had laid under us. Then we both got in the shower, washed each other, and just enjoyed looking at each other naked.

I said, "I don't think a wedding night could be more perfect if we had been at the Ritz Hotel in Paris."

He laughed and asked how in the heck did I know about the Ritz.

I told him I loved reading books and learning all I could.

He laughed and said, "Oh, how I love you, honey!"

We woke up about nine in the morning and made love again.

Clarence said, "Honey, I think I could lie in this bed with you for the whole five days I have off, but no matter what they say, man cannot live on love only. I don't know about you, but I'm feeling pretty hungry after the night and morning we've just had."

I said I could use a bite to eat also. "Do you think Kathleen could deliver us a big pile of those danish?" I told him I was certainly going to miss her cooking, but not nearly as much as I loved being married to the most wonderful man alive.

He laughed and said, "Do we want to go out, or would you trust me to make breakfast?"

I told him I trusted him completely. Then I thought, now is as good a time as I'll ever have to tell him my problem. "Clarence, honey, before you start breakfast, can I talk to you about something very important?"

He sat back down, leaned over, and kissed me a long slow kiss, and I said, "Hey, we can't start this again, or we'll both waste away to nothing." We laughed, and it made the moment a bit lighter, so I just blurted it out. "Clarence, I have never cooked one thing in my entire life. How am I ever going to be a good wife if I can't even have your dinner ready after you've worked a long day?"

He took me in his arms and held me tight, then he said, "Do you think I didn't know that?"

I looked at him with a shocked look on my face.

He said, "I saw how hard you worked every day, and your poor mama cooking for all you kids on a campfire. How could you possibly have learned to cook when you were pulling cotton till your precious hands bled every single day? I wanted to have your old man locked up just for treating all of his children the way he did. When we have children, they will be treated with the best of everything we can possibly give them, but back to the subject at hand. In time, watching me and helping me, you will learn to cook and be just as good at it as you are at everything else." He leaned over and patted my bottom.

I said, "Okay, husband, cook my breakfast, and I will watch every detail."

We had bacon, eggs, fried potatoes, and toast. It was just as good as anything Kathleen had ever cooked—well, maybe not her danish. I should have been getting up really early, and I'm sure she would have taught me how to make things. "I really hadn't thought until the morning of our wedding right after I ate breakfast, brought to me on a tray, just how spoiled I had been while living there. I started crying and told Annie that I couldn't cook or even boil water. She said the same thing you did. She was quite sure since you had met me when I was at home working so hard that you were bound to know that I hadn't ever cooked."

Clarence said it was no problem because he had been cooking his own meals since college.

I asked him how he learned, and he said he used to love watching his mother cook, and she had a houseful of children too, so she was always happy to have him help her. "I was the oldest of all my brothers and sisters. Mom never treated me any different than she did her own children, and that meant so much to me. So anyway, that is how you will learn. By watching and helping. I will show you the best places to shop for groceries, and I always look at the paper to see what's on sale and who has the best price on the items we need. It's quite easy once you get the hang of it. I mean cooking and shopping. I will always leave you with plenty of money for what you need to buy.

"And by the way, there is a secondhand bookstore right around the corner. We can go for a walk later, and I'll show you the stores; there are just so many things you can do during the day while I am at work. I know you said you love to read, and the books are really cheap. I buy a lot of their westerns, and they even have a trade-in deal where once you have read the book, you can trade it for another. You'll be a college graduate before we know it. Book-wise, I mean."

We had five beautiful days of making love, cooking, and taking long walks. When our last free night was here already, I told him I didn't know how I was going to live without him for nine whole hours every day. He kissed me and said the days would go by fast if I found some good books. I told him I would go to the bookstore tomorrow.

I had learned so much about my husband's many talents in the past few days—some I won't mention—but I will say, "He is an excellent husband, an amazing lover, and just the very best cook and teacher that I could ever have imagined."

He made cooking and learning how to cook so easy. I was actually looking forward to having a delicious meal ready for him when he arrived home from work on Thursday. I wasn't sure what I would cook yet, but he had taught me so much in such a short time. Especially since we spent so much of our five days making love. We never seemed to be able to get enough of each other. It seemed so silly now that I was worried about not knowing what to do and not knowing anything about it. When Lola said, "You will see; it will all come natural to you after you are married," she certainly knew what she was talking about. Someday I would tell her. I sure didn't want to write that in a letter and have my beautiful nieces, Glenda or Joyce, get their hands on it. Lola was so proper all of the time; this would just mortify her since they were still so young, not old enough to be asking questions about these things for many years.

Thursday morning got here way too soon, but when Clarence's alarm went off, we quickly made love again. He said he could grab something to eat on his way to work, but he couldn't imagine waiting all day to do this again. I sure wasn't going to complain because I felt the same. I couldn't get enough of him, and the thought of him leaving without our making love was just more than I wanted to think of.

As Clarence showered and shaved in the bathroom, I quickly ran in the kitchen and fried a large sausage patty and two eggs just the way he had shown me. The toast popped up, and I put this all together and had it ready by the time he got out of the bathroom.

He smiled and said he was so impressed and that I was such a good student.

I kissed him and told him, "It was all the teacher's doings." I held my breath as he tasted it.

He opened his mouth up right away, and I knew I had done something wrong. He said it was delicious, but I had forgotten the salt and pepper. I guess I wasn't such a good student after all. He leaned down, kissed me, and said, "Listen, honey, not many women would even get up and fix their husband's breakfast, let alone make love first."

I laughed and said, "Anytime, sir."

I hadn't mastered making coffee yet, but thank goodness Clarence loved milk and I had poured him a big glass. As he finished, he took me in his strong arms and said nine hours sure seemed like a long time from now.

I swatted him and told him to get to work before he started something he didn't have time to finish. I told him as he was going out the door that he was taking my heart with him and I loved him so much.

He said the feeling was mutual, and he would be home just as soon as possible. He warned me that since he had been off for three days this week, they possibly could be a little behind, so if he wasn't home by four twenty, he would probably be working a little overtime; we could sure use the money.

I said I was going to try and have dinner ready when he got home, and he said, as he was driving away, not to worry about dinner. We had other things to do first, and then we could make dinner together.

As it happened, he only had to work one hour over, so he was home sharply at five twenty. I was wearing my little red nightie, the one that one of the ladies had bought me for my shower. They weren't kidding when they said I would know what to do quick enough. I ran and lay down real quick on our bed as soon I heard his car drive up. I pretended I was reading and didn't notice when he unlocked the door and opened it.

He whistled and said, "Where is my wife? Some little vixen has taken her place."

I said, "Oh, you're home, honey. I missed you so much, but I just got so involved with this book, I didn't hear you drive up."

He said, "Do you usually read your books upside down?"

I looked down at the book and laughed, then tossed it aside.

It took Clarence all of five seconds to get his clothes off. Then he asked me to stand up so he could admire this beautiful little vixen.

I stood up and slowly turned around in a full circle. He said, "That is gorgeous. Now let's see how quickly you can get it off."

In about an hour, we were lying there, and we both decided it was time to get up and think of something to make for dinner. I told him I had looked at the cookbook he had and was thinking of trying to make a meatloaf. He said that would take too much time now, so we could just make hamburgers, and then we would have plenty of time before going to sleep for other things. I laughed and said, "You are a real sexy guy, you know." He agreed and laughed, then said, "I just can't get my fill of you."

As I fell asleep in his arms that night, I thought of how Mrs. Peterson had told me how fast time goes by and not to waste a minute of it once we were married. I thought we were handling that topic very well.

The next month went by so fast I barely remember anything except that I had never been so happy in all my life. I couldn't ever think of anything before that compared to our love. It was so intense. We just stayed home mostly, because we only wanted to be alone and be able to do whatever we wanted, when we wanted. It seemed to me that I loved Clarence more every day, and I couldn't see how this could keep happening, since I had loved him so much when we had married. I thought if this love kept increasing, we would just be one person. How could that be? I wondered. I just had too much time to think during the long days while Clarence was at work.

I was getting pretty good at looking at the newspaper and watching closely for the things I knew we were low on and then writing them down on our grocery list. I also had learned to cook several things that Clarence seemed to really enjoy. He liked my meatloaf, and I did a pretty good job of mashing the potatoes, but Clarence always had to make the gravy, because I just couldn't get the hang of that.

I tried to make fried chicken one night when I knew he would be home on time. He took one look at it and said, "Oh, honey, thank you so much for trying different things to cook—I really do appreciate it—but this chicken isn't nearly done enough, and we could get very sick. It's really important that chicken and pork are cooked until completely done."

I asked him how he could tell by just looking at it.

He said there was a bit of blood coming out of the breast part, and that cooks the fastest.

I started to cry.

He put his arms around me and said, "I am so sorry. I wasn't yelling at you; I was just trying to tell you it's important, and you certainly can't be expected to be able to cook everything in one month." He then ran back to his car and brought in a bunch of beautiful pink daisies.

I said, "Thank you, honey. They are so pretty." I went over to the cabinet, got a vase out, put them in, and added water. I wanted them in water so they would live as long as possible. Then I hugged his neck and kissed him so long we both had to gasp for air. I said how sorry I was about the chicken and that I had wrecked it.

He said, "It's not wrecked. It is still warm, and the oil just has to be heated back up and we'll fry it a little longer. I'll show you how to tell when it's done. By the way, happy one-month anniversary."

Then I started to cry again, because I hadn't known what the date was.

He said, "How could you know, sweetheart? There is no calendar in here."

I told him I read the newspaper every day, and I was sure that it was dated.

He held me again until I stopped crying, and then said, "We have to get this chicken back on to cook, or it will be wrecked." Then he laughed. He heated the oil back to hot and added the legs and thighs. He said, "You always cook the dark meat first for at least ten minutes, then add the breasts. You can tell that the that the thighs and legs are done when you see that they are separating from the bone a little. Then put the fork into the breast and slightly pull up at the edge, and it should pull away easily."

I had already mashed the potatoes, and they were still very warm. Clarence poured most of the grease into an old can he kept just for that. Then he put in several tablespoons of flour and got it well mixed with the little bit of grease and crumbles from the chicken. After the flour started to brown just a little, he added the milk slowly and kept the lumps mashed quickly so the gravy wouldn't be lumpy. I was watching every move so I could make it again one day in a week or so, and actually have everything done when he got home. While I was watching him, I reheated the green beans.

Dinner turned out delicious, and after washing all the dishes and cleaning up, we spent the rest of the evening just talking and making love. Then we showered and made love again in the shower.

"That's our first time doing this," I said. I told him he was so strong to be able to hold me up with my legs wrapped around him.

He said, "You are so light, but you were also up against the wall, so that helped hold you up." He asked if I had enjoyed making love that way.

I told him I loved making love to him any way, but I had already told him I liked being on top best. He also liked it best because I did, and it excited him so much to see how much pleasure I got from being on top. I told him I had climaxed every single time we had made love, so "all ways are wonderful, and you are wonderful, my handsome husband. And also happy anniversary to you." We had finished drying each other by now and raced to the cozy bed. We soon feel asleep.

CHAPTER 10

Finally Open our Gift

The next Saturday Clarence didn't have to work, I reminded him we had never gone over to Mrs. Peterson's to open our wedding presents like we had said we would in a few days. And we had to get thank-you notes in the mail soon, or we would be considered rude. I certainly didn't want Mrs. Peterson, of all people, to have her friends thinking badly of us. He agreed completely, saying how much she had done for us and we should have gone over that week like we had said. "I just don't know where this month has gone." "I do," I said, and laughed. He swatted my behind and said we had better get going before something else got started. "Get in the car, wife."

As we drove up in front of her beautiful mansion, I told him that I would trade all the wonderful nights and days that I spent in that gorgeous place for one night I've spent in our home. "It's ours, and I love it, and I love you."

We walked up and rang the bell.

Annie answered and started screaming our names and hugging us both, and by the time she had said thank you several times, I realized she was referring to Mike. Clarence had told me right after going back to work that Mike had told him that they had a couple of dates and she was just the sweetest girl he had ever met. Then last week he said they were going out several times a week now.

Mrs. Peterson got to the door in record time, and she started hugging and kissing us both and saying she was wondering if we had forgotten all of them so soon.

I explained how I just didn't know where the time had gone.

She laughed and said she understood and was only kidding. She reminded me of what she had told me: "Time flies when you're married and so in love."

By this time Kathleen was out of the kitchen, and after hugging us both, she said, "What do you want for dinner? I must get started so everything is perfect."

We told her we only came by to open our wedding presents like we should have a month ago. She looked to Mrs. Peterson for backup, and she got it.

Mrs. Peterson said, "You must stay for dinner, or Kathleen will never forgive any of us," so we finally agreed.

"Anything you cook, Kathleen, will be absolutely delicious. So go for it," Clarence said.

We all laughed as we were so happy to see these wonderful friends who had all done so much for us.

Mrs. Peterson called her driver, who lived above the garage in a place called a carriage house. She asked him if he was busy. Of course he was not busy for anything she needed, so he came running. It's funny, but I never knew his name. He was just her driver.

When he knocked on the door, we were all still standing in the large foyer, chatting back and forth about everything that had been going on. Mrs. Peterson said, "Tony, I'm sure you remember Mr. and Mrs. Clarence Rader? He smiled, shook Clarence's hand, and just sort of bowed just a bit to me. "And this is Stella; I feel quite sure you remember her." After all the introductions, she asked him to carry all the gifts that were hidden away in my room downstairs. In a matter of minutes, he had a huge stack of presents in the parlor, where she had told him to take them. He said, "Will that be all, ma'am?"

She said yes, "but thank you so much for being so quick, and on your day off especially."

We said thank you also, and he was out the door.

"That man can really move," I said.

Mrs. Peterson said, "Yes, he certainly can, and he is a man of few words."

Annie spoke up and said, "I've lived here almost twelve years now, and maybe I have heard him say twenty words, and that's probably an overstatement."

Mrs. Peterson said, "Harry hired him as a very young man who looked hungry and asked if we had any work we needed done. He asked him if he knew how to drive, and he said very politely, 'Yes, sir, I do.' So Harry hired him on the spot, and he has lived in the carriage house ever since. The cook rings a bell they fixed somehow years ago, and he comes to the back and she gives him his very hearty meals. He's a very private man, but he is always johnny-on-the-spot and never questions anything—just does his job. We never asked what his problems were, and he never offered to tell us. He keeps the limo spotless and shiny, and that's all we ever asked of him, except of course to drive us to where we were going and wait. He reads all the time while he is waiting for us, and that is about all I know about Tony. He's a good man in my book."

We were in the parlor, and Annie said, "Well, are you going to take care of these? I have been so excited to see everything you got."

Clarence and I looked at each other in amazement at all the presents. Before I could even think of what was in them all, I all of a sudden realized all these people probably wondered why they had received no thank-you note. Annie said she would write down each present, describe it, and put their address after each present. I thanked her. She said Mrs. Peterson had thought of it, and she had kept the address list from the wedding. I was so thankful Clarence wrote so beautifully and fast, because people would not be able to read my handwriting, even though I was trying to practice and was getting better at it. I felt it was important that I write at least well enough that it could be understood. All that being settled, we started opening our gifts.

The first package we opened was from one of Clarence's coworkers. It was a really nice toaster. Clarence laughed, and we all looked at him with a why on our faces. He said that Jack was with him when he bought the toaster we had now at a secondhand store for twenty-five cents. Jack laughed and said, "You'll never get that thing to working." Well, he did, but not really well, so the new one would be so appreciated.

As we kept opening presents, we realized we didn't even know a lot of these people. How were we going to get their addresses to send thank-you notes? Mrs. Peterson said that most of the packages had return addresses on them; she had saved the addresses and made notes of which packages they had come with.

We received so many beautiful things—big fluffy towels like the one I had dried on here. And lots of nice things for the kitchen, which we really needed.

As I opened some of the kitchen things, it reminded me to tell Annie that Clarence was teaching me to cook, "and I'm doing okay, aren't I, honey?"

He laughed and said, "Yes, if you call trying to kill me with raw chicken okay." He quickly added, "I'm just kidding. She is doing a great job; the raw chicken was only one time."

I punched him lightly, and he winked at me so everyone knew we were doing fine.

Mrs. Peterson said some of the gifts were from a few of her friends that I had not met, but they had seen the article in the paper and just sent a gift for our wedding. She said she felt quite sure that was why several people came to the wedding that she did not know. The mayor and his wife sent a set of beautiful crystal stemware. They were so beautiful, and I said I would be afraid to wash them for fear of breaking one. They were just gorgeous. Mrs. Peterson pointed out to me that each glass had Waterford on it, which meant they were just about the best quality you could buy. Now I was really afraid to use them. Annie helped me wrap them very carefully and get them back in the box.

We opened a very small box, and in it was a gift certificate at the nicest furniture store in town. Mrs. Peterson said, "Buy yourself the nicest, most comfortable bed you can find, and then you will appreciate your next gift."

Annie handed us the big box that had been over in the corner. It was a gorgeous set of purple satin sheets and a big furry blanket to match them, and then at the bottom were new down feather pillows and a comforter with large purple flowers all over it and a dust ruffle of a light purple shade to match some of the flowers.

Mrs. Peterson said, "Clarence, when I bought all this bedding, I had met you several times and knew you were man enough to not be bothered by pretty things."

Clarence got up, picked her up, and gave her a huge hug and kiss on the cheek. He said, "If Stella loves it and it makes her happy, we can paint my car purple." We all got a big laugh from that.

I kissed Mrs. Peterson and told her I loved it so much that I wouldn't want to crawl out of bed on cold mornings. She said the comforter was down filled, and she had her friend make it so it should last many years. The other blanket would be just right for these summer nights.

We had so many beautiful new things, I didn't think we would ever have to buy anything again. We had a whole new bedroom set, new sheets, a new dish towel set, oven mitts, and dozens of new fluffy towels, as well as a new set of dishes. Clarence had picked up a few things at the secondhand store when he first got the room, but very few things matched. Our new dishes were so pretty. They had little yellow roses all around the edges. Clarence said his boss remembered him coming to work the next morning after painting the room and kitchen and he still had paint in his hair. So he know what color to have his wife buy. And the best thing, our new beautiful bedspread had tiny yellow roses here and there around all the big purple flowers of many shades of purple.

It was like everyone went shopping together so that our whole little apartment matched. I was just so excited. I was hugging Annie and Mrs. Peterson over and over—between kissing Clarence, of course. I said, "We are going to have the prettiest apartment ever."

Annie had bought four of the really fluffy towels and then had our initials sewn on the ends. I had never seen this before and just could not get over how pretty they were. Another set that was really pretty had "His" and "Hers" sewn on them. It was all just too much and too exciting.

"Is all this going to fit in our car, honey?" I asked.

Clarence said, "I'll pack it very carefully in the backseat and in the trunk."

About the time we finished carrying out everything and getting it all squeezed in, Kathleen came in and said, "Hey, where are all the gifts? I didn't get to see a thing." We told her how sorry we were and told her to come over to our apartment and Clarence could fry her the best chicken dinner she ever ate. She asked if she could bring her new man. We told her she could bring everyone in the house, and then she wouldn't have to cook that night. "Sounds like a plan to me, but I need to get back in the kitchen and watch to see my danish doesn't burn. I made a whole big new batch for you two lovebirds to take home with you."

Clarence went over, picked her up, twirled her around, and kissed both cheeks.

She laughed and said, "You'd better watch out. I happen to know a judge that might not like that." And into the kitchen she fled.

Mrs. Peterson excused herself and said she was going up to her room for just a little bit to freshen up for dinner. I'm sure Kathleen outdid herself.

Clarence and I were alone sitting in the parlor with Annie, and she got real excited and told us that Mike had asked her to marry him last night.

I said, "Well, how did you answer him?"

She got kind of quiet, as if she was worried someone might hear. She said, "I told him I loved him and didn't ever want to marry anyone else, but I can't just leave Mrs. Peterson here all by herself."

I said, "Kathleen is here."

But Annie said that was just not enough. "I am the one that helps her with so many little things that no one else could do."

Clarence and I both looked at each other, and then I said, "What did Mike say?"

"He said he could wait as long as I needed; after all, it's only been six weeks today since we met."

I said, "Oh my, how the time flies when you're having fun." I told her I knew the first time I saw Clarence that I wanted to marry him, and he spoke up and said the feeling was mutual. "Love doesn't happen that fast for all, so you'd better not keep him waiting too awfully long."

Mrs. Peterson came in at that very moment and said, "Keep who waiting?"

Annie got very quiet, and Clarence and I certainly weren't going to answer.

Mrs. Peterson stood there with a rather stern look on her face and said, "Well, who's being kept waiting?" for the second time.

Finally, Annie spoke up and said, "Mike asked me to marry him last night, and I told him someday I would, but not now."

She said, "You listen to me, young lady. You have been cooped up in this place without a boyfriend or any man since you have been grown, and I won't have you staying around here on my account."

Annie got up, hugged her, and told her she just couldn't leave her or here.

I laughed and said, "Oh, now, I know the real reason."

Annie looked at me strangely and said, "Why?"

"You just don't want to leave that paradise on top of the world."

She laughed and said, "Well, that would be awfully hard."

Mrs. Peterson said, "Listen to me, Annie. You have been in this house with no one but Kathleen and I for eleven years now. It's about time you had a life of your own. You're almost twenty-six years old, and it's about time you start raising a family. You tell Mike tomorrow that you would love to marry him—if that's what you want, of course."

Annie said with tears in her eyes that she loved him very much, but she just could not leave Mrs. Peterson by herself.

Mrs. Peterson said, "I was here alone with just Kathleen and I for quite a few years when you came along like a little lost lamb. Kathleen and I will be just fine."

Annie said, "What if Judge Daniels asks Kathleen to get married? Then where would you be?"

"Kathleen and I have already discussed that, and it has been settled. She says she has no desire to get married, and she and the judge have talked about that, and he says he is not ready for anything like that yet. He loved his first wife with all his heart and soul, and for now it's just nice to have a very nice woman to go to dinner with once in a while and out to the theater and things like that, which are no fun to do alone. But he has a life away from here. He has three children and seven grandchildren and another one on the way, and 'I sure don't want to be taking care of a bunch of kids,' Kathleen said. We had a good laugh at that. So my sweet darling Annie, you tell that man of yours, yes, you will marry him. I think I did pretty good having ten days to plan a wedding. Just think what I can do in, say, six months!"

Annie laughed and said, "I knew you weren't in a hurry to get rid of me."

I laughed and told them I didn't think either one of them was wanting to get rid of the other—one just fell in love.

Mrs. Peterson spoke up and said, "Oh, by the way, Miss Annie, your wedding present is all upstairs in your room. I'll have everything in your room shipped to your place with Mike. Hope he is as much a man as Clarence and doesn't mind purple."

"He loves my room."

At that Mrs. Peterson said, "What?"

Annie quickly said, "I only took him up there to show him my room, for at most three minutes. You know me better than that," and they went to each other and hugged. They were more like mother and daughter than anything else, and I know they felt that way; it was so evident in everything they said to each other.

The only thing I wondered about, and being me couldn't keep my thoughts to myself, so I finally worked up the nerve and asked, "Why is it that Annie has never been to any of your parties and introduced as I was?"

Mrs. Peterson answered, "It was what Annie wanted. She was so shy as a teenager, and I always thought that she was worried someone might be here who would recognize her."

Annie said, "You know me better than I know myself."

Kathleen came in and said dinner would be ready in a few minutes.

Mrs. Peterson said, "Kathleen, would you mind setting the table for two more, please?"

"Of course; whatever you say."

We all went into the dining room, and Annie headed for the kitchen.

"Annie, ask Kathleen if she will come in here please," said Mrs. Peterson. Kathleen was there in seconds. Mrs. Peterson continued, "I think it is about time we all eat together. Kathleen and Annie, bring all the food in here, and we will pass it around, just like a normal family. You see, I know these things as I was in a normal family growing up, until I met my Harry, and he had always been raised to be served, which is fine, but I feel that we are all family here and should eat together."

Kathleen said, "What about Tony? He will be coming for his meal in just a little bit."

Mrs. Peterson said, "I know him well enough to know he would not come in here and sit with us without being chained to the table. I don't know much about him, except he is a very quiet and private man. After we have our soup, you can fix his meal real quick, and as always, make sure to give him plenty."

Kathleen said, "I always do." She smiled like she had just let something out of the bag.

"I know you do, Kathleen; I was just reminding you since you will be hurrying."

I could see how excited Kathleen and Annie both were. Annie often ate with Mrs. Peterson, but Kathleen always stayed in the kitchen and served. She said that was what she was hired to do.

In just a matter of minutes, Kathleen and Annie had carried all the dinner into the dining room and set things on the table.

After they took their seats at the table, Mrs. Peterson said, "I would like to say a quick blessing on this special meal now." We all took one another's hands and bowed our heads. She began by saying, "Heavenly Father, please bless everyone at this table as they are all so special to me, and I know in my heart that each person here is a Christian and loves you as I do. Please take care of our troops being sent overseas to fight a war I don't understand, but we pray it won't last long. Let them capture this man they call Hitler, so that things can return to normal. Bless this meal prepared by our own special Kathleen and bring happiness to Stella and Clarence for all their married life and let Annie find happiness with Mike. In Jesus's name, Amen."

We all repeated Amen and began passing plates of delicious-looking food around; each of us filled our plates with roasted chicken and dressing, mashed potatoes, candied yams, homegrown green beans, and fresh homemade yeast rolls along with butter and jams made by Kathleen, of course. As we all started eating and talking and laughing, I thought to myself, this is how all families should share their meals. The thought had no sooner left my head when Clarence spoke up and said this was how his family always had their dinners, and he really missed his mom and dad and all his younger brothers and sisters. He said he hoped before too long he and I would start a family. I said, "I second that!"

Annie quietly said, "This is the only family I've ever had, and I think you are all pretty wonderful."

Kathleen said that she couldn't complain about anything, because growing up she had spent many dinners like this with her family. She said, "We were all so close, but then when both my parents died, my brothers were both married and moved to other areas with their new wives, and I just decided, 'I'm going to America,' so here I am, and I've been made to feel a part of this family every since."

Now it was Mrs. Peterson's turn to talk, and she said when she was growing up, her father, whom she adored, worked long hard hours, and when he was at home, it was usually time for her to go to bed. "Mother fixed the meals, and I sat and ate while she fixed a plate for Dad. I guess Mom would eat as she was cooking; she rarely sat down to the table and ate with me. Once in a while, Daddy would be home on a Sunday, and that was the only time we dined together.

Meals were always quiet, as Mother said, 'We are at the table to eat, not chitchat.' My dad would come up and tuck me in and tell me how much he loved me, and I knew he did. My mother loved me to, but she was a very quiet woman and never really showed her emotions, so I looked forward to Daddy coming home at night.

"I studied hard in school, so I could get a good job, but I no sooner got my college degree, when I was in town one day and my whole life changed. I met my Harry, and it was a whirlwind, perfect romance. We had a beautiful wedding, and my father walked me down the aisle. Both my parents were older when then finally had me, their only child! And they didn't live long enough for me to even have them over to my beautiful home for dinner. You see, Harry and I were so much in love, and we took a long honeymoon and life turned into heaven for me, except while we were gone, my dad had a stroke, and Mom died shortly after. So it was always just Harry and I, until Kathleen came along, and we always treated her like family. We tried to get her to sit and have meals with us, but she said she was doing her job and wanted to do it right."

Kathleen chimed in and said, "Now you know how very much I love you and Mr. Peterson."

Mrs. Peterson said, "Of course, we always knew how you felt, my dear Kathleen. And you, sweet Annie, are like my own daughter, and I hope you know that. You will have a beautiful wedding, and it will be such a happy day for all of us."

For dessert, we had a delicious golden cake with fluffy icing on it that was just heavenly!

While Clarence and I were driving home, we talked about how truly special Mrs. Peterson, Kathleen, and Annie were to us.

I said, "If not for Mrs. Peterson, there is no telling what might have happened to me; I might never have found you. Oh, I just can't think of how awful that would have been; I am so very happy. I just wish that we had Tony to help carry all these beautiful gifts into our little home. He managed to load them all in our car in what seemed like minutes. I can't help but wonder why he is so quiet and private about his life. Something terrible must have happened to him for him to just stay in his room all the time; I think it must have been something like Annie's terrible childhood. What else could possibly make him like that?"

Clarence patted me on the leg and said, "Honey, it could be a lot of reasons we don't know. You are just so loving and care so much about everyone—that is why I know you are going to be the best mother to our children, and I hope we have a bunch of them."

I said, "Me too, but I don't think I want twelve like my mama had."

Clarence said, "That is a lot for sure."

We pulled up in front of our home and started unloading the carful of our wonderful presents. I was so happy and excited that it didn't seem hard at all. When we finally had everything in, we realized how small our little room was.

I said, "This is going to be a job, figuring where to put all this."

Clarence said, "I think it's time to find larger housing." We both laughed, and he continued, "We'll see how things are after we've put this all in its place. I do hate to think of moving already, especially since overtime has slowed down and work seems to be slowing down, period! But don't worry, honey; I've promised to always take care of you, and that is a promise I will never break. I love you more every minute that we are together."

We stood there looking at each other, and in seconds we both had our clothes off and were in the shower washing each other in every possible place. I loved exploring his body, just as much as he did mine. When we were all dried off, we got into our bed and made love over and over during the night. We just couldn't get enough of each other. Just a slight touch during the night would have us awake and making love again. Our love was so beautiful. Sometimes I just lay there in our bed and wondered, how did I get so lucky as to have our tent next to Clarence's?

The next morning, as soon as Clarence left for work, I starting rearranging everything in our kitchen with all of our new items. Everything we no longer needed, I put to one side. I thought that more than likely, they could be of use for a while longer to someone else with little money, as Clarence was when trying to save every penny he could to send to me.

When Clarence came home after work, we could take them back to the secondhand store and donate them. That was the right thing to do.

After I finished the kitchen, I took our new sheets and towels and walked around the corner to the laundry place. I washed them all and then put them in the drying machine. I couldn't wait to get back and get them on our bed. I had been working so hard and so fast that I forgot to eat anything. By the time I folded everything and walked back with my arms loaded, I thought I would pass out. I guess the past few months had made me soft. I wasn't used to hard work anymore. I lay down for a few minutes and then got up and made myself a quick sandwich. After eating I felt much better. I quickly took off the sheets on the bed and remade it with all of our new things. It looked so beautiful. I went into the bathroom and took all the old towels down and hung our fresh new ones with "His" and "Hers" on them. It made me shiver with happiness. I looked around, and everything looked so different and so beautiful that Clarence would think he had come to the wrong room. I giggled at the thought. He would be so pleased that I had done so much today.

Then I remembered I had better think of something for dinner. There were a couple of pork chops in the icebox; I took them out and added salt and pepper as I had watched Clarence do. Then I peeled a few potatoes, cut them up, and put them on to fry and then started cooking the chops in another pan. I was learning these things pretty quickly, and it also helped that Clarence was so easy to please. As long as he had potatoes and gravy, he was a happy man. I watched the chops and potatoes closely, so they wouldn't burn. I glanced around the room and was so happy with the way these things had changed the look. It had looked just fine before, but now it looked beautiful. I hoped Clarence was as happy with everything as I was.

Just as I put some green beans on to cook, Clarence walked in the door. He came over to me and said, "How in the world did you get all this done in one day all by yourself?"

I told him I just worked hard and did it.

He said it looked like a room fit for a king and queen.

I said, "Well, what do you think we are?"

He swung me around and kissed me, and then I said, "The dinner is going to burn." He said, "Oh, my love, how quickly you change." I kissed him quickly and said I hadn't changed at all, but we couldn't afford to be burning up food if we were going to get a larger place. He agreed and said he was starving anyway, so his stomach was taking first place for now.

He started making the gravy after making sure the chops were done. Within a matter of a half hour, all the food had been eaten and the dishes washed. I asked if we could run all these things over to the secondhand store and donate them. He kissed me again and said what a big heart I had. I said I just thought how great it was that he had found a few things that we needed, and now maybe someone else might need them. So we loaded up the car and ran them up there.

They were very pleased and remembered Clarence very well. They said, "So this is your beautiful girl you talked about nonstop." He smiled, put his arm around me, and said, "This is Stella, my wife now." They asked if he didn't need this stuff anymore, and he told them about all our great wedding presents. They said they were so happy for us and someone else would be happy to get these things for a bargain again. They thanked us very much, and then we drove back to our new home.

Clarence went in to take a shower, and I was right behind him since I had worked so hard today. We just stood there soaping each other and kissing mostly. Before long, one thing led to another, and we made love in the shower again. Afterward we washed up again, got out, and dried on our new towels.

Clarence asked if there was anything I wanted to do tonight. I said, "Whatever you want to do is fine with me." Together, we pulled down the fancy bedspread, and Clarence picked me up as if this were our first night and carefully laid me on our beautiful new sheets. He just stood there staring at me and finally said, "Stella Rader, do you have any idea how happy you have made me?" I said, "Probably about as happy as you have made me. Sometimes when I am here by myself during the day, I just think how short a time it has been, really, since we first met outside of our tents, and how lucky I am that you had the tent next to ours. I shiver at the thought of that day never happening. Sometimes I think this must all be some magically made-up fairy tale."

He lay down next to me and ran his hands up and down my body, then said, "Does this feel real?"

I reached down and felt the hardness pressed up against my body and said, "Oh, yes, this is definitely real; it's no fairy tale."

After an hour or so, I still lay there touching his body and feeling how strong he was. Muscles just rippled his whole body. He said he had always worked hard and played sports as a kid and in college.

I told him how much I envied the fact that he was always able to go to school. And then that reminded me that he had received a letter from Oklahoma today. I said, "I am so sorry, but in the excitement and being in such a hurry all day, it completely slipped my mind." I ran over to the desk and brought it to him.

He started reading it without even thinking, and then said, "I'm sorry, honey, this is yours just as much as mine." He started over and read it to me. His mother and daddy were just so happy for us, and all his brothers and sisters wanted to know when we could come home to meet them. The letter went on to say that they were so happy that Clarence had found a woman who truly made him this happy. His mom said she could tell by even the way he wrote that he was different and finally complete. Now they were just looking forward to a bunch of grandbabies.

I spoke up and said, "No more than I am."

He rolled over and said, "I guess we'd better work on that."

We both laughed and just lay there talking about how many children we wanted. We both agreed that we would have as many as the good Lord gave us, and we didn't care whether we had boys or girls first, so long as they were healthy. And another thing we always talked about was how we were going to see to it that they had everything they could possibly want within reason, of course. He said he had a very nice childhood; comparing it to mine, he said his was perfect. I agreed mine could not have been much worse. I said I really didn't want to think of those terrible times right now when I was filled to the brim with happiness and it was all him. We just lay there holding each other for a while and saying nothing; just feeling was enough.

After a while I remembered the new radio that someone had bought us. We set it on the night table next to our bed, and Clarence said it was a really nice one. He tuned in a baseball game and said, "Yes, very nice." I said, "Seriously, are you going to lie here and listen to a whole baseball game?" He fell back and laughed about the hardest I'd ever heard him laugh. I said, "What is so funny?" He said he just wished he'd had this when he was lying here alone night after night worrying himself sick about where I was or what might be happening to me. "Now I have a radio and a beautiful wife I can't keep my hands off of, and I have to decide which is more important." I really punched him at that, and he laughed again and said he would find some news or some music, whichever I preferred. I said, "Music would be nice for a while, and I don't care if you listen to ball games once in a while. We can take turns; that's the only fair thing to do."

Weeks went by so fast that before we knew it, we had been married close to three months. We lay there listening to our new radio on our new bed that had been delivered weeks ago. Such a special present from Mrs. Peterson! It had been fun the day we went and picked it out, lying on one bed, then another, until we both agreed on one that was just right for both of us.

I said, "Do you think on Saturday, we could go and visit for just a little while and see how the wedding plans are coming along?"

Clarence said, "Sure, honey, I was just thinking we needed to go and thank her personally for such a great present and tell her how much we are enjoying it." He laughed and said, "I mean how well we are sleeping on this very comfortable new bed she bought for us. My back never hurts from all the lumps anymore. Of course, you knew what I meant—you just have a one-track mind, and it's not on comfort."

I rolled over, felt him, and said, "I think someone else's mind is on other things than the lumps that were in that old mattress."

So there we were again, enjoying our new bed in every way possible.

Saturday came, and we slept in a little, then woke up feeling hungry for food and for each other as usual, and as usual, we satisfied ourselves first. We made a big breakfast and ate till we couldn't hold another bite—like there was anything left to eat. We both did the dishes; I washed, and Clarence dried. I kept some of our old dishes because I wanted to keep the good ones for dinners and company. I always tried to make the dinner table look real pretty for when Clarence came in the door to a beautiful room and something good cooking. I was learning more each week. I even bought a cookbook at the secondhand bookstore, where I loved spending my mornings after everything was cleaned up. It had some different things to cook, but it seemed like we always went back to the old faithfuls.

We got in the car and drove over to Mrs. Peterson's. Outside, Tony was washing the limo. He even looked happy to see us. We went up the stairs and rang the bell. We waited only seconds. It was as if they knew we were coming and were standing at the door. Within minutes, Kathleen and Mrs. Peterson were in the foyer, and we were all hugging and kissing and Kathleen was asking if we were hungry. We assured her we were still stuffed from a late breakfast.

We stood there for just a moment more before Mrs. Peterson said, "Oh, you have news for us, I can tell."

We both said at the same time that we loved our new bed and we wanted to thank her in person.

She said, "That's wonderful, but I mean the real news." We both looked confused, and she said, "Don't be coy with me. I can tell; Stella has a glow all over her."

Clarence looked at me and said I was just as beautiful as always.

CHAPTER 11

We're having a Baby

Mrs. Peterson said, "I've been around a long time, kids, and I'm telling you that Stella is expecting a baby."

We both looked at each other and said, "Well, I guess it's possible."

Clarence added, "If not, it's not for lack of trying."

I punched him, and I know my face was twenty shades of red.

Mrs. Peterson said, "Listen, Stella, I've been a bride, and I know what goes on. I'm not that old, but I still assure you that you are pregnant."

I went into the parlor and tried to count in my mind when I'd had my last period; I was definitely a couple of weeks late, but I just hadn't thought about it. I turned to Clarence and said, "Honey, I think she is right. We are the last to know. There have just been so many things going on that I haven't kept track of my periods. Now that I am counting back, I think I'm about three weeks late, so we're going to have a baby."

Annie and Kathleen were dancing around like a couple of schoolkids, and Mrs. Peterson and Clarence were doing a bit of a jig themselves. So we all knew about the same time.

"It's a good thing we came over," Clarence said. "Stella might have been as big as a basketball before we knew it."

I said, "I think I would have noticed a while sooner than that."

Mrs. Peterson said, "I will make you an appointment with my doctor. He is wonderful, and you will love him."

Clarence said, "I need to check with my boss and see if our plan covers babies."

"Of course it does if you have insurance," Mrs. Peterson said.

He said he did. So now they just all stood around looking stunned and excited at the same time.

I said, "You know, I have been feeling awfully hungry lately. Kathleen, you don't have any danish left from breakfast by any chance, do you?"

She said, "Is the Pope Catholic?" At that she took off for the kitchen, yelling if I wanted tea or coffee with those danish.

I said, "Some tea for me, and maybe a big glass of milk too."

Everyone was laughing. All of a sudden it got stone-cold quiet, and Clarence came over and sat down next to me and put his hand on my stomach. He looked at me and said, "We really are going to have a baby." I nodded, and he leaned over and gave me the sweetest soft kiss, like I would break all of a sudden. "Life couldn't get any better than this," he said, with a tear rolling down his cheek. Again he said, "Really?" I said, "Really!"

We only stayed for just long enough to have tea and danish—and my milk, of course! Now I had to remember to drink plenty of it. We visited for just a little while. They all begged us to stay for dinner, but we said we really needed to go and get some laundry done. We just wanted to be alone right now; we didn't tell them that, but I'm sure they knew. It was such a special time for us.

As we lay in bed that evening after dinner, Clarence just kept touching me so carefully. I told him that nothing had to change with our lovemaking or anything as far as that was concerned. As an example, I told him my mother had twelve children and worked herself to an old woman already and she really wasn't that old. She was only in her forties but looked to be at least sixty already. It was because she had been beaten so many times and mistreated in every way possible all her married life—mentally, physically, and verbally abused constantly. I told Clarence that I knew I would never go through any of that; I would just be a normal happy pregnant woman with an adoring husband. And I knew he would be the best father ever to our children.

He assured me that was all so very true. We made love, and it was so beautiful and sweet that it almost made me cry. As we lay there as close together as two people could be in every way, we fell asleep as content as we could possibly be, feeling such happiness knowing we were going to be parents.

I wrote to my mama the next day, a nice long letter telling her how happy Clarence and I were at the fact we had just discovered we were going to have our first baby; we could not be any happier if someone had given us a million dollars. "This baby is so much more important than money." I asked about all my brothers and sisters and told her to tell them I missed them so much, "and also I miss you, Mama. But I am so happy. I never believed I would have such a perfect happy marriage after all I had been through. It breaks my heart that you are all going through this life still. I pray, Mama, that things will get better for you. How can Daddy stay so mean for so many years, I wonder?."

I mailed this letter to Lola, told her to read it first, and make sure she got it to Mama when Daddy wasn't around. I knew she would.

As the next couple of months went by, we visited Mrs. Peterson and everyone on a more regular basis. It was so wonderful having people who loved us and were so happy for us.

I told them that I had just received a letter from my mama, and she was so happy for Clarence and me. She said Daddy was just the same and probably always would be, but she also told me she was pregnant again also. Just a little further along than I was. She said Maxine, W. K., and Velma missed me so much; Garner was too young to know the difference. I really thought that Garner would be her last baby. How much could one little body take? I realized for the first time how really strong my mama had to be to go through all she did and still find good in things. She felt so strongly about the Lord, and I'm sure it was God who gave her all of her strength within; inside she knew it was all going to be okay.

Mrs. Peterson said, "I just don't know how she does it. The poor dear having another baby at her age. As badly as my Harry and I had wanted children, I don't think I could have had twelve."

Annie agreed. She said that she and Mike had already decided that they thought two would be plenty to have, and be able to give them all they wanted.

I said I was glad the wedding was soon, or I wouldn't be able to fit into my bridesmaid dress. I laughed and told her I would try to quit eating so much.

She said, "I don't think you're eating that much; you don't even seem to be gaining any weight."

I told her that hopefully I would be one of those women who got their figure right back after their little bundle was born.

Before we knew it, Thanksgiving was coming upon us, and Mrs. Peterson said we would be at her house for Thanksgiving dinner, and she would hear no different. So that's where we spent our first Thanksgiving.

Clarence told me his mother was the best cook, and they always had a big turkey and all the trimmings. We had no idea if that was what they cooked at the Peterson house, but we would be finding out tomorrow. We kept offering to bring something, but she wouldn't hear of it. She said everything was taken care of, and help was coming in for Kathleen, as much as she complained about it.

So Thursday we showed up with a pretty bunch of fall-colored flowers. We knew she would have a beautiful centerpiece, but we had to bring something. She said she loved them and put them in a vase immediately before they could wilt; to our surprise, she then put them right in the center of the beautifully decorated dining table. Of course, Mrs. Peterson had different china for Thanksgiving. It was so pretty with fall colors, and in the center was a cute little turkey.

Mike showed up a few minutes later, and Annie was so excited every time she saw him. She could hardly wait for their wedding right after Christmas on January 14. They wanted to get married before Christmas, but Mrs. Peterson said it just couldn't be arranged that soon. Too much to do and too many things to pick out and the time would fly. And it was flying by fast.

Kathleen said dinner was ready, so we all headed for the dining room. What a feast we had before us. Clarence said, "I thought my mother fixed a lot, but it was nothing compared to this." There was the biggest turkey I had ever seen. Of course I had really never seen one cooked except in pictures, and all over the stores they had pictures of dinner tables, turkey fixed with all the trimmings, but they hadn't seen this table. Besides the huge turkey, we had mashed potatoes, stuffing, gravy, candied yams, and several different kinds of salads—a fruit salad, a regular green salad, and a couple of Jell-O molds with different things in them—and then of course, we had a mountain of yeast rolls.

After saying the blessing and going all around the table so all of us could say what we were thankful for, we started passing everything around the table. A large man came out dressed in a tux. He took the turkey over to the buffet and had it carved and sliced beautifully in a matter of minutes. It was then passed around also. Dinner was just as delicious as every other meal we had eaten there. Nothing but perfection for Mrs. Peterson, and no one deserved it more. She was the sweetest lady ever. As we told her over and over, we would never be able to repay her. She said it was her pleasure to do all she had done for us. Within a half hour we were all so stuffed we felt like that turkey must have felt not long ago in the oven. When the maid came in with three kinds of pies, we all agreed they were going to have to wait. So she set them on the buffet and left.

We all went into the parlor and said we needed a nap. But instead, we discussed Christmas. We made them all promise on their lives that we would not be exchanging gifts because we had to save all our money for this new baby, and there was hardly any left each week for even that. So everyone agreed that Christmas would be just another day of friends getting together and enjoying each other's company and celebrating our Lord's birth, as it should be.

After an hour or so passed, we headed back to the dining room for pie and coffee. Kathleen had made apple, pumpkin, and mincemeat, so we all had to try a little of each, and more of our favorite. Mine was the apple; Clarence loved them all but wanted more mincemeat. What a wonderful day it had been, and in just barely four weeks, we would be doing it all again.

I said I wasn't sure about getting into my bridesmaid dress after all this. Annie said, "Oh, Stella, you barely have a bump there." I said, "Yes, but it's six weeks till the wedding." She said the dress had a full chiffon skirt and would hide it all. I hoped so.

On Annie's wedding day, we were all dressed to the nines. Mrs. Peterson had planned the wedding of the decade. Everyone in town was invited, I think. Not really, but it was a large wedding. Clarence, Tony, and of course Mike were all in tuxedos. Mrs. Peterson, Kathleen, and I were all in beautiful rose-pink dresses, all different styles, yet still looking alike for the most part.

I think Annie was more nervous than I had been, if that was possible. As we helped her dress, she kept laughing, then crying.

Mrs. Peterson said to her, quite sternly, yet in a motherly fashion, "Listen, missy, I'm paying a lot of money for my special hair lady to come to do your hair and makeup, and I won't have you making a mess of it. She will do the rest of us first, so you can have some quiet time and rest before the wedding."

Annie promised to compose herself. Kathleen and I went to my old room, and the hair lady came and fixed my hair, then Kathleen's; she then went to Mrs. Peterson's room, where she had been resting.

After Mrs. Peterson was finished, we all went into the other guest room on the second floor, where Annie was dressing. We all looked at one another and bragged about how gorgeous we were. I laughed and said, "We aren't too proud, are we?" Mrs. Peterson said we had a right to be proud and brag. "Look at us; we couldn't look any better if we tried," she added.

When Annie got into her dress, we all just stood there in amazement. She looked like an angel, blond curls and all. Her dress took up half of the room.

Mrs. Peterson said, "Oh dear, what was I thinking? We should have dressed in the church. How in the world are you going to get that beautiful dress in the limo? Tony will have to take us first and come back for you. It will only take a few minutes to drive back and get you. Now it's time for the four must-haves."

Annie said, "Well, I'm all new, so that's taken care of."

Kathleen stepped as close to her as she could and gave her a beautiful beaded coin purse; she said, "This is your something old. It was my mother's, and I have always treasured it. Now I want you to have it; I know you will treasure it as I have." As Annie started to say something, Kathleen stopped her and said, "You remember, no more tears; we are all too beautiful." That made us all laugh as we were about to tear up.

I stepped forward and gave her a fancy blue garter to wear, which, of course, the groom would throw out to all the bachelors later at the reception. Then I handed her my pearls and said she could borrow them for the wedding. "Just put them in your beautiful coin purse for good luck. So now you have something old, something new, something borrowed, and something blue, so you're set."

Mrs. Peterson said, "Not quite yet." She got as close to Annie as she could and said, "Don't you dare cry, or I will and we'll all be a mess. Just take my wedding gift to you and love it as I always have." She stepped around behind Annie and fastened her diamond necklace around her neck. "Now everything is perfect. You are my daughter in all ways that matter. In our hearts. And this is my and Harry's gift to you." Annie looked in the mirror at herself and started to tear up. Mrs. Peterson said, "Don't you dare, I said."

Tony came to the door, walked each one of us to the limo, and said to each of us separately how beautiful we looked. When he had all three of us in the car, he drove us to the church, around to the side door where we could enter privately. He then left to go back for Annie. It took at least fifteen minutes for them to return, and we were starting to panic. Tony apologized, but said it took several minutes to get Miss Annie in the limo and make sure her dress didn't get any wrinkles. "I had to have her stand up, and I got in and made sure she sat carefully so as not to make a mess anywhere on her beautiful dress. I knew you would want that, Mrs. Peterson." She looked at Tony and thanked him so much for being so thoughtful. Tony had been so different since Annie had asked him to walk her down the aisle. He said he had never been so honored to do something in his whole life.

First Mrs. Peterson was walked down the aisle and placed in the mother of the bride's place, just as she had been at my wedding. Then Kathleen and the judge walked down together and stepped up on the first step on separate sides of the church as they had practiced. Then it was my and Clarence's turn to walk down and step up on the next step, Clarence next to Mike as his best man.

Then the "Wedding March" started to play. Tony and Annie stood at the back of the church for just a few seconds, long enough for the people to stand and turn to watch the bride being walked down the aisle. Mike looked like he was going to run to her, he was so excited. As soon as they got to the steps, Mike walked down and took her hand.

The minister said, "Who gives this bride to be married?"

Tony said in a very refined deep voice, "I do." Tony then took a seat next to Mrs. Peterson.

Then Mike and Annie walked back up the steps to the minister. After all was finished, all the vows said, and Mike had kissed his bride, they turned and were introduced for the first time as Mr. and Mrs. Michael Adams.

Everyone clapped as they walked down the aisle to get into the limo to be taken to the huge ballroom at the finest hotel in town. It was a wedding fit for a princess. But I loved our smaller wedding more. The only thing I wished different was that we had remembered a photographer. It would be etched in our minds forever anyway.

There were several photographers taking pictures all over the place for Annie's wedding, and the cake was big enough to feed everyone in town I think. It had five layers, the bottom layer had to be at least three feet in diameter, and each layer was three layers deep, so you can just imagine how tall it was. It was so delicious—a white cake with a lemon custard filling. Each layer had a different flavor filling between the layers. It tasted incredible! But we had eaten so much food before, it was all I could do to finish my piece. Clarence had a few bites to help me.

There were so many presents at the house and twice that many at the church. It would take Tony five trips to get them all back to the house.

Mike and Annie were going to fly to Jamaica tonight for three weeks. Another gift from Mrs. Peterson, of course.

When Mike took off her garter and tossed it over his head, of all people to catch it was the judge. And of course, Kathleen caught the bouquet. But they both insisted they were just good friends who loved each other's company.

It was a perfect wedding, and everyone had a wonderful time dancing and eating and dancing some more. Mrs. Peterson looked very tired, and I was worried about her. Clarence said he thought she was just going to miss Annie so much, and it was just hitting her that Annie was actually gone. I wasn't so sure. I asked her if she would like Clarence and I to come over for a while after the wedding, but she said she felt way too tired. She was just going to take a long hot bath and fall asleep without her usual reading. So Clarence and I went home.

The next few days, I kept worrying about how Mrs. Peterson was, so finally we decided we would drive over again on Saturday to check on her. It was nearly noon by the time we arrived there after doing all our morning chores.

Kathleen answered and said that Mrs. Peterson was lying down.

I said, "Isn't that pretty strange for her this early in the day?"

Kathleen agreed it was not normal, but she had been extratired ever since the wedding.

I asked Kathleen if she was concerned. She said she had tried to get Mrs. Peterson to go see her doctor a few days ago, but she had just shrugged it off, saying she had just been working so hard on the wedding and also trying to keep up with her Red Cross work, and it had finally gotten to her. She insisted she would be fine when she caught up on her rest. The Red Cross had been a lot of extra work as the war continued to get worse over in Germany. "The talk of things over there is just plain scary if you ask me," Kathleen said. I agreed it was, as I had been listening to the news on the radio in the mornings while I cleaned up. I asked if Kathleen thought it would do any good for me to ask Mrs. Peterson to go to the doctor. She said, "No. If she thinks we're all ganging up on her, she'll have a fit." I said, "Yes, I know how independent she is."

Clarence and I had walked back to the kitchen with Kathleen when we first arrived, and sure enough, she started heating a pile of her danish.

I said, "What in the world do you do with all these if we don't come by or someone else doesn't drop in?"

Kathleen said she gave them to Tony, "and what he doesn't eat, he takes over to some homeless people he's been friends with for years."

I said, "I wonder if he was homeless at one time," and Kathleen said, "Yes, I've wondered the same thing many times. He has no family, and besides taking things like that and other leftovers I give him, he is just around here all the time. He fixes things for me from time to time here in the kitchen. I know Mrs. Peterson could afford to pay to have them fixed, but it makes him feel good to know he is helping, and he figures it pays for the things he take to his friends. Sometimes Mrs. Peterson doesn't go anywhere for days, and sometimes just on Sunday to church, so he has nothing to do but be on call and keep the limo spotless. And he does all this very well. I've never seen so much as a water spot on that car. You could eat off the seats and carpet as clean as he keeps them. I think he was so thankful for getting this job all those years ago, he wants to make sure he earns his keep. And he certainly does. I've never seen such a hard worker."

As we sat there eating the danish and drinking the tea, Mrs. Peterson walked in. She said when she came down the stairs, she thought she noticed a car out front that looked familiar. I got up and hugged her, and Clarence was on his feet the second she walked in. He gave her a big hug too, and then she said, "Come on out here to the parlor, and we can chat. You are welcome also, Kathleen." I could tell how less formal things had become since we had all become such great friends. But Kathleen still made sure that her work was always done and meals were on time. She talked about how hard Tony worked, but I think she had him beat by a bunch. But I also knew how much she loved her job. Cooking to her wasn't even work, she said, since she enjoyed it so much; she would go nuts without all the meals she fixed. I guess that's why she was so very good at it.

Mrs. Peterson asked what had brought us over to her side of town today, and I quickly told her we were just a little bored after all the wedding plans were over, so we came for a visit with our favorite person in the whole world.

She said, "Oh fiddle, you two are so in love, I doubt you get bored with each other so easily. You have just come to check up on me."

I said, "Okay, you caught us, but we just thought you looked extratired after the wedding."

She said, "Well, weren't you tired after all that?"

I said, "Oh my goodness, I danced till my feet felt like they were going to fall off. And there were so many people to talk with so as not to be rude. But I really didn't know half the people there. You were busy all day talking with everyone there and making sure everyone was introduced to one another. How in the world do you know so many people?"

She said with her Red Cross work, there were so many people she had to work with, and she was still on the board of Harry's business and that was a huge company. "I am in the process now of selling my shares of the company, as I am getting older, and I wouldn't want to leave anything left undone as I get older. Also, I want to let go before I'm just too old to do it and they force me out. I doubt they would ever do that, since Harry was loved by all, and they all knew how much he loved me and likewise. So I've always kept up on exactly what was happening in the business so that I knew how to vote on anything that might come up. They really think I should stay because I do so well at keeping everyone on their feet, but I just feel like it's time. But I do love the business and will always care what happens to Harry's company. Too bad we didn't have a son to take over, but we didn't, so that's that."

Clarence said that construction was really dropping off, and he wouldn't be surprised if they started laying some of the men off. "Maybe when Mike and Annie get back from their honeymoon, he could help you some. He is a very smart man and could probably learn anything fast."

I wasn't worried about Clarence too much, because a friend of his from college had just written him and asked if he could come and run his milk farm. The man that had been the foreman had been drafted. So we would be moving to Oregon if Clarence were laid off. I personally thought that Clarence was way too smart to be doing what he was doing and even to be running a milk farm, even though it was important that the farm was run well and people got their milk as times got rough. But Clarence was such a loyal friend, he felt obligated since he had been asked.

If it hadn't been for all Mrs. Peterson had already done for us, knowing us for such a short while when she paid for our whole wedding plus all she had bought me before Clarence was even found and all she bought us for wedding presents— if we had known her much longer, I would have suggested Clarence. He was brilliant as far as I was concerned. He graduated from Texas A&M at the top of his class and paid for all his own education except for his scholarship from high school. He had to work to pay for his living expenses and all that, plus he graduated as valedictorian of his class. But still, Clarence had never mentioned working for Mrs. Peterson's company, even when today would have been a perfect opportunity. He just wasn't that kind of man, and that was why I loved him so. Even though the thoughts were running through my head of how perfect he would be for her company, I would have been embarrassed had he asked for a job. It was just too much to ask of a woman who not only had taken such wonderful care of his bride-to-be; she went above and beyond by throwing us a dream wedding when we were about to go to the justice of the peace and get married.

This woman was a saint as far as we were both concerned. And we were both more worried about her now than before they got there. No matter how or what she was saying or the way she was putting it, the fact remained: she was putting her affairs in order. A woman who loved her work and enjoyed doing it all didn't just quit for no reason. Although she went on to say she was going to be rather bored when all the paperwork was finished and she had no more board meetings to go to, she still thought she was doing the best thing for Harry's company.

Clarence had just suggested Mike to work for the company, because he knew Mike would never say anything himself, even after being laid off and having a new bride. At least Mike was a somewhat son-in-law. Maybe not in fact, but for all that mattered he was. So the seed had been planted, and when Mike and Annie returned if he had no job, Mrs. Peterson just might remember what Clarence had said about him, which was all very true. Mike was a very smart man. After talking a while longer, we all said our good-byes, so as not to further tire Mrs. Peterson.

As we drove away from the house, we were both very quiet for a change.

After a short while, Clarence spoke up and said, "Are you thinking what I'm thinking?"

I said, "I'm afraid I am. She is putting her affairs in order, and I don't like the sound of that at all. She has been so special to both of us, and I don't want to lose her."

"Me either, honey, but there's not much we can do but visit more often."

I said, "I know! Why don't I ask if we can have just a family dinner for them when Mike and Annie are to return home? Kathleen would just be doing what she loves to do, and maybe us all being there would perk her up a little."

Clarence said that sounded like a good idea, so the plan was in motion. We would go visit again next Saturday, and I would say that why we came over was to ask about throwing a family party for Mike and Annie when they returned. We were so excited to hear all about their honeymoon, and also it would be so fun to watch them open some of their wedding presents. It would take them many days to open all the presents that were stacked up in the ballroom. But I knew from experience that it was more fun than work. Even though Annie had everything she could possibly want for the past eleven years, it was still fun to open gifts that were hers and Mike's.

I said, "I guess I'm taking things for granted that it would be just a family dinner since technically we aren't really family, but I really believe that Mrs. Peterson considers us family, don't you, honey?"

Clarence said, "Of course she does. She has shown us in every way possible since the first night I met her."

That made me feel better. If Clarence felt it too, then I knew it to be the truth. He was just too smart to think any different if it weren't so.

Saturday morning right after breakfast, we started out for the other side of town and were met quickly at the door by Kathleen. She said, "So what did we do to deserve a visit two weeks in a row from you newlyweds?" We said, "We had an idea we would like to run by Mrs. Peterson and you, of course." She said, "Come right in. Mrs. Peterson is just sitting out in the sunroom enjoying the beautiful day. Fall is in the air, but it's so pretty out today."

When we walked into the sunroom, Mrs. Peterson immediately perked up, which made us feel good. We got right to the point before she could think we were checking up on her again. She thought it sounded like a wonderful idea and was especially thrilled that we called ourselves family.

I said, "I hope it wasn't too much of us to say that."

She said, "Don't be silly; you two are a very important part of this family, isn't that so, Kathleen?"

"Definitely," Kathleen said. "They have been from day one. I fell in love with Stella when she used to come down early and spend time with me in the kitchen."

Clarence asked, "Why the heck didn't you teach her to make those danish?"

Kathleen laughed and said, "We didn't have that much time, and they were always already made when she got up. I am an early bird, and it takes not only time, but lots of experience to learn to make them right. I started watching my mother when I was just barely high enough to see the countertop. She would slowly show me each process. I guess by the time I finished high school, I had learned the art pretty well. If not for wanting to learn all that Mother could teach me, I might not have learned before she suddenly died just before I was to go away to college. Within weeks, my father died. Of a broken heart, they said. He and my mother had always loved each other beyond anything the rest of us could conceive. My older brothers were both married and lived a ways from our home, and I had always wanted to go to America. So I did. And I've not been sorry for even a day. So now we must decide what to have for our dinner feast when Mike and Annie get home. I haven't fixed enough meals for Mike to know his favorites."

Clarence told her he had gone for meals with him enough to know that Mike loved everything as long as it was food.

So Kathleen said she would decide, and we would all love it, she promised.

The next weekend Mike and Annie returned home as expected on Friday night. A note had been left for them to come right over to Mrs. Peterson's on Saturday afternoon. They showed up right after lunch, which they said they figured was "afternoon."

We were there already and told them of the family dinner for them that Kathleen was making special and no one was allowed in the kitchen.

Mrs. Peterson came rushing in and hugged Annie and told her how much she missed her. Then she hugged Mike and said she was so happy they were back. "It seemed like three months instead of three weeks."

Annie started rambling on sixty miles an hour talking about how beautiful it was and what a wonderful time they had. We all laughed and said it was so good to see them and it had seemed like a long time. Mike said it seemed to them that they had just left. He said the days flew by so fast, and on Thursday night they couldn't believe they had to leave already the next morning.

Clarence and I had already half filled the parlor with gifts, with the help of Tony. When we all walked in, Annie's eyes got really big, and she said, "Are all these ours?" We laughed and said this was only about a quarter of the presents. She said, "Can we start opening now, or do we have to wait until after dinner?" Mrs. Peterson said, "You can start in just a few minutes, after I call in the crew." She stuck her head in the kitchen and told Kathleen to get Tony.

In a couple of minutes, we were all sitting around them and told them to start. Clarence was writing down the presents and who they were from. I told them that way they would be able to read the list.

Annie starting tearing into the packages, and they just couldn't believe all the beautiful things they were getting. They had a waffle iron and six different toasters (I guessed they would be returning some and having store credits). "You have so many sets of beautiful fluffy towels," I said, "you shouldn't have to buy any for the rest of your lives." There were many beautiful figurines with fancy names I wasn't familiar with, beautiful sets of Waterford glasses, and a gorgeous decanter to match one of the sets. I think it came with a pretty set of brandy snifters, whatever that means. They had very nice things to hang on walls and pretty throw rugs for bathrooms and the kitchen, and a few really fancy ones for foyers or parlors, I presumed.

I guess people thought they would have a house as big as this. Oh well, the thoughts were certainly meant well, I'm sure. They had a lovely set of everyday dishes and a full set of the most beautiful pattern in some gorgeous Bavarian bone china I have ever seen—like I've seen so much. I kept chuckling to myself at some of my silly thoughts.

They kept opening presents, and it never seemed to end. Tony and Clarence kept carrying in more. There were so many cards without gifts, and they laid them all aside to open later. They received quite a few gift cards from fancy department stores so they could go and pick out what they still needed, which I couldn't imagine what that could possibly be with all the things they had received. I actually lost count, but I know they received at least eight or nine really nice sheet sets—every color you could think of. I never knew sheets came in so many colors—even a purple set. Annie held them up and yelled, "Yeah!"

Kathleen ran in to check on dinner; she had a couple of people to help her today. Mrs. Peterson couldn't believe she had agreed to it, but Kathleen didn't want to miss out on the opening of the presents.

So while Kathleen was gone, they decided to open some cards and read them. Every card so far had at least fifty dollars in it, and some had a hundred, and several had five hundred. There were checks and savings bonds and lots of cash. When they were about halfway through the cards, Clarence said, "You have just a little over four thousand and fifty dollars already." Mike looked up at him and said, "How the heck do you know that?" Clarence said he just had a good head for numbers, and he kept track in his head as they opened the cards. Annie and Mike looked at each other in amazement. It was just too much to take in right now. They said they needed a break.

About that time Kathleen said for everyone to take their place at the table. She said, "Before we say the blessing, I thought I would tell you that I knew Annie and Mike liked simple food, and so do Clarence and Stella, and Tony, who is eating with us for the first time, loves everything. So I decided against the fancy French foods that I had been thinking of and just stuck to the basics." We all said, "Sounds wonderful!"

After the blessing was said, Kathleen went to the kitchen door and said, "We are ready for dinner to start." They came out carrying a delicious soup, followed by a big salad with fruit and nuts and several kinds of greens, all tossed in a semisweet dressing. It was quite delicious, and I could have stopped then and just eaten more salad, it was so good, but I knew there was more to come. Next was a large bowl of baked potatoes and fancy piles of butter made to look like wedding bells. Then we had filet mignon, fresh asparagus, and a huge bowl of Kathleen's fresh yeast rolls, which always melted in your mouth.

We all had a wonderful time chatting during the meal and just enjoying one another's company. Tony was kind of quiet, so Mrs. Peterson tried coaxing him into the conversation. For the first time in over twenty years, she asked him where he had come from and had he always lived in California.

He got really quiet and said he had no idea where he had come from. His first memory was being a very little boy and being fed by a group of homeless people who found food in garbage bins or wherever they could find it. "I finally decided one day to clean up as best I could and look for a job. It just didn't seem right for that to be my whole life. That's when I walked by and saw Mr. Peterson and asked if he needed any work done. He asked if I could drive, and I lied and said yes, so he said he'd give me a try. I used to go to the library and read books when I was bored. And I had read all about how to drive a car."

Mrs. Peterson said with a shocked look on her face, "You mean you had never actually driven a car the first time you took us somewhere?"

He said, "I'm so sorry I lied, but I really wanted to work."

She said she remembered it so well, him driving them to their favorite restaurant up in town. He asked if he had not done things right. She said it seemed flawless. "I would never have guessed," she added. We were all quite shocked that he could learn to drive by just reading about it.

He went on to say that he still saw the old men who had fed and raised him. "That's who I take all the leftovers to. It's okay, isn't it?" Mrs. Peterson said that was fine and how happy they had always been with his wonderful service and his willingness to do any job that was asked of him. He said, "My goodness, why wouldn't I? You pay me so well for doing so little."

Kathleen said, "I don't think you begin to realize how many things you fix for me in the kitchen all the time."

And Mrs. Peterson said, "You are always ready to do anything asked of you." She then said, "I have only one request."

He said, "Sure; what is it?"

She asked if she could go with him and speak to the men who had raised him. He looked puzzled and said he didn't think they would mind "after all the years of getting delicious leftovers—and they are crazy about your danish especially, Kathleen. And oh, I have to admit, while I was waiting to take you and Mr. Peterson to dinner that first night, I practiced driving the car up and down the driveway."

We all laughed.

In just a few minutes more, we were all finished with dinner, and the table had been cleared. Now it was time for dessert. One of the ladies came in carrying Kathleen's famous chocolate cake, and behind her, the other lady had a huge tub of homemade vanilla ice cream. Needless to say, everyone had seconds of both. Oh, it was so good, and I felt like my stomach was growing by the second. I said, "I think there must be two babies in here. It sure looks like it now." Clarence reached over, rubbed my belly, and said he had never seen anything more beautiful!

We sat and talked a while before heading back to the parlor. I was amazed that they were close to being finished opening presents. Annie was like a whirlwind going through presents. She said, "This is just about the most fun ever—except for our honeymoon, of course." When they finished all the rest of the presents, they started opening the rest of the cards and reading each one out loud. Annie got choked up and almost cried a couple of times at the beautiful things that people had written and all their well wishes.

When they finished with all the cards and had set all the checks into a bowl, Clarence told them they now had $6,750.

Mike and Annie, who were both sitting in the middle of the parlor, just fell over backward and said, "We are filthy rich."

We all laughed until we cried. Clarence, Kathleen, and Tony started picking up all the wrappings and bows and, carefully making sure it was all trash, then put all the paper in a big bag to be burned.

Clarence said to Annie, "You know, I heard once that every string broken when opening presents from a wedding meant how many children you're going to have. I don't think you two will live that long. There must be a couple hundred broken ribbons here."

Annie said, "Oh phooey, Mike and I have already decided to have one boy and one girl."

We all laughed, and Clarence said, "You can't order them like that, I'm sure."

I was very tired and I could definitely tell Mrs. Peterson was also, so I told Clarence it was time we headed home.

On our way home, I asked Clarence why he hadn't mentioned the layoff and the fact that we were moving in a couple of weeks to Oregon. He said he just didn't think it was necessary to spoil the party. I agreed.

Clarence said, "We will have to go back in a day or two and tell them. Mike will find out Monday about the layoff when he goes to work and they give him his last paycheck. I doubt they will be too strapped for money for a while."

When we arrived home, we went straight to the shower and took our time washing each other's back and massaging out all the knots from the long day. It was really an amazing fun-filled day, but nothing compared to our fun-filled nights. We just couldn't keep our hands off each other when we were alone. There was just no doubt that God had made us for each other. We took turns rubbing each other with the great-smelling lotions that Mrs. Peterson kept giving me.

I told Clarence that when we moved to Oregon, these lotions were what I would miss most about California. I did love it here though. Being in this beautiful little town right on the ocean was always lovely and cool. I had grown up with too many hot days working all day in the sun, so this was like heaven to me. I would miss it, but Clarence told me how beautiful Oregon was also, and I would be happy anywhere as long as he was there also.

The next morning we started packing the things that we knew we wouldn't need in the next couple weeks. After we packed until we ran out of boxes and packing paper, we decided to go over to the police station and say good-bye to Officer Joe.

When we walked in, he saw us from his office and came running up front like he had just seen his long-lost friends. He said, "Where in the heck have you two been?"

We told him we had been very busy helping out with Annie's wedding, and we were very sorry we had not come by before now.

He took one close look at me and said, "You have been busy. When are you due?"

I told him as close as I could figure, we would be parents right around our first anniversary. "It's so exciting; I can hardly wait."

He said, "Yes, I understand that completely. I have three of the little rug rats myself and wouldn't take the world for them."

We asked him if we could take him to a late lunch. He said, "Sorry, I would, but my wife is not feeling well, and I told her I would be home shortly, just before you guys walked in. But I am so glad I was here and able to say good-bye, and I hope it is not for the last time I see you two. You have both been very important to me, and it means so much to me that I did bring Clarence back to you. Stella, you were just about the saddest-looking little girl I'd ever seen when you walked in here that night, and it broke my heart, until I was able to find Clarence for you." He took me in his arms and gave me a big bear hug.

We both thanked him a million times over and told him he saved us. Clarence said, "Thank you so much for taking such good care of her and finding a wonderful place for her to stay. It means so much." Clarence grabbed him and hugged him too and told him he was the best policeman ever. "The Lord definitely sent Stella to you. I hate to think what could have happened to her without you." He said, "I was just so happy I was here and able to help." With tears in all our eyes, we said what might be our final good-bye to a very special man!

So with that sad task finished, we went by the market and found more boxes and packing paper so we could get on with our packing.

As we arrived back at our house, Mike was there and said that Mrs. Peterson had been taken to the hospital. We got back in the car and followed him as quickly as possible without getting pulled over. When we went upstairs to her room, the door was closed, and Annie, Kathleen, and Tony were all standing there with very worried looks on their faces. Annie held onto Mike and said the doctor was in with her and said he didn't want them in his way. She said, "I don't think I like him." Mike said that if he could help her, that was all he cared. We all agreed.

After about thirty minutes, the doctor came out and said we could go in and talk with her for just a minute. He said that he wasn't sure he was able to help; she seemed to be in heart failure. He also said to try and stay as calm as possible so as not to upset her; she was extremely weak.

We all went in, and she looked so tiny and frail. Each one of us gave her a gentle hug and said something like, "No more scares like this, do you hear me?" as Annie put it.

Mrs. Peterson smiled and told us how very much each one of us meant to her. She said in her office in the second drawer on the right-hand side of the desk was a copy of her will.

Annie said, "I don't want to hear talk like that."

But Mrs. Peterson said to Kathleen, "You know where all my important numbers are, don't you?"

Kathleen quietly said, "Of course I do, but why do we need them?"

Mrs. Peterson said, "Just in case something happens, I want to make sure my attorney is contacted immediately. I have been meaning to contact him for over a month, but the days kept getting away from me. I have been wanting to change a few things and add a few things, but if I don't get the chance, don't think for a minute, Stella and Clarence, that you are not important to me or I love you any less than the others. My will was all written before I ever met you and before Annie met Mike."

She took a deep breath and said she thought maybe we should go home, get her attorney's number, call him, and ask him to come down here immediately. We all said we were staying right here and whatever had been written was just fine. She could change whatever she wanted when she returned home.

She smiled very slightly and said, "You are all my family, and I love each one of you with all my heart and soul."

We all said, "We know that, and we all feel the same for you." We stood there being very quiet, as it looked like she might need to go to sleep. In just a few seconds, the monitor started making loud siren sounds. The doctor rushed in and tried to pump her heart, but after a few minutes, he turned and said he was so sorry; he had done everything possible, but her heart was just tired and gave out. No doctor could have done more. He looked sincerely so sad. But not half as sad as we all were.

It just didn't seem possible that she was gone. She had always seemed bigger than life until just the past couple of weeks when Clarence and I started noticing how easily she got tired. I wish I had said something to Kathleen, and maybe she could have gotten her to see a doctor sooner. But all the maybes and what-ifs were not helping now.

All of us quietly got in our cars after hugging one another, and Kathleen said, "All of you come over to the house. I have some danish I can warm up, and I'll make a pot of coffee and a pot of tea."

CHAPTER 12

Our angel has passed

So we all went back to the house feeling lost and like we had ourselves partly died.

"Lord, why take her now? We all love her so much," I said as we were taking our cups from Kathleen—poor Kathleen, she looked as if she were moving in slow motion. I told her to sit down, and I would finish serving and get the danish out of the oven. She quietly sat down, and I poured everyone what they wanted and got the butter and danish all on the table. We all ate in silence, and Kathleen just quietly sobbed until there were no more tears left. We were all cried out for the moment.

The next day the attorney, Mr. Morgan, was called and was at the house within an hour. He said he had adored Sarah since the moment Harry had brought her to his office to introduce them. I guess Kathleen and probably even Tony had known her first name, but it just never even entered my mind to ask since everyone else had also called her Mrs. Peterson from the first day I was invited into this house. I suppose it was out of respect, but now thinking back, I should have at least asked out of curiosity.

These thoughts are silly right now, but I was so upset and hurting so much, there were no sane thoughts going through my head. I can only imagine how the rest of these people were hanging on. They all seemed to be going on just sheer energy. Especially Kathleen and Annie. They were both family as much as any family could be. Blood simply doesn't matter when it come to love. Only the love they felt was keeping them going right now.

Mr. Morgan asked everyone involved to come in to the dining room. Kathleen said that she knew with all her heart that Mrs. Peterson would want Clarence and Stella to be in the room also. Mr. Morgan said it was fine with him if they all wanted them in the room. So it started.

Mr. Morgan said it was Sarah Peterson's wish to have her will read immediately after her death, mainly, he said, so that nothing changed in the household. He then asked if they wanted to hear all the legal language, or did they just want the facts as they were written in layman terms. They all said they just needed to hear her wishes and what she wanted each of them to do—not knowing for sure how quickly they were going to be moving or what.

So he started. Sarah Peterson left her home and everything in it to Annie Peterson, because this was how she thought of

Annie, as her real and true daughter. But, he said, there were conditions that had to be met. Annie listened to every word carefully even as she cried quietly. Sarah's terms were as follows: Kathleen is to stay in the only home she has known since being in America. It is up to Kathleen if she ever wants to move and also if she wants to continue to cook for the household. Kathleen is to be given $100,000, and as long as she continues to be the cook, her salary will stay the same. As for Tony, he will also be given $100,000 and be allowed to live in his home over the garage for as long as he lives. If he wants to continue to be the driver for the household, as he has been, and handyman for Kathleen, then he too shall continue to get his salary as usual. Sarah wrote in her will, "As for the rest of the cash in my account, it shall be used to pay all household bills as usual, including groceries, until such time when Kathleen or Tony or both leave, either by choice or by death. At that time, all the rest of the money in my account shall be put into Annie's name alone. Also, anyone in the household who needs clothing or whatever else, it shall be paid for from my account while those people are still living in Annie's home." We all sat there in silence, not knowing what to say or what to do.

Finally, Mr. Morgan said, "Are there any questions?"

Annie asked, "Is there enough money in Mrs. Peterson's account to last for very long?"

Mr. Morgan chuckled slightly, almost to himself. He said, "There is enough money to last until you are all old and gone. In her account after the cash given to Kathleen and Tony, the approximate amount, and I say approximate because there may still be some outstanding bills I do not know of, that being said, the amount in her account is three million, six hundred thousand, nine hundred and twenty-six dollars and some odd cents."

We all sat there with our mouths open and in complete silence.

After what seemed to be an eternity, Annie said, "Mrs. Peterson said that she had been meaning to call you to add something and make a change." He said, "I can say, knowing her as well as I do, that she probably intended to add your husband now that you are married." Annie said, "I am sure she intended to give something to Clarence and Stella. She said to change something and to add something. So what else could it have been?" He said, "I have no way of knowing that, so there is nothing I can do." Annie asked, "So when do I have control of the account to do with as I please?" He said, "As I said, any money that you, Kathleen, or Tony need for any purchases you need to make, it will be paid for out of the account, but except for that, and I am sure that would include anything you buy for your husband, the account will not be officially in your name until the death of Kathleen and Tony or until they decide to leave the household."

Annie just started sobbing and could not be consoled even by Mike. Finally she said, "I just know she wanted Clarence and Stella to be given a sizable amount. Is there nothing that can be done about that?" Mr. Morgan said, "I wish I could say what she might have wanted, but as much as I tend to agree with you, I can only go by her will of record."

At that, Kathleen said, "I am able to do with my money as I wish?" And then Tony asked the same. When they were both told it was their money to do with as they pleased, they both stated they would give a portion of their money to Stella and Clarence. Annie said, "Please, Stella, you know how much Mrs. Peterson loved you and then Clarence as she came to know him. She would do anything for both of you."

But Stella and Clarence insisted that they just would not accept money meant for Kathleen and Tony. They had both lived there and worked for Mrs. Peterson for most of their lives, and they deserved the money given them.

Annie said, "I would give you at least the same amount if I had control of the account, but I have control of nothing for many years."

I got up, put my arms around Annie, and hugged her, and then went to both Kathleen and Tony and hugged them both and told all of them how much Clarence and I both appreciated their offers, but "we just can't take them."

Annie said, "You and Clarence can move in here to the room you loved or even Mrs. Peterson's room, which is larger. It is my home, and I can make that offer. Am I correct, Mr. Morgan?" He said, "Of course, Annie, it is your home now."

Again Clarence spoke up, this time before Stella had a chance, and said he wouldn't hear of it. Stella was his wife and they were expecting their first child, and he wanted to be in his own home and raise his family.

Annie almost begged. She said to Clarence, "Please, there are so many rooms in this house not being used. You and Stella could have a whole wing to raise your family."

He said, "Annie dear, I love you for this offer, but I am already committed to a job in Oregon starting the first of March; we are already half packed."

They all sat there in silence.

Finally Kathleen said, "When were you going to tell us all this?"

I said, "We had planned to come over on Saturday and tell all of you. We figured Annie and Mike would be here, so we could tell you all at the same time. We would have told you last Saturday, but we didn't want to put a damper on your coming-home party. I am so glad now that we didn't, since it was the last time we saw her."

We stayed for Mrs. Peterson's funeral, and I think the whole town was there. We were seated with family over to one side, with a sheer curtain covering us. I was glad because I think it was just hitting Kathleen, Annie, and Tony. They were all three just a few moments from nervous breakdowns. Thank goodness that Annie had Mike. But Kathleen just looked like she might never smile again. Tony also was just sick–looking, even though he was just as clean as always. I wondered how they were going to get through this.

I had only known Mrs. Peterson for seven months, and I was wondering how I would ever get over knowing this precious woman, who had such a zest of life and loved doing for others above herself. I could not imagine what might have happened to me had I not gone to the police station that first night—and what if it had not been Officer Joe on duty? What might some other officer have done? Especially because he would most likely not have been such a good friend to Mrs. Peterson. I just felt like God had been sitting next to me from the day I got on that bus without any money, and he continued to put someone in my path to help me all along the way until Clarence was found.

As the church filled up, they kept bringing folding chairs for one place or another, and pretty soon there was no place to put another chair. People just stood outside the church's front doors and got as close together as possible to just get a view inside and possibly be able to hear. The service was beautiful, with so many of her good friends getting up to say some funny thing she did or something she had done for them, of which there were many. Several beautiful hymns were sung, and the minister, who had known her since she was a child, had to fight to hold back his own tears, but he gave an absolutely beautiful eulogy. I would love for my mama to have met her just once.

When the service was over, each row got up, went around, and said their last good-byes to her, then they started coming from outside, and there were as many outside as were inside. Some could barely stand as they said their last farewell to the great lady of town. I had no idea I was living with royalty all those weeks. I just knew it only took me days to love her, so

I felt so sorry for people who had known her for years and decades. Kathleen just fell apart when it was our turn to go up and view her. If Tony had not caught her, she would have been on the floor and probably not able to get up without help. Tony helped her into the hearse, and then Annie and Mike got in, followed by Clarence and I.

Almost half of the people came to the graveside. We sat there until the last person went by and put a rose on her casket. It was covered with large beautiful lavender roses. I had never seen anything like this and probably never would again.

Close friends were invited over to the house, and I wasn't surprised to see that Kathleen had called the caterers. They had quite a spread of food ready as people started arriving. Surprisingly, not too many ate much; I didn't blame them—I had no appetite either. Tony fixed a plate and took it to Kathleen and insisted she eat. He said, "You haven't eaten a bite in two days, Kathleen. You have to eat something, or you're going to get very sick." She took the plate and put a few bites into her mouth and chewed as if it were work. Clarence and Mike both got up and fixed Annie and me plates and pretty much gave us the same orders, except Clarence reminded me the baby needed food too. I ate for that reason only; I sure didn't feel hungry. The guys then all fixed themselves plates and ate a little of everything.

Slowly the people started leaving. The mayor and his wife came by and said how very sorry they were and wished us all well. "She was a grand lady," said the mayor. Then they also left.

Soon it was just us, and suddenly the house seemed small without her presence.

Clarence and I left after a couple of hours. There just were no more words to say. We all hugged, and then we drove away, promising to come by in the morning as we were headed for Oregon. Annie tried again to talk us out of moving, but Clarence told her he had already given his word he would be there, and his word was as good as a contract to him.

The next morning we got up early, even after a long night of making love, mainly because we got into bed and then couldn't stop even if we had wanted to, but also it helped ease the pain to show each other how much our love meant to us both and how much we loved each other. When we got up, the reality of this being our last night in this, our first home together, was a little sad, but everything seemed a little more sad than usual knowing Mrs. Peterson was gone and Kathleen, Annie, and Tony were going to be having such a difficult time for quite a while. At least Annie had Mike and they were very much in love, but just knowing all of that house and money was theirs had to be so confusing to them both, as just the day before her death, they were setting up their own little love nest.

We finished packing up the last of everything after having breakfast and getting the dishes finished. Now the car was all loaded. We were pulling a trailer with all our furniture, which was covered tightly, just in case we ran into rain. The last thing before leaving was to go by and say our last good-byes, and that was going to be heartbreaking to say the least.

Annie answered the door when we arrived before we had a chance to ring the bell. She grabbed me and held me so tight, like maybe we would change our minds if she held on tight enough. Kathleen quickly came out of the kitchen and asked if we were hungry. We told her we had eaten breakfast earlier, but she said at least have some danish and coffee or tea. It didn't take much to convince us of that. We sat eating the delicious rolls with such a void at the table, I'm sure it was felt by all.

CHAPTER 13

Headed for Oregon

After just a little while, we got up and said we had a long drive ahead of us, so we'd better be on our way. Of course, Kathleen came running out with a huge basket filled with sandwiches, fruit, and more danish. It was enough food for a five-day trip, with a half dozen people traveling. We thanked her, hugged everyone, and promised to write them regularly. And off we were to our next adventure.

It was a long ride, and Clarence stopped often so I could use a restroom somewhere. Being this pregnant and traveling was a bit hard on my already cramped bladder. I told Clarence I was sure it was a boy because he kicked so hard. He laughed and said he didn't care as long as the baby was healthy and beautiful like his mother. I said I wanted him to look just like his father. So for an hour or so, we talked about names. He said he definitely didn't want him to be a junior, if it was a boy, and I said no little girl of mine would be named Stella. He said he loved my name, but I assured him I did not. So after a while, that got old, and we decided to wait until this precious little bundle arrived and then think of a name.

We stopped alongside the road in a really pretty place and ate lunch. Kathleen's sandwiches were very good and much appreciated. It saved us money, as we didn't have to stop at restaurants. Clarence said, as he was studying the map, that as close as he could figure, it should take about five more hours. I said, "Oh, that's not too bad." The day had gone by much faster than I had thought it would. I told him the only traveling I had done was cramped up by lots of brothers and sisters, and all of us hungry, quite different from this. And my bus ride, which could have been terrible had God not put Hazel on that bus to save my life. Maybe literally!

We got back in the car, and Clarence had taken a small pillow out of the things packed in the backseat. He said, "This will help your back if it gets to bothering you again." He was so thoughtful and worried so much about me and the baby. After a while I laid my head on his shoulder, and before I knew it, I was sleeping.

When I woke up, Clarence said he hadn't had the heart to wake me just to show me the sign saying we had entered Oregon. I asked how long I had slept, and he said about two and a half hours. I couldn't believe I had slept that long. He told me pregnant women needed more sleep than usual. I asked him how he got so smart about everything. He said he had read a lot of books about a lot of different things. I was so glad that I loved to read and was learning more all the time. At least I hoped I would remember all I had read.

I asked Clarence if he was hungry again yet, and he said, "Maybe in a little while. Why—are you?" I giggled and said just a little. He said, "Well, you are eating for two, you know." So in a little while, we stopped at another pretty rest stop and ate another sandwich, had an apple, and shared a Coca-Cola. Then we were back on the road.

It seemed like we got there before we hardly got back in the car. Clarence's college friend and his wife were both so nice—Alan and Mary Nelson. They insisted we come in and spend the night with them, as they had plenty of room, and in the morning there would be a whole crew that could get our trailer and car unloaded within less than a half hour. There was just no reason to even try in the dark. Mary said dinner was just about ready, and she had fixed plenty for us, since this was about the time they figured we would be here. So that was that; we were both too tired to argue.

Mary showed us to our room, which was nicely decorated and very clean. She said we had our own bath, so we could wash up if we wanted to, and I did. I felt very sticky, having had no water to wash with after we'd eaten a few hours before.

In just a bit, Mary said dinner was ready. She said it was just meat loaf; she hoped we liked that. We both said we were not picky and that it sounded great. And it was really great. They said that having the ranch made it nice—they could always have the best beef. I said it seemed to really make a difference, because I had never tasted any beef with such a fresh flavor. Mary said, "Thank you, but that's the beef, not me." The mashed potatoes were so fluffy, and her corn had been homegrown and taken off the cob and frozen right away to seal in the freshness.

"Everything was just wonderful," I told her as we washed the dishes together. She asked me how far along I was and if I needed a name of a good doctor. I told her I was almost six months and that I had not seen a doctor at all. I told her Mrs. Peterson had wanted me to go to one she knew, but I had felt fine, so I just didn't think it was necessary. Mary said, "Oh yes, you need to be seen by a doctor. They can help you so much with questions and things you should be doing."

I asked her how many children she had, and she got really quiet and said she had lost three babies in the last two years. "They didn't know why, other than my body just doesn't seem able to carry full term. They want me to wait at least six months before trying again." I asked how far along she was each time, and she said she never made it past four months for some reason. "But I won't give up. It's not my nature."

Just as we finished the dishes, Alan and Clarence came in. Alan said, "We thought we'd better be checking on you women to see what all the gossip is." Mary said, "We were not gossiping about anyone. We were discussing how important it is that Stella see a doctor and get checked out."

I said, "I will look for a doctor as soon as we unpack and get settled in."

Mary said, "I really don't want to be pushy, but I just know you would love my doctor. He is so understanding and very easy to talk to. Do you mind if I call him tomorrow and see when he could fit you in?"

I said, "No, that is fine with me, as I would have no idea who to call."

Alan said, "Now that that is settled, do you two like to play cards?"

Clarence said he didn't think there was a card game he had not played, and I said I had never played any cards. Clarence put his arm around me and said, "That's okay, honey. We can start with some real easy games, and as sharp as you are, I just know you will learn fast."

So I said, "Fine with me."

Alan opened up a top cupboard and got a large can of pennies down. He said, "How much do you each want?" Clarence pulled two dollars out of his pocket and said a dollar each should start us off good. So Alan counted us out our pennies, and we got started. After a while Clarence and I both had a pretty good pile in front of us.

Alan said, "You two are probably tired after driving all day long. I don't know what I was thinking." He looked at his watch and said, "It's way past our usual bedtime also." We had been playing for a little over two hours; I couldn't believe that much time had passed. Alan said, "We'll call it a night when this hand is over."

Clarence said, "Oh sure, you just don't want to lose the ranch."

We all laughed. They had both had to buy more pennies a couple of times. When we finished and counted up our pennies, I was surprised to see Clarence and I had won over two dollars each. "Here you go—four dollars and eighty-five cents," Mary said.

I said, "Wow, this is fun."

Mary laughed and said, "We'll get it back one of these nights."

So off to bed we went. As soon as the door was closed and locked, we both stripped off our clothes and headed for the shower. Surprise! There was no shower, just a large, deep tub. Clarence said, "This is going to be different." We filled the tub with water as hot as we could stand it, and I put in some of Mrs. Peterson's bath salts that I had in my bag. We got in, and I just lay back against Clarence; we were just relaxing and soaking out the sore muscles from the long day we'd had.

It wasn't long before I felt something poking in my back. I giggled quietly and said, "Whatever could that be?" He said, "Turn around here, and I'll show you." So I carefully turned myself around, and Clarence soaped up my whole front and massaged my breasts gently. I said, "Okay, you're killing me." I already had my legs wrapped around him, but I pulled myself up onto him, and almost as soon as his penis touched my insides, I climaxed. It was so strong and such a wonderful feeling that I couldn't believe it happened so fast. But as we moved up and down gently in the water, it wasn't long before we both climaxed together, as we did often.

Clarence said, "I sure hope there is one of these tubs in our house, or we might just have to come and ask if we can take a bath a few times a week. That would be okay, don't you think?" I laughed and said it might be a little embarrassing.

We got out of the tub and did our usual drying each other off, which sometimes got us into another round of lovemaking, but tonight we were extra tired and crawled into bed, and both of us went right to sleep.

Just before the sun came up, Clarence was ready, and I was willing. We were so in love that it never seemed to be enough. We were so good together that we couldn't get enough of each other is what I mean. We lay there talking about the baby again and how anxious we were to see if it was a boy or girl. It wouldn't be long now. We got up and got all our things back in our bags and carried them out to the living room.

Alan said, "Boy, you two slept in."

Clarence looked at his watch and said, "It's only seven o'clock."

Alan said, "Our days around here start at five."

I said, "In the morning?"

"I'm just kidding," Alan said.

Mary said, "Don't listen to him. Come on in the kitchen, and I'll make you breakfast."

Clarence asked what time the crew would get there to help him unload the trailer.

Alan said, "You're too late, buddy; they have it unloaded and your car also. It's all in your house down the road a bit. Hope you don't mind."

Clarence said, "Not at all; thank you very much."

Alan said, "I figured you two had a long day yesterday and needed the rest."

After a big country breakfast, we followed Alan down to our place. It was a lot smaller than their house, of course, but still twice the size of our little place in Carmel. Our furniture looked a little sparse in this place, but it would be easier to clean without having to move things out of the way to vacuum. I said, "It is so nice; I love it."

Clarence agreed and said, "The place is great, Alan. Now tell me about the job."

I went into the kitchen and started unpacking and putting things away. I ran my hands over the bottoms of the cabinets and could tell they had been cleaned well, so I put things away as I unwrapped. It seemed so nice to actually have a place to put everything in a cabinet. I was so used to having appliances sitting wherever we could find a place for them.

Just as I finished the kitchen, Clarence came in after his work talk with Alan.

He asked what he could do to help. I said, thank you honey, it would be great to get all these empty boxes out of the way. In about three minutes he had broken down all the boxes and was back for more orders. All that's left to do is the bedroom and bath. We headed to the bedroom and stopped to look at the bathroom, and to our delight, the tub was the exact same tub that had been in the guest room where we slept last night. Clarence got this gleam in his eyes and I said, hold on honey, I really would like to get unpacked and get our bed put together, then we can play. He gave me this pouty look and then laughed, what are we waiting for, to the bedroom, my bride. We opened the door and had a great surprise. They had put our bed together for us. I was amazed at all the work they had accomplished in such a short time this morning. So, we started unpacking all our bedding. I immediately got very teary eyed, the first look at all our beautiful bedding brought back dear Mrs. Peterson to my mind. I thought of almost everything in this room and she had bought it all for us, including our new bed which was so comfortable. Without her, none of these things would have been possible. She gave us a beautiful wedding and reception and we received so many gifts from all who attended our wedding, but there were so many presents sent from people we had never even met. Mrs. Peterson putting our story in the newspaper hit the hearts of many people in town and they sent the nicest gifts letting us know how happy they were that we finally found each other. Clarence agreed and we both said how much we would miss this wonderful generous woman. We would forever be grateful, for all she had done for us. We opened the box marked bedding, and first Clarence had to lift the mattress up so I could get the bed ruffle where it belonged, then we put the mattress cover on, then our new sheets, and the beautiful soft and fluffy blanket, and then, the beautiful comforter in the gorgeous purple flowers of many different kinds. We stepped back and admired how different it made our bedroom look. On to the bathroom, there were so many cabinets and built in drawers, which made it so easy to get everything put away in record time. There were double mirrors which each had very deep shelves. All my toiletries and other women things fit in my side easily, and Clarence's shaving things and after shave and colognes all fit with room to spare. Now we went into the living room and arranged what little furniture we owned and if I did say so myself, it looked real nice.

Clarence said, after all your work I am sure a long soothing bath is what the doctor ordered. I agreed completely and he said, he would always try to know what would make me feel the best possible. We filled the tub with very warm water, I had read that too hot of water might possibly harm the baby when I was as far along as I was, so to stay on the safe side we decided it was better to bath in warm water. I put in bath salts and we sat in the tub for almost an hour just relaxing and letting the water soak out the sore and tired muscles from not only driving all day yesterday, and now completely getting everything unpacked and put away. Clarence said, I don't want you working this hard anymore honey, you are in the last of your pregnancy. We wouldn't want to hurt our precious baby in any way. I agreed and promised to take it easy for the remainder of my time with our little bundle of joy in here, I said as I patted my quickly growing belly. It seemed to grow more by the day lately. I had read every book they had at our little store around the corner from our first home together. But I had to admit I was glad I was seeing a doctor soon, I would feel better when told everything about my pregnancy looked normal and the baby was growing well. I knew in my mind that everything was fine, because I had felt movement very early and the baby was very active these days. After a little longer, we let out the water and refilled it with new water a little warmer and I turned around and put my legs around Clarence and let him wash my front again. I just loved the way I felt when he was soaping up my breasts and gently massaging them. They seemed to get more sensitive with every passing day. It wasn't long before he entered me and again I was so ready for him. He made me feel like I was going to die from pleasure and I told him so. He said, honey I'll try my best to always make sure your completely satisfied. That's been my main goal in life since the moment I meet you. I wrapped my arms around his neck and told him he had already made me the happiest woman on earth. I thought back and it seemed like yesterday that I was just a young girl, and now I couldn't feel more like a woman. We both stood up and reached for towels, I quickly told him the ones on that side were just for show and these over here that say Mr. and Mrs. were the pretty fluffy ones Annie had given us. We only needed one towel, because we always took turns drying each other and the towels were so big and soft, they just soaked up all the moisture so fast.

After we were dressed in clean clothes, all of a sudden, I realized I hadn't even asked, what Alan and he had talked about concerning his duties. Clarence said, he thought the job sounded very easy really, he had to get up early every morning and make sure the men were doing their jobs properly. Then in the late afternoon the same thing over again. They had to get the cows milked quickly and then it had to go through several processes before it was safe to sell to markets, and to milkmen who delivered it to homes. I asked how early he had to get up and he said, about 4:30 in the morning. I said, oh my goodness, that is the middle of the night. He said the cows had to be milked twice a day on a very regular basis so they kept producing the same amount of milk. If they aren't completely emptied, then they produce less milk after a while, so it is every twelve hours for just a couple of hours every day. I said I was just kidding about the middle of the night, all my life if daddy was around, he had everyone up and working by 6 o'clock, I have just got lazy this past year being pampered by, Mrs. Peterson and then even more so by you, my sweet darling. He laughed and said he wouldn't wake me when he got up, if possible. I told him he could leave without kissing me goodbye. He said, I get Sunday off. Alan will do it that then, because he is not working at his regular job. I said I didn't understand why Alan had another job if he could be running his own milk farm. Clarence said when Alan first graduated from Texas

A&M College with a degree in mathematics, his father was still alive and healthy, so he kept the farm running, and Alan went on to become an investment broker. It was almost ten years before his father died and his mother died of a broken heart just a few months later. Being an only child, the will was read and the farm was his. Even though he knew exactly how to do everything since he had worked the farm on summers since he was 12 years old, he made so much more at his other job, because he had so many people whose money he was responsible for, so he took a little time off to train a foreman. The man had stayed with him for many years and now he has gone. Clarence made it clear to Alan that he would only stay long enough to train another foreman.

The next morning while Clarence was working, Mary came by and told me that she got me in to see the doctor today. I was shocked, that she had been able to get me an appointment the next day, but I told her I could be ready in ten minutes. So, I told her to have a seat and I would hurry. I threw on a nice dress and shoes and ran a brush threw my hair. When I grabbed my purse, I said oh wait, I need to leave Clarence a note, or he would be worried to death coming home and me not here, especially since I know only you and Alan. I quickly wrote a note and explained that Mary had got me in to see the doctor this morning and I would be home soon after. I Love you, Stella. Mary had a very nice car and it was a comfortable ride into town. Mary said Dr. Brody was a very nice man and a great doctor, she was sure I would like him. She said only the first visit will feel a bit uncomfortable, but after that everything just seem natural. She said she was real nervous her first time, but I seemed very calm. I told her I had never been to a doctor before for anything, so I really don't know what to expect. She briefly explained what would happen, and now I was nervous. Mary said how sorry she was and that she should have kept her mouth shut. I said not to worry, I'm a tough girl, you have no idea the things I've been through. When we went into the office, they handed me a stack of papers to fill out. I asked what I was supposed to write on them. They said, just your previous doctors and illness's and so on. I told them this was the first doctor appointment I'd been to in my whole life. The lady behind the counter looked like she was hearing things. So, I just signed the few things that needed my signature and I was finished. A few minutes a door open and they called Stella Rader, I said Yes. She said, follow me and I'll take you to the examining room. She then handed me a gown and said, everything needs to come off and put the gown on opened at the back, and then get up on that table and sit on the end of it. I said even my bra and underpants? She said it would be real hard for the doctor to examine me with them on. I was shocked, but did as I was told. I wished I would have read about doctor visits so I had known what to expect. After what seemed like forever, the doctor came in and shook my hand and said, Hi Mrs. Rader, I am Dr. Brody and I am going to examine you and be as gentle as possible. I understand this is your first time seeing a doctor, I never like to hurt anyone. He first had me lay down and he checked my breasts and asked if they were extra tender? I told him no, not really. He said soon they would probably start getting more tender as my milk glands started forming. He asked if I had planned to nurse my own baby and I said of course, who else would do it? He said some women liked to have a wet nurse and then proceeded to explain. He asked me if having intercourse was painful? I told him not at all. He said that was good. Then he asked me to put my feet into the metal things on each side of the table and let my knees relax and fall to the sides. This is so embarrassing, does every woman having a baby, have to do this? He said Yes, I am afraid this is the only way we can see the cervix and make sure the baby is secure in there. He tried to be as gentle as possible, but I felt like I could just cry. I wished Clarence was here with me. The Dr. said you need to relax Stella, or I can't examine you. So Finally, I let my knees spread apart and tried not to think of what was happening to me. The Dr. Put his finger inside me real deep and moved it all around. He then put his finger in my behind hole and I almost jumped off the table. He said relax Stella this is almost over. After he took off his gloves that had been well lubricated, he pushed gently all around my belly. When he finished, he said, all over now you can get dressed and come into my office so we can talk about your baby. I dressed as fast as I could and waited for the nurse to come in and tell me where his office was. After a minute or two, I opened the door and looked out. At the end of the hall I could see the Dr. sitting at a big desk, so I walked into his office and was told to sit down. He then asked me a few questions about when I had my last period, I told him I wasn't real sure of the date but I got married July 17th and I had two periods after getting married. He took a little chart out of his desk and looked at it for a minute or so, and then said it looks like you will be delivering a healthy baby within a week or so around your 1ˢᵗ anniversary. Everything looks fine and your cervix is just as it should be. I told him we didn't have any insurance and he looked at me and said, I think you better talk to Mary because she told the office that you had been on their insurance policy since April 1ˢᵗ. I got a surprised look on my face and he said it was normal for them with all their employee's to be started on their policy their 1ˢᵗ day of work. I felt very relieved as I didn't want to start running up bills just after we moved. The Dr. said for me to make another appointment in 6 weeks. I said okay and thanked him.

As we drove home, I told Mary I had no idea he would do those personal things to me. She said how sorry she was that she hadn't explained, but she figured that I knew they always had to do pelvic exams. I said, well it's over for now and I lived through it. He said the baby looked very healthy and the right weight for me being in my third trimester. I said I wonder how they can tell these things. Mary said, they go to school for a very long time and then, after as many babies as he has delivered, they get a good idea, by feeling around the stomach the size of your baby. I told her I was anxious to tell Clarence as soon as I got home, and then I thought to thank her for the use of the lovely home and how much I liked it. There are so many cabinets, and it was so easy to unpack because there was a place for everything. She said I was very welcome and it was the house built for our former foreman and his wife had helped design it. I said, Thank the Lord for her, she did an excellent job.

As soon as I walked in the door, Clarence ran to me and said how sorry he was that he had not explained about my doctor visits. I just explained that Mary had come by this morning and said her Dr. could fit me in this morning, so I quickly dressed and went with her. I would like to have known what to expect, but it's my fault, not yours honey, why should you be sorry, I should have read more books. He said because he was so much older and had even heard of the exams from friends who had children. and he always thought he would be the one taking me to my doctor appointments. I told him not to worry, that it had frightened me at first, but Dr. Brody had been so professional about everything and it was over before I had much time to worry. And best of all he said, the baby looked just the right weight and I looked healthy. So, all is fine and I don't have to go back for six weeks. He said when you make another appointment, make it around lunch time, then I can take you and hear what the doctor says. I promised him I would. He was just as excited as I was about the baby, and wanted to be included in everything. I asked him how his first morning was and he said everything went very well and he thought there would be no problem training a new foreman when we decided we wanted to move back.

When Clarence had his first day off, we took a long drive and saw how beautiful Oregon was. there were streams and rivers everywhere you looked and everything was so green. We went into town to buy some groceries and ended up in a furniture store that was going out of business and both of us just fell in love with the prettiest bedroom set. We discussed how much money we had in our savings and how much the doctor bills were going to be, and I could have just punched myself. I had forgot to tell him that we were on the farm's insurance policy from the first day he was hired. So, all our Dr. and hospital bills would be paid. He picked me up and swung me around, gently of course. We talked about it and decided that we needed some bedroom furniture and this was on sale for a real great price and we both loved it, so the next day it was delivered. Now we could quit living out of our beautiful luggage. I lined the drawers with pretty paper and then very neatly organized our clothes in all the drawers. We also bought a very inexpensive lamp to sit on the nightstand. And our fancy radio fit right on the side next to the lamp. When the bed was all made up with our beautiful bedspread, it all just looked amazing. As soon as Clarence got home from work, I took him right into the bedroom to see it, he could believe they would get it here so soon, but he agreed that everything looked complete now. He could only see one problem. I said, what's wrong honey? He just said, he wished that bed didn't look so perfect because it would be a shame to mess it up doing what was on his mind. I laughed and pulled off the comforter and pulled the blanket and sheets down in about twenty seconds and said, how's that for fast? He said, have I told you how much I love you, sweet darling wife of my dreams? I said, I think you could show me better as I already had my clothes off and had laid down on the bed. It took him all of five seconds for him to join me. As he lay next to me he just raised up and stared at me. He said I was the most beautiful woman he had ever seen and he knew from the second he had seen me come out of that tent, he knew he had to have me for the rest of his life. I said I felt the exact same thing. I guess our minds were joined at that moment. He took his time going up and down my body with kisses, lingering at each breast and nibbling each one gently. He ran his whole hand around my breast and asked if I had noticed how large they were becoming? I said I had thought my bras were awfully tight lately. He said I'm going to have to take you to the Sears and Roebuck in town and get you some maternity clothes. Your belly is too precious to be squished in those cotton panties. You need some with some stretch. Then without another thought, he put his legs over mine and started kissing me with so much passion that I felt I was going to bust if he didn't enter me quickly. I reached down and felt he was rock hard and knew that with my touch he wouldn't be able to not hold out much longer. He put his finger down just barely touching my inside and I told him to stop teasing and satisfy his bride now. We climaxed together almost as soon as he entered me, but he was still hard and we moved together in such perfect rhythm it wasn't long before we both climaxed again. It felt so good I thought I might just float away. How could anything ever be as wonderful as we are together. Clarence said the he knew God had made us for each other. He just got mixed up on the ages a little. I told him to stop that talk right now. I loved him the way he was and the age he was. We are perfect together and that's all that counts.

The next day Clarence and I went into town as soon as he got home from the morning milk. We went right to Sears and asked for the maternity department which just excited me to even ask for the it. Now that I was growing so quickly and felt so much movement, it was becoming so real that I was really going to have our own precious little baby. When mama had all my younger siblings, I hardly ever got to hold them or play with them because I was working or being told to do something by daddy, whether it really needed being done or not. Mama was always nursing a baby, for my whole childhood, that I could remember. There was no baby food they could afford, so whatever she ate had to nourish the babies also. As soon as they were old enough, she would mash up potatoes or beans, or whatever vegetables she could find. We all lived, so I guess it is true that beans and potatoes are healthy. Poor mama would walk around wherever we lived sweeping the floors or peeling potatoes or whatever she was doing, with a baby attached to her hip. I was going to sit quietly and nurse my baby, hopefully in a rocking chair if we could find a nice one used somewhere. We probably shouldn't have bought ourselves the bedroom set, but we were so tired of things looking wrinkled from being in the suitcase. We hung everything possible, but closets are only so big. And the baby's thing would go in our chest of drawers. So, we really had needed the set and the price was so good. I was thrilled we could pay cash for it. But most of all, I was just so excited to have my own baby to love and raise properly. We got to the maternity department and I looked at the panties first. They came in packages of three, so I said that was all I needed, because I could wash them by hand. Then we looked at the dresses. Clarence picked out a beautiful pink set. A skirt and a real pretty top that had a fancy ruffled collar that looked so feminine. I said I loved it when I tried it on, it fit very loose. The sales lady said, if they fit you tight dear, you wouldn't be able to wear it next week probably. She said, I would be surprised how fast I started growing these last two months. We had already told her I was just about seven months. I said I should get just a couple of cheap dresses to wear around the house. Clarence said, don't be silly sweetheart, no wife of mine is going to be in some cheapie looking dress when I make plenty of money to buy you what you like. So, I picked out a very nice yellow and white dress and Clarence said, pick out at least one more, you can't wear two things every day for two more months. I went carefully through the racks and avoiding the expensive ones. Finally, Clarence said I like this one, so try these two on. I did and they both had plenty of room to grow. I came out of the dressing room with the pretty bright blue one on and Clarence said I looked like a vision. I laughed and said what, a vision of a fat lady. He said, don't ever say that about yourself. Your pregnant and there is nothing more beautiful than you look right now. You are glowing all over, isn't she? He said, to the sales lady. She said, I must agree, you look beautiful, and you are a beautiful woman. I thanked her, and Clarence said, See I told you. So, I tried on the yellow and white and hated it on me. So back to the racks to look some more. Then I spotted a real cute navy colored dress with white polka dot and a little white collar. It had a rounded neckline and when I tried it on my cleavage showed as my breasts were getting so large. Clarence said he loved it and we would take those three for now, but I still had to try on a bra that would fit. The sales lady asked what size I was wearing now. I told her it was my normal size, a 32D. She said, I suggest you just buy a couple of nursing bras, as they are a little higher, but you will be able to wear them the whole time your nursing, so you get your money's worth. It's silly to spend money on a bra that you will outgrow in a month. So, I tried on the size she thought would be okay for now, but allowed for growing. It fit fine, so I told her two would be plenty, because I could wash one while wearing one. We spent a total of thirty-three dollars. I said wow, that's a lot and Clarence said, sweetheart, you worry too much. You let me make the money and you take care of the house. I said okay for now, but I must do something to help. He said, you are, you're giving me a baby. I said, silly, that's for both of us.

A few weeks passed and I received a letter from my mama, she had another little boy and she said, he had white hair just like Velma's, and she had named him Kenneth. He was born on April 9th. He is the cutest little guy. She said, she better stop writing now, before your daddy comes in and catches me, in case your daddy comes in and catches me sitting down. He's been meaner than an old yard dog lately. He and Velma get into it all the time. I wish she would just keep her thoughts to herself, like Maxine and W.K. does. But she's got your temper, and a mouth that you just can't shut up. My love to you and to Clarence bye- bye for now, Mama. My poor mama, how many more children did daddy think she could keep having. She was not quite forty and her body had been through more than any woman and mother should have to endure. I hate that man so much and wish I could help mama somehow. I don't know why she stayed with him. Being on relief would be much better, but mama was so proud. She had said, that one time we had been on relief she felt so awful letting someone else taking care of her kids. She just didn't realize how much better off we were. At least we had real beds to sleep in and enough food to eat to keep us healthy. But mama thought she was doing her best. And that's all she can do, I guess.

I was growing so fast now that all my new maternity clothes were getting tight. It was the end of June so I should be able to stay in them for another few weeks. Mary had given me a shower and I met several ladies who were married to other workers at the farm. They were all very nice and I was so surprised when I walked into Mary's house and they all yelled "Surprise". It was such a nice shower and I received so many nice gifts which were all needed. Lots of diapers and little outfits that were just soft and cute and could be used for boy or girl. I was so thankful and told them all so. Clarence, being the perfectionist that he was, got all their addresses and wrote out the thank you notes. He is so wonderful, and is getting to the point where he won't let me do anything lately. I am ordered not to start dinner anymore. He said he will do it before he goes back for the late afternoon milking. I think I truly must have the most perfect husband in the whole world. Our love just gets stronger every day. Thank you Lord for sending this man to save me from the life I was living. I must say this prayer at the very least, ten times every day.

The next week a truck pulled up and I saw it stop right in front of our door, so I walked or I should say waddled, because that's about all I could do these days, to the door. The bell rang and they said they had a delivery for Clarence and Stella Rader. I told them I was Stella, and he said, sign here. I asked what I was signing for he said a gift from friends is all the message said. So, I signed and they started unloading every possible baby thing ever made, I think. There was the most beautiful crib, already put together and a stroller and high chair. All these things were top of the line and I put two and two together and immediately knew all this was from Kathleen, Tony, Mike and Annie who I'm sure was the instigator. They just kept coming in and out carrying boxes of who knows what. Clarence and I had a crib all picked out, we were just waiting for his next paycheck to pick it up. The one we had picked out was probably about a tenth of what this one cost. It was just beautiful. All of a sudden, I started to cry, which I did a lot these days. I don't understand why because I could not have been any happier. Just the way it goes in the life of a very pregnant woman. Just as the truck was finally finished and pulling away from the house, Clarence drove up. I was still standing there in shock, and I greeted him with our usual minute long kiss. He came in and said what is all this and where did it come from? I told him he had one guess, and that's all it took. We started opening boxes and found cases of diapers and beautiful soft expensive blankets in pink and in blue and yellow one and even a pretty checked one with all the pastels you could name. There were soft little pajamas and at least thirty receiving blankets in all colors. At the bottom of one of the boxes was a letter from Annie.

She said, Dear Clarence and Stella, I thought it was about time to get all these things to you before that baby beats me to it. I have sent everything you could possibly need for a boy or a girl. Whatever you can't use, save it for the next one, or give it to someone else who has the need. I wanted you both to have the very best as you know in your heart, Mrs. Peterson would have given you had she not left us too soon. Please don't feel like you're getting too much because you're not. You're getting just a little of what you both deserve and I only wish I was there giving it to you in person. I really had thought of driving up there so that I was there when it was all delivered, but I am having quite a bad time with morning sickness. I giggled as I read that part. Annie pregnant, wow, how exciting. Clarence said keep reading. She said you were so lucky to have never had this problem. Anyway, we all here in Carmel, miss and love you both so much and want to hear about what you had as soon as the baby arrives. Clarence, you call us collect from the hospital and I mean it. I am just so excited and wanted to be there so bad. Kathleen had thought about driving up with me, but she said who would cook for Mr. Mike if I left too. She is so funny, we can't convince her she doesn't have to cook for us every day, but she said, as long as she was getting a paycheck, she sure does. And by the way, she sent a special box all sealed up for you two, just from her. She still goes out with that judge, once in a while. I can tell they are crazy about each other, but both feel they are too old to start that kind of relationship. I told her you're never too old. But I get nowhere, so I've quite trying. I just can't wait to hear all about your beautiful baby. Closing for now with all our Love, Mike, Annie, Kathleen and Tony. Clarence and I started opening boxes and putting things in the different stacks, pink or blue. Then we started opening the real big box that had been brought in last, it was a beautiful chest of drawers that matched the crib. I told Clarence, I think God knew exactly what he was doing when he had me leave Texas early and through that, all of this has happened. Had I not ran away when I did, I would never have met Mrs. Peterson and Annie and Kathleen and Tony. Our lives would be so different now. I know we could not be any more in love or we would not have had a wonderful life anyway, but God just tested our love and made it better because we passed his test. Clarence said, sweetheart, I think you just might be right. We continued opening boxes and finally came to one that was all in blue things. All soft and pretty little boy outfits and just a note form Kathleen saying, I know you are having a boy, I have known it from the first day I told you that you were pregnant. Don't ask how I know, I just feel it so strong, that it must be so. Anyway, You're a wonderful couple I love and miss you so much and at the bottom of this box is your present. We dug to the bottom and opened the box that was all taped up airtight. Inside were dozens of danish. We laughed so hard I almost peed my pants, which was getting to be the norm lately. I mean not literally, but it was getting harder and harder not to. When we finally finished opening and stacking things, Clarence said, I hate to tell you, but it's too late to start dinner now, so when I get back home after second milking, we'll go into town and have dinner at that little café. I said that sounded wonderful, because I was exhausted. I was going to lay down for just a little while, then I get all these things carried into the baby's room. He said you will do no such thing. You just rest until

I get back and after we have had a nice dinner, we will do it together. Okay, I promised.

We went in to town and as Clarence helped me out of the car, who do we see but Mary and Alan going into the café also. We yelled hey, wait for us. They turned and were delighted to see us, so we got a table together and enjoyed a very nice meal. Alan said, Mary had just found out she was pregnant again and they were celebrating. She said, I just hope I get to the waddling stage like you are now. I told her I would pray very hard for her and I truly believe God answered prayers. On our way home, I told Clarence I couldn't understand since my mama was so good and such a wonderful women, and she prayed so much, how God could let all these terrible things happen to her year after year. He said he didn't understand it all either, but God knew what he was doing and there must be a reason, but he said, as for me, I sure can't figure that one out either.

In an hour or so we had taken everything into the baby's room. All the beautiful things just waiting for a baby to fill them. I told Clarence I would have to wash everything as soon as I get home from the hospital. For now, I will just wash a few receiving blankets that are yellow and green so the baby has something to wear home from the hospital. We went to bed early and laid there holding each other and kissing and just a bit of messing around as best we could.

The doctor had told us last visit, absolutely no intercourse anymore until 6 weeks after the baby was born. neither one of us could imagine waiting that long, and it had only been a couple of weeks. It seemed like years. Laying together and not being able to make love was pure torture. We did all we could without doing something that might hurt the baby. I at least tried to make sure Clarence was relieved every night. He gently massaged me with his fingers and I would almost instantly have a climax. I said that feels so good, I can't see how it could hurt the baby. He said, the doctor just said no intercourse, he didn't say, no messing around. He kissed me and said goodnight. He got as close as he could and we laid there, his front to my back. I couldn't lay anyway that was comfortable except on my side. Next week our anniversary was a beautiful evening, Annie had the top of our cake flown in and we went out to dinner and then came home and had Alan and Mary over and we ate cake and had coffee. Mary was having a bit of trouble with morning sickness like Annie was. But for Mary all she could think about was the fact that she was almost 4 months pregnant and so far, no signs of problems. She was on top of the world. I was so happy for her. As I sit there trying to eat my cake, all I could think about was that I wish I could sit up straight. This precious little one was trying hard to kick it's was out through my ribs. I had thought I would be holding our baby by now, but the baby had a mind of its own. I excused myself to go to the restroom. I had to pee every time I drank an ounce. I don't mean to sound like I am complaining, because I am not. If I had to be pregnant another month then so be it, I was just so anxious to know if I was going to have a daughter or a son. Clarence was just worried because he could see how hard it was for me to sit still and be comfortable. I told him that I was fine, it's just that my stomach was so full of baby that there was no room for anything else. He said, don't worry sweetheart, it can't possibly be much longer. The doctor said that the head is down and ready for a perfect delivery any day now and that was several days ago, so now it was just a waiting game. We were ready to go, a suitcase all packed and all we needed was a pain or two. As we talked with Alan and Mary, all I could do was pray that she got to this stage. Somehow I just knew she was going to carry full term this time.

Clarence and Stella right after he proposed to her

Stella, her Mama, Maxine, Joyce, W.K., Garner, Velma.
The whole family lived in that tent behind them.

Older picture. Alvis and Lola standing on each side of their Mama. Stella is on her Daddy's lap. Maxine standing next to her Mama who is very pregnant with W.K., Birdie is on far right and J.E. and Preston in front.

Picture of Clarence and Stella taken with a group of friends from Northrop Aircraft in 1942.

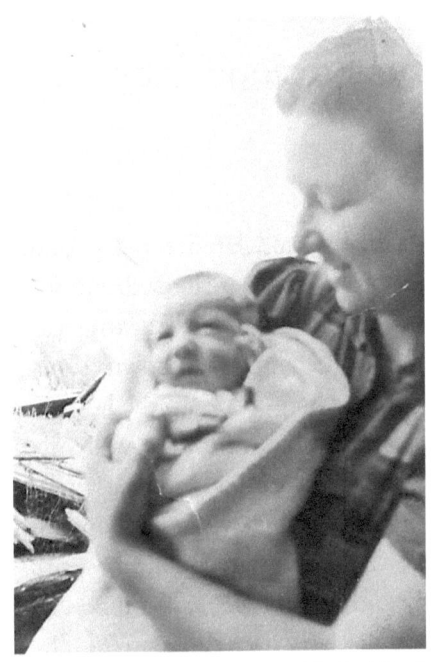

Stella holding newborn Ronald Carl Rader

CHAPTER 14

Our Precious Baby arrives

Five nights later, I woke Clarence and said, honey I think my water just broke or I wet the bed. He threw the cover down and said that is not pee Sweetheart, let's get you to the hospital. While you change your gown, I'll call the doctor and tell him we are on our way to the hospital. He tried to look very calm, but I knew him too well and could tell he was a nervous wreck. It almost made me laugh because I was just relieved that we were having our baby. About 13 hours later, we were the proud parents of a beautiful little boy. I was so happy and I could see tears rolling down Clarence's face. He could not have been more proud if he tried. When they took the baby away to get cleaned up and weighed. He was 7 pounds and 13 ounces and 21 inches long. We talked about what his name would be. We had talked and talked about names for months, but until we knew what he was, we couldn't really make this decision. I told him I wanted at least his middle name for the baby and he agreed to that. But we didn't think Carl Rader sounded good enough for this beautiful baby. I said I really liked Ronald and Clarence kidded with me that I had just fell in love with that actor we had seen in a movie last week at the theater. I said he was the only man in the world for me and that would never change. He agreed that Ronald Carl Rader sounded like a very great name, so that is who our baby is. I was falling asleep as we spoke, so Clarence said he had a phone call to make, then he was going to stop by the nursery and take another look at Ronald before he went home. He said he would be back the first thing in the morning. I asked who was doing his job, and he said there were several of the guys capable of handling the job and Alan said to take a few days off and take care of my family. He left, and I feel asleep before I had time to think. It was exhausting going thru labor, but the rewards were well worth the pain. That was my last thought before I woke up to them handing me my baby to feed. The nurse said he seems like a hungry little guy which is excellent. Some babies we have to wake up, and try to get them to eat, but not this little one. His mouth keeps opening and he is wide awake. I took down the front of my gown and put him to my breast and he took all of 5 seconds to take hold and start sucking. It hurt and felt wonderful at the same time. I guess I should be glad that Clarence had always been a nibbler, because it had toughened my nipples up to where this was not hard getting used to it at all. The nurse said the pains in my stomach were normal and I should be thankful because it pulled on the stomach muscles and made the tummy get back to being flat faster. I said that's a good thing. In just a little while they let Clarence come in to the room. The nurse said that he was lucky that they didn't know the baby was in the room. They worry about germs being brought in. He assured her that he had just showered and his clothes were all clean so our baby would get no germs from him. He was just enjoying watching his son eat and seeing his family all together for the first time. The nurse said she would be back in twenty minutes and be sure and change breasts in five minutes. You need to have both sides having milk come in at the same time. Right now, he was just getting a little fluid which would help him develop antibodies to fight off any sickness while he is little. Clarence and I both just starred at our little miracle and could not believe how perfect and beautiful he was. Clarence quickly untucked the blanket and looked at his perfect little feet. He got him all tucked back in before he got caught. I said, look at this perfect face. His eyebrows look like thy have been painted on by an artist and his eyes look like two black marbles. He is the most beautiful and perfect baby in all the world. Clarence said, stick with me, Sweetheart and we have a few more just like him before we know it. I said I would like to have a few months to enjoy Ronald first, if you don't mind. He said, don't remind me, about waiting six weeks before we can make love. I think I'm going to bust waiting that long. I said it was hard for me too, but maybe I won't be sore for a whole six weeks and I winked at him. I had to stay two full days in the hospital before they would let me go home even though I told them I felt fine the first day after. To deaf ears I was talking, they said I was lucky, some women had to stay three or four days. Clarence said when he called Annie, and she answered like she had been sitting on the phone. She said, I wasn't far off, since she had been so nervous waiting this past week expecting a call every day. Kathleen got on the phone and said I told you it was a boy, didn't I, Mr. Clarence. I asked her where this Mr. came from and she said she was just excited and nervous and so happy for us both and she loved his name. she said she had just seen the best movie last week with the judge, and the actor was so handsome and his name was Ronald. He laughed and said, you women are all alike. She was too happy to even get the idea. Annie said she couldn't wait until her baby was born and they could all come visit us. We told them we were looking forward to it.

On July 25th, 1940 we walked into our home with the most precious package ever. Ronald was just the best baby, he hardly ever fussed and Clarence said who would, if they got to suck on one on those all day. I laughed and said he would get his turn again soon. He smiled the first day he was home and I knew it was a smile and not gas like they said in some books. He was looking right at me after I had burped him and laid him in my lap while I was hooking up both my bra straps tight to help me keep from leaking. My milk had come in and I was looked like a milk cow. My breasts had doubled in size. Clarence said it looked fine to him. I kicked at him and told him they felt like they were rock hard. I'm glad he likes to eat often or I might bust. About that time there was a knock on the door. I had told Clarence I didn't want any company for at least a week, so Ronald didn't get any germs, but here was Mary, and she was so excited to see the baby, we just didn't have the heart to say no. She came in a said she promised she had washed everything she was wearing and had washed her hands three times. She just wanted to hold him for one minute, almost begging so I picked him up off my lap and handed him to her. She held him like a pro, kept his little head held high and said, hi there you beautiful little guy. And there he went again, a big smile. Mary said, did you see that, he recognized my voice. I said he should, you have sure talked to him a lot. She couldn't help herself, she raised him up gently to her cheek and said he was the softest most beautiful thing she had ever seen. I thanked her and said I couldn't argue about that since I felt the same. Mary handed him back to me and said she was sorry she just burst in on us with no notice, but she couldn't stand not seeing him for another minute. I told her it was fine, but I really was tired and needed to go lay down for a while. She jumped up and said again how sorry she was, I told her to stop that, it was perfectly okay and I would have done the same thing had the dates been reversed. She left and Clarence took Ronald so I could get up and go to the bathroom. I could hear him talking to him telling how they would go fishing and play baseball and he would help him with his studies when he started school. I wish I had a way of recording the conversation. It was just priceless. I went in and laid down on the bed and Clarence carried Ronald in and laid him next to me, then laid down with us. We both just marveled at how perfect he was. I'm sure all parents think this, but he really was perfect in all ways. I guess mama's babies were a bit fussy sometimes, because she hardly ever got to just sit and enjoy them. She was back on her feet working in a day or so after each baby, and always had another one barely two, that still needed attention. It made me so sad for her that she never got a day like this where she could lay on a clean bed and have a loving husband lay with her, and they both enjoyed the beauty of their baby. As long as I could remember, she was working and nursing at the same time. It was so sad thinking back on that memory, when I had this beautiful memory here to think about. Life could not be more perfect. I fell asleep and Clarence got up quietly and started a quick dinner. He came back in to find me holding Ronald's little hand and kissing it. He asked if I had slept at all and I told him I had just woke up and found this little guy wide awake and looking around like he was checking out the place. I said I just can't get over how beautiful he is. Clarence said, you are sure not going to get an argument from me. He had seen a lot of babies, but never one this perfect and so handsome. He said we had to quit calling him beautiful or he might be a little sissy. I told him not to be so silly, I would call him beautiful because he was, and no one could tell me different.

The next couple of months seemed to fly by and Ronald stayed the same good baby, hardly ever fussing unless he was wet or hungry. Mary came by every couple of days and held him for an hour sometimes. I would get dinner started while she was enjoying herself. And she was she happy because she had started her seventh month and her baby was very active. Br. Brody assured her everything was going fine this time. I was so happy for her and Alan. They were great people and deserved this baby so much. I told her I sure wish my prayers had helped my daddy be a good person like it helped her pregnancy. She said she was so sorry for how terrible my life had been before I met Clarence. We had talked about it a few times when she came over in the afternoons. I never told her half of the real bad stuff or she would be even more sorry. She said she hoped her baby was just half as good and happy as Ronald was. I told her I knew God had really blessed us with this perfect little guy. Almost every day when Clarence came home we would just lay on the bed with him between us and watch him learn new things each day. Now he was learning to watch his little hands. It was so darn cute to see him study his little fists like he was willing them to do something. Clarence would pick him up and gently fly him around ever his head. That didn't happen too many times after he puked on his head. I laughed so hard. I said I told you he had just finished nursing and his little tummy was very full, but he hadn't listened and now he was taking my burp cloth and wiping his face. I said, wait till you change his diaper and he pees in your face. Clarence said no thanks. I'll just stick to playing with this little hulk. Look at that fat belly, he said as he rubbed his hands over Ronald's tight little belly. You're going to be so strong soon and we will be able to play ball on the floor and all kinds of things. Your Aunt Annie keeps sending you every baby toy known to man.

Annie was due in about another six weeks and Mary about eight weeks. Someday they will all be playing together. At least I hoped so, but Clarence was getting unhappy, not being able to use his brain with this easy job. And he knew Alan had his eye on two of the guys for foreman. He would just keep Clarence, as long as he was willing to stay. I knew Clarence wanted to go back to California and get a job at one of the big aircraft companies so he could use his brains. It's hard for a smart man to let his mind be idle for so long and he knew that they really needed men to work at big companies now that so any were off in Germany with this terrible war. But Clarence didn't want to move while Ronald was so little. He said we'll give him another month to grow strong and then I'll give Alan a few weeks of notice before leaving. Then he can pick out which one he thinks will be the best foreman.

Ronald continued to amaze us with all the things he was learning. I would lay a big blanket down on the floor and he would lay there and just watch everything that was going on in the room. He was just starting to find his feet. It was the cutest thing ever. His feet would go up in the air as he was kicking and his little hands would try to catch them. Finally, he did and would not let go. I wish so much I had got film for the camera, Annie had sent us. It came loaded but we weren't sure how to work it and went through a whole load of film and probably only got a couple of pictures. I had to drop off the roll and buy another one at the drug store next time we went into town. And I was going to ask the man to show me a few things about the camera so I didn't miss anymore cute pictures like today. He was growing like a little weed so fast he would be rolling over soon I could tell by the way re rocked himself back and forth with such a mission to accomplish in his eyes. He was so smart just like his daddy. We were just about the proudest happy parents ever. He was even almost sleeping through the night in his beautiful crib. Some nights I would nurse him at eleven o'clock and he would sleep until Clarence got up at five. Clarence would bring him to me and bring me a clean diaper and a warm wash cloth. What a wonderful daddy Clarence was. He was such a help to me, and it was so great to be able to make love every night again and sometimes catch Ronald asleep when he came home from early milk and we would not let a chance get past us. I had read in a book while still in Carmel that when couples have a baby they lose interest in each other for a while and not to worry because it was perfectly normal. That sure wasn't the case with us, we could keep our hands off each other, and made love every chance we got, we certainly took it.

The next week Ronald came down with a little cold. For the life of me I didn't know where he caught it. I was so careful to keep him bundled up when we went to the store, I always kept a loose blanket over him and Mary and Alan had been the only people over and they hadn't had a cold. I took him to see Dr. Brody and he said sometimes babies just get colds and not to worry. He said to keep him inside and keep him away from any drafts. I checked the window in his room and it was airtight. In the next couple of days, he seemed to not want to eat as much and his little chest sounded congested, so I told Clarence to go into town and call Dr. Brody even thought it was Sunday, I couldn't bear to listen to him all night like this. I was so frightened. I rubbed vicks medicine on his chest and that's all I could think of to do. Clarence said his answering service was all he got and they said to take him into the emergency room and have him checked. We bundled him up good and the car was already warm so we took off for the hospital. They checked him and said, he has a low fever, but his breathing is not right, so they would put him in under a tent and it may help his breathing. The nurse took Ronald from me and started to walk off. I said I am going with him. She told me that only the staff was allowed in the children's wing except during visiting hours which were an hour in the morning from nine to ten and the evening from six to seven.

I was crying so hard and Clarence tried his best to console me, but he was just as upset as I was. We asked to talk to someone in charge and they sent out some of guy, who said we had to follow the rules if we wanted our baby helped. I told him Ronald would be so frightened, and he had never been with anyone but his dad and I. But my begging and crying was to deaf ears. The man just said, come back in the morning please and turned and walked away. I told Clarence I wanted to just get him and take him home and he agreed. We were told that once we had signed him in, he had to stay at least 24 hours or they could be held responsible if something happened. I was ready to just go take him but the glass door would not open. I was crying so hard that I just fell to the floor. Clarence picked me up and said I was going to make myself sick and then who would feed Ronald? That made me cry even harder because I realized that Ronald had never had a bottle, only my breast milk, what would happen to my poor little boy if he wouldn't drink from a bottle. It had been hard to even get him to nurse. I was going to die if they didn't let me in to my baby. Please Lord, let them take me to my baby. Clarence was holding me tight, but no one was coming when we banged on the glass. I wanted to call the police, it had worked for me before in Carmel. But we hadn't even brought any change with us. All we thought of was getting Ronald some help, never thinking they would just take him from us. We got in the car and drove to Alan and Mary's. They answered the door right away even thought it was night and not knowing who it might be. Bad things just didn't happen here or at least we thought it didn't. Mary was so big now, but she almost ran to me when she saw me without Ronald, what happened she said, through many tears we explained what the hospital had done to us. Mary said that is why she had told Alan she wanted to a hospital in a bigger town like I had. Yes, that is why Dr. Brody didn't want me to delivery Ronald there. Alan called the police station and they told him that was the hospital's policy and we should have read what we signed. They said he's in the hospital, what better place for a sick baby? Alan hung up on them and said this was just unacceptable. He called the hospital and they hung up on him when he started talking and mentioned the Rader baby.

Now all I could do was wait until morning. I was there at seven thirty and hoped they would let me in early, but we sat there for an hour and a half before the glass doors opened. A nurse came and told us to follow her, when we got to a big room there were at least eight cribs all around in the room and I immediately saw Ronald laying there in nothing but a diaper, and it was not warm at all in here. I went to pick him up and the nurse said that was not allowed. I said what do you mean? not allowed this is my baby. She said, we are responsible for him while he is in here and if you dropped him, we could be held liable. I picked him up anyway and held him tight to me. Clarence told them they had better not even try to take him away and we were leaving with him now. They said it's only been a little over 12 hours and we have him on strong antibiotics which would be very dangerous to take him off right away. Clarence said, very sternly, then give us the antibiotics so we can give them to him. The nurse said they are controlled medicine and can only be given in the hospital. Ronald seemed so much worse than when we had left him. I couldn't even get him to open his little mouth to nurse. I asked if he had had anything to eat during the night or this morning. They said he refuses the bottles that the nurse tried to give him. I told you people last night he had only nursed and that's all. I sat there rocking and talking to him softly so as not to frighten him, but he just lay on my arms like a rag doll. I couldn't stop crying and Clarence was so mad, but he was crying too. He pulled up another chair and sat there rubbing Ronald's little leg. I asked why he had nothing on but a diaper. They said that is the way we keep all the babies. It is healthier than being all rolled up with blankets where they can't breathe. I said I'll decide what my baby has on and I want the blankets he had when we brought him in here. They are being sterilized and will be back in here when you come back tonight. I said we are not leaving him again. She said it is almost ten now, and you have to go, or be taken out by the guards. Clarence said, Stella sweetheart, it is only 9 hours before we can come and get him. So, let's go or we will cause a big stink and the baby will be frightened. I said they had better take good care of my baby and put a blanket over him as soon as it came back from being sterilized.

CHAPTER 15

Why us, Lord?

At three o'clock that afternoon the police car pulled up in front of the house. Clarence said they better not be trying to cause trouble for us. He opened the door and the policeman said, Mr. Rader and Clarence said yes that's me, what do you want. He said, can we come in? Clarence stepped aside and let them in. I had been crying all morning so I'm sure I looked terrible, but I didn't care, I just wanted them gone. They sat on the sofa and asked Clarence to please sit down. He did, and the policeman said very quietly that our Baby, Ronald had died at two fifteen this afternoon from pneumonia. I looked at him like he was crazy. I said no, we were just there at ten this morning. The policeman said he was so sorry, but there was no mistake. I said I want to go see my baby right this minute Clarence. He looked at the police and they shook their heads and said how very sorry they were, but the hospital did all they could. I told the police that if he was gone it was the hospital's fault, but I didn't believe that my baby was dead, he can't be. I guess by then Clarence believed them and he took me in his arms and tried his best to console me. I twisted away from him and hit the policeman in the chest and said tell me the truth, who has my Baby and I want to be taken to him right now. The policeman just let me hit him over and over until Clarence pulled me away. It was finally sinking in and I knew my Precious little baby was gone. I fell to the floor and just cried and cried and heard nothing that was being said to me. All I could think of was that my baby was gone. Then I would think I must be dreaming all of this, because my little Ronald was such a good healthy baby. Clarence showed the policeman out and sat there on the floor with me. He was crying also and took me in his arms and said he couldn't think right now, but somehow, we would get through this together. I told him I wanted to see Ronald. Please take me to see Ronald, will you? He said we could go to the hospital, but he didn't think that Ronald would still be there. We would probably have to go to the morgue. That just made me drop to the floor again. This time I just lay there like I was in a trance. I could tell Clarence was saying things to me, but I had no idea what he was saying. I heard him answer the door, but didn't move. I heard Mary's voice and thought she must be talking to me but why did she sound so sad? I don't remember how or when, but I woke up and was lying on our bed. I could hear the sound of soft voices in the other room, but nothing was registering with my head what was going on. Why was I in bed while company was here? As I tried to hear what was being said, I heard Clarence say Ronald's name. Where was Ronald and why did he make it sound like he wasn't here. I just don't understand. A moment later Clarence came into our room and said, Hi Sweetheart, your awake I see. Do you want something to eat or drink? It's been quite a while since you have had anything. I said, why do we have company and why did I hear you say something about Ronald? Clarence lay down beside me and wrapped me in his strong arms, and said, do you not remember the police coming by earlier? I said why ever would the police be here and what has that got to do with my baby? Clarence said softly, sweetheart, Ronald is gone. I squeezed myself out of his arms and sat up feeling very angry. What do you mean Ronald is gone, who took him? Clarence stood up and pulled me into his arms again and I could see he was crying. I pulled back for a second and said, why aren't you answering me, where is Ronald? He looked at me and again, very softly he said, he is gone. Remember, we took him to the hospital because he was sick, and the police came by and said Ronald had died early this afternoon. You have been sleeping for several hours since then, but you must remember. I started crying very hard again and said, I don't want to remember, I just want my baby. By then Clarence was crying as hard as I was and said I want him to Darling, but he is gone, and there is nothing we can do to bring him back or I would and you know that. I would do anything in the world to stop this hurting that you and I both are feeling, but the fact remains, Ronald is dead. I went limp again as slid down on the bed.

Clarence called for Mary to come in, and immediately there she was. He asked her if she could sit with me while he got me a bite to eat and something to drink. I asked her if she was okay, because her stomach was huge, and she looked as if she could pop at any moment. She sat down next to me and said, oh Stella, I am fine, we are here to help you and Clarence in any way we can. I said, why, what's wrong with us? I asked her if she could bring Ronald in to me. He needs to nurse, my breasts are leaking and I need to feed him. Then she started crying and said how much she wished she could do that, but he was gone. Somewhere in my head, I knew what she was telling me and what Clarence had told me was true, but I just didn't want to believe it. I felt as if I just wanted to lay down and die so none of this could be happening. Mary put her arms around me and said, she knew what I was feeling just a little, from losing three babies before they were old enough to be live, but what I was living through must be unbearable. I pulled away from her and said quietly, why are you really here? She said that she had seen the police cars here at our house early this afternoon and called Alan and asked him to come home quickly. He was home in five minute, thinking I was ready to deliver. I hadn't even thought to tell him it wasn't me, but you and Clarence, I was concerned about knowing Ronald was so sick in the hospital. Remember, you were both at our house late last night, because they wouldn't let you bring Ronald home with you. I said, he is so cold, and they have him only wearing a diaper and no blanket on him. He is bound to get worse if he they don't keep him warm. Clarence came in carrying a bowl of soup and a coke, which was my favorite drink. He said, you must be a little bit hungry by now. I said I will eat as soon as I nurse Ronald, my breasts are throbbing from being so full of milk. Clarence was still crying, I could see the tears rolling down his handsome cheeks and I wanted so much to console him, but for some reason, all I could think about was feeding my baby.

Mary said she had tried to make me understand, but my mind was just not remembering. She said, I had blocked it all from my mind to keep the pain from being there. I am sure she knows, somewhere in her mind, she knows, she just can't accept the fact right now. I said, would you two quit talking about me as if I were not in the room. Clarence sat down next to me and just asked me to eat some soup, he was holding a spoon full in front of my lips. I started to open my mouth to take the bite, then my head started spinning around, at least I felt like it was spinning. I looked at Clarence with tears rolling uncontrollably down his face and I said, why did my baby die, I can't eat, I just want my baby to be here in my arms where he supposed to be. Clarence put the spoon back in the bowl and set it on the night stand. He pulled me close to him and said there is nothing I want more than that also, but he is really gone sweetheart and there is nothing we can do but accept it and start making his funeral arrangements. I said, you mean put our baby in the ground? All I could think of at that moment was W.K. being just a little boy, and Mama asking him to dig a deep hole and she wrapped her dead baby in the blanket he had brought to her, and the three of us covering up the hole after Mama laid him in the deep hole. We stood there, all three of us crying as Mama said a prayer. W.K. and I were crying because Mama was, we were too young to really under how terrible this was for Mama. I remember

Velma was only three, so I had to be almost nine and W.K. five years old and here we were burying a dead baby in a dirt hole.

How can you expect me to put my baby in a dirt hole Clarence? We were both crying and he said, that's not how Ronald will be buried sweetheart, he will have a beautiful service with the minister praying and the angels will be singing as they accept out precious little Ronald to Heaven. Only his little body will be in a beautiful little coffin, but his soul is already in heaven, where we will see him again one day when we are old and we die. I said I want to die now so I can be with him. Clarence said, Look at me Stella. Do you mean you could just leave me here by myself to grieve our precious baby? He said, I want him so bad, that my whole body is hurting, but my love for you is still so strong that nothing can tear us apart. Please tell me that you feel the same. I looked at this face, that I loved more than life itself, and I held him tight and said, I love you Clarence and I never want to be without you, but how are we going to get through this? He said all we can do is take it one day at a time and hope that as time passes it will get each day will get easier. I stood up and walked into the living room where Alan and Mary sat. They were both crying and stood up, Alan put his arms around me and said how very sorry he was and how much he wished he could somehow take all this pain away that Clarence and I were going through. I asked Mary if she was alright. She was due anytime now, and all this can't be good for your baby. She said she was fine except she was hurting so bad for us and feeling so helpless because there is nothing we can do. I said no one can help, it is just too much to think about. I am so sorry I snapped at you in the bedroom a while ago. I just can't think about Ronald being gone forever. It's just more than I can bear right now. You and Alan should go home so you can rest. You want to have a healthy baby, don't you? We were both crying because there was nothing we could do to stop the tears. It was just too much to think about and accept that it was real. I still wanted to go to his beautiful room and see his beautiful little face sleeping peacefully, but my mind was trying to realize it wasn't going to ever happen again.

As the days passed, nothing seemed to get easier, we had a beautiful service at the little church where just a month before we had the minister dedicate Ronald to the Lord. I hadn't meant He could take him so soon from us. I was trying to remember verses in the Bible that Mama had read to us so many times, and understand God's will, was not to be questioned, but that was just too hard right now. Everyone we knew in town came to the Service, all the men and their wives which Clarence worked with. They all kept bringing food to the house. We had so many casseroles and cakes and pies. We asked them all to come to the house after the service so they could help us eat all their wonderful food they had prepared. Dr. Brody was there also and he came to the house afterward also. He said how very sorry he was that he had been out of town visiting family a few hours away, so he had not been able to take care of Ronald.

He seemed to be carrying so much guilt and even though I was hurting so much I almost felt numb to everything and everybody, I could see the terrible pain that Dr. Brody was feeling and I told him I understood that he had no possible way of knowing Ronald was sick, and I knew that had he known, he would have helped. I sat down next to him and told him that awful hospital was completely responsible for Ronald's death and no one else. We should never have left him there at that terrible place. But they never told us their stupid rules, that we could not take him home after we had signed him in. We signed papers for him to be examined and thought we would be able to stay there or at least bring him home when we could see how he was not being treated well at all. Dr. Brody promised to look into it for us but he was not really affiliated with the hospital. I asked him where he sent his patients to, if they needed to go to a hospital or have surgery. He said, how very sorry he was again, and he should have told us that he always used the hospital where he had delivered Ronald. I told him we just wanted to get him to the hospital quick and thought they would all be the same. Ronald was born in a hospital in the next town over, which was a larger town and a larger nicer hospital. But when Ronald was so sick and not nursing at all for a while we thought it was best to take him to the closest. He put his arm around me and said he would give anything to change things but we both knew that was not possible. Everyone at the house kept coming over and saying how sorry they were, and all of it was like a broken record to me. My need was to get off my feet right, and I kept telling them, I knew by talking, they were only trying to help, when I really just wanted to tell them to get something to eat and go home.

I knew that would be so rude, and I was thankful that my head was being smarter than my heart. After a couple of hours, finally everyone gradually started leaving. All except Alan and Mary, who were being our rocks. Without them to help in all this nightmare, I don't know how Clarence and I would be coping. Mary was at the sinking washing all the dishes and Alan was picking up napkins and cups and anything he could find out of place and taking it into the kitchen for Mary to wash. He put all the trash outside in a large can to be picked up in the morning. I went into the kitchen and told Mary she had gone above and beyond being a wonderful friend. She said she would not leave me with dishes in the sink. I told her that she had been on her feet far too long and I looked down and saw that her ankles were swollen. I said washing dishes would give me something else to think about and she really needed to get off her feet or those ankles were going to really swell. She looked down and said, okay you win, my feet are killing me and the dishes are almost done. She went over to the sofa and sat down next to Clarence. He seemed to be in a trance. Tears were rolling down his face. He quietly said, evenings are the worst, because I enjoyed playing with Ronald as soon as I got home. Stella had always finished nursing him and bathed him, so that I could have this special time with him all for me. As soon as she would finish a few things to be ready with our dinner, she would come in and lay on the bed with us and we would just marvel at this most perfect little precious baby that we had both created from our love. We would laugh at his every cute little thing that he had learned that day. He was so smart and so ahead for his age. Dr. Brody said, he was just about the smartest little guy he had ever seen. He probably told all parents the same thing, but to us he truly was the smartest baby ever born.

Mary said, I know when I was over during the mornings while you were at first milking, I was amazed at the things he could already do. He was a beautiful healthy baby and I can only imagine the pain you two are going through. Just keep loving each other and you will get through this together. I won't even begin to say it will be easy, but knowing you two and how much you love each other, I know you'll be okay. Alan came in and sat down and told Clarence to take as much time off as he needed to help Stella and himself get through this. Clarence said that they had funeral bills to pay so he need to get back to work soon. About that time Stella walked in and said dishes done, and what did I walk in on? Alan said, I was just telling Clarence that he could take as much time off as he needed. Clarence spoke up and said, that I told him I needed to get back to work so we could get the funeral bill out of the way. Stella looked at me and said, whatever you want to do. He came over and put his arms around me and said I'll stay home as long as you need me. I said, I will always need you, but I can be alone for a few hours, a couple of times a day and not fall apart. I agree that Clarence should get back to work as soon as he can. Alone, Clarence and I sat there holding on to each other. We still made love because we loved each other so much and knew that our love was the only thing holding us together. I don't mean that's why we were together, we were together because we truly loved each other and making love was just our way of showing each other that. But dealing with the loss of Ronald would be more than either of us could bear without each other. We were each other's rock now.

Clarence went back to work on Monday after the funeral on Friday. It was almost a relief for him to be gone, so I could cry and feel all the pain that I was feeling without dragging Clarence down and him feeling he had to be there with me every minute. I looked at every beautiful little outfit that he had ever worn and thought of the day he wore it and what we did that day. I sat in his room in the beautiful rocking chair that Annie had sent as a special present the day he was born. I held the soft blue blanket that Kathleen had sent and reread the letter she had in her box. I needed to see these wonderful friends now very much, but most of all I needed to hug my mama and have her tell me that I would be okay, like she has so many times after daddy had beat me so bad. I thought to myself, that animal of a man could just keep having babies and make them work their butts off as soon as they were old enough to hold a bucket or do anything that would give him whiskey money, but for some reason God chose to take our baby who was loved so very much by his mother and his father. Two parents could not have been happier or more in love with their child. Why us, Lord? I kept asking this question over and over. I finally decided to write mama and my siblings a letter and tell them about Ronald. I had written and, told them how beautiful and perfect he was a week or so after he was born and promised to send a picture as soon as we had a roll developed. I said

I hoped that some of them turned out because it was a new fancy camera our good friends had bought us and we weren't sure how to work it and had probably over exposed some of the pictures. I was just keeping my fingers crossed that a few turned out, because they just had to see how beautiful he was. We had just got the roll back the day before Ronald got sick, and I barely looked at them, because I was so concerned about how fast Ronald seemed to be getting worse. If only I had call Dr. Brody that first day while he was still in his office. That thought had gone through my mind a million time in the past week. After I finished writing the letter, I went over to our little desk and opened the drawer and sat there looking at the envelope from the drug store. I had barely looked at the pictures when we picked them up because Ronald was starting to coo and talk to us when we talked to him and that was more important than looking at a picture I could look at any time. When he did things for the first time we never wanted to miss a thing. We were both so in love with out Perfect little guy. I opened up the envelope and looked at the pictures. Just as I had thought, most were over-developed or doubled exposed because we would forget to roll the film to the next picture. I looked at one of me holding Ronald and there were two almost exactly the same, so I put one of them in with my letter to Mama. I quickly put a stamp in it and took it out just as the mailman was coming. It was gone now, so there was no changing my mind. I went back in and looked at the one I had kept and then one of just Ronald with his fat little belly looking so darn cute. I took both pictures and went back to my rocking chair in his room and picked up the fuzzy soft blue blanket and sat there looking at the picture and cried myself to sleep.

Clarence came home before I woke up and kneeled down next to me and said, Stella sweetheart, this is just as hard for me, but you are going to make yourself very sick if you don't remember to eat and take care of you. Do you realize what it would do to me if I lost you, after the terrible loss of our precious Ronald? I couldn't think of any way I could get through that. Please try to take care of you, my only precious gift I have left in this world. You are my world, sweetheart. Try to remember us and how important we are together. One couldn't survive without the other. I love you so very much. Please for me, come out into the living room and have a bite to eat. I will fix you whatever you want. I told him I loved him very much too, but I just can't eat. It would just come back up I know. He said how about a nice cup of tea. I told him that sounded good and he said please come to the kitchen table and sit with me. So, I got up and followed him to the kitchen. He had a plate of snack foods that people were still bringing by. Without even thinking about it, I picked up a cute little sandwich with the crust cut off and nibbled at it. Clarence sat my tea in front of me and I added sugar and stirred it a while to help it cool. Clarence ate two or three of the sandwiches and said, these are really good, I wonder what they are made from. I told him they were a chicken salad. We had made them for soldiers at Mrs. Peterson's house also. I picked up another one and Clarence had a couple more too. I said that they had been one of my favorites also. We just sat there mostly in silence, because it was just so hard to talk about it. Clarence got up and put a few homemade cookies and some cupcakes on a plate and sat them on the table. He ate a cupcake and I picked up an oatmeal cookie. It still seemed so amazing to me how used to eating good things came so easy, after never having them my whole life until just a little over a year before. I drank my tea and Clarence had a cup of warmed up coffee from this morning. I realized that I had not been doing anything lately but sitting in Ronald's room. I knew in my head it wasn't good for me, but I didn't seem to care, because it's what my heart wanted to do and it's the only thing that made me feel close to Ronald. Feeling his clothes and holding his favorite toys and his favorite blue blanket. I hurt inside so much and the only thing that made me even feel alive was when Clarence and I made love. That was so natural and felt so right that I wished that only the nights existed, so I didn't have the days to be alone.

Another few days passed all seeming like the last, until Clarence came home from early milk and said that Mary had her baby during the night and it was a little girl. I asked if she was okay. He said that Alan said that she and the baby were wonderful. He was so happy and tried to calm it down for my sake. I told him to knock it off, that we were very happy for them and wished them our very best. I hope I didn't speak out of turn for you. I said, of course not. Mary has been through so much waiting for this baby. I want you to have Alan send his guys over to pick up all those beautiful little girl things that Annie sent. He said that is a wonderful idea. He asked if I would like to call Mary and tell her. I told him he could do it. My poor wonderful husband was trying so hard to help me, there was just nothing but him that helped. For that I was very thankful, just knowing out love was strong to withstand this terrible loss and knowing he was hurting just as much as I was. Ronald had been so very important to us both. He had been our world for over four months now and even before he was born looking forward to him had brought us closer together than even before which I didn't think possible, since we were so very happy with just each other, but being with Ronald had made life just a bit of heaven. Now he was gone and learning to be without him was almost more than I could bare. Without Clarence, I know I would have just died. He was my only reason for living now and when he wasn't here, all I wanted to do was sit in Ronald's room with all his beautiful happy things. It made sense to me, even if no one else understood. I just didn't care.

When the crew came to pick up all the beautiful little girl clothes and blankets and dolls and just everything you might think of to buy a little girl, Annie had bought. It broke my heart to see it go, because somewhere in my head I had thought I might be pregnant by now with another baby. Clarence and I had talked about wanting at least four or five children and since he was so much older we didn't want to put it off. I know four, well almost five months now since Ronald had been born, I had been nursing and I had read that you sometimes you didn't need to practice any birth control methods because you wouldn't get pregnant anyway. Thinking about having another baby now hurt badly, in many ways because I knew no baby could ever replace him. I knew I wanted more children so much and so did Clarence, but I really didn't know how I would feel when I became pregnant again. Maybe I would be happy, but nothing could replace my precious perfect little

Ronald. He had been such a joy to us from the minute he was born. All the wonderful new little things he learned to do every day just thrilled us. My mind was consumed by my thoughts of him. I hurt more than any pain my Daddy had inflicted on me. The pain just went so much deeper. I felt so completely empty, sitting here all alone when I knew I should be playing with my baby and washing his diapers and giving him baths, which he loved so much. That was when he had first laughed out loud, while learning to splash the water with his little hands. His face just lit up with joy. I would give anything to just be able close my eyes and sleep without any dreams, but my mind wouldn't shut off.

Clarence came home a little earlier than usual this evening and I had promised myself that I would try hard to be in the kitchen preparing a meal for my wonderful husband when he came home, but no there I was rocking Ronald's blanket as if he were in it. He came in and looked so deep in pain seeing me like this, I could tell it was making it harder for him than it already was, and I really hadn't wanted to be here when he got home. I said, Hi honey, how was your work this afternoon, you're home so early. He took my hands and pulled me up to him and held me tight, he said that the guys were well trained now and could handle things without him. Then he said he had brought in the mail and there were so many more cards to read. He said let's go in and sit on the sofa together and read them. It will never be any easier sweetheart, and our friends just want to show they are thinking of us. I saw that there are some from my family in

Oklahoma and one from Ft. Worth, Texas too. I said okay, but will you read them to me. My eyes just can't stop the tears and then I can't even see what I am reading. He said, of course I will read them to you. So, there we sat in the living room together on the sofa, and before he picked up the first letter, I was crying. Clarence said, oh my precious darling, I would give anything to bring him back, you know I would, but somehow together we have to go on without him as bad as it hurts, there is just nothing to do but grieve him and remember all the wonderful moments God gave to us with him. I said, why did he have to take our baby, he was so good and so perfect and we were such good parents to him, why, I just can't make myself understand. Mama always told us God would take care of things. How is this taking care of anything. Ronald is gone and my heart hurts so much, and my arms want to hold him and rock him quietly while he nurses. When will it stop hurting?

Clarence took me in his arms and said, sweetheart, I can tell you that I honestly don't know for sure about anything, but I think it will always hurt, because we loved him so much and he was a part of us and our love for each other, but I do know that we are still alive and we still love each other just the same as always from the first moment I saw you and we must go on living. We will have more babies and none of them will be Ronald, but we will love them the exact same way we loved him. So, I am going to help pack up his things and we will give them to one of the guys that just had a baby boy. They don't have much, or the money to go out and buy a lot of things and Ronald is gone and can't use them anymore. It's the best thing we can do sweetheart. I know it hurts and you think you need his things, but they are making you not think clearly. I sat down and thought to myself, how can he give Ronald's things away. Then my normal head knew it was the only thing to do. Ronald was not coming back no matter how much I cried or how much I prayed. The fact was, he was gone. I said okay, but I have to save just a couple of his little things to keep him always in my heart. So, Clarence said, now sit down and let me read these cards and letters.

The first one he opened was from his mother and dad, they said how very sorry they were for our pain and would be praying for us. They went on to talk about his younger brothers and sisters and how sad they were that they never got to meet their only nephew. It was a very nice letter and his mother seemed to be such a nice woman. The next was a card from one of the guy that he worked with. They just gave their sincere feelings about our loss and most of them added that we were in their prayers.

Finally, he opened the letter from Lola, she went on and on about what a tragedy it was and then she said she thought she would drive out to the camp where Mama and the kids were and tell them in person. But she said, she no sooner got there, when daddy drove up and got out of his old car and waved a letter around saying Stella had sent a picture of her and her new kid. She said Maxine, W.K., Velma and all the rest of them were saying come on Daddy, let us see the picture and mama, was saying please can I read her letter? Then he announced, that none of them would ever see her kid anyway, because he was dead. So, that's how my mama had to hear about Ronald. I hated that man with every fiber in my body. I knew the Bible said not to hate, but when someone has done the things he had done your whole life, I just couldn't feel any other way.

The next letter was from Annie, Mike, Kathleen and Tony. They each wrote a little and it was just so obvious that every word they said was from their heart. As, I'm sure Clarence's family's letter was also, it's just that I knew them. Annie was just like me and always wore her heart on her sleeve, so the things she said had me crying my eyes out, yet somehow made me feel better. After all the sad parts from each of them saying how they couldn't imagine the pain we both must be in, they finally had to say that Annie had a little boy last week just about the time Ronald had died. They named him Jacob Michael. I said that's a beautiful name, don't you think, honey? He said yes, it's a beautiful name. I hope we get to meet him one day. So do I. We finished reading all the cards, or I should say Clarence read and I listened, kind of numb after a while, they all sounded the same. Nothing against any of them, It's just that there are only so many things you can say to a couple who has just lost their little baby.

Clarence finished up the week and when he came in Friday evening, I actually, had a meal ready for him. I know he was happy, but also quite surprised. I made fried chicken, mashed potatoes, gravy and green beans with a pan of biscuits. I was getting better at making them, they even raised this time. While we were eating, Clarence told me that he had sent an employment application in to Northrop Aircraft in

Southern California. He said they were in desperate need of engineers from all he had heard. I said when did you send it to them? He said, I just mailed it off today. Why, doesn't that sound okay to you, sweetheart? I said it was fine, as long as we were together along for the ride. He said, you are very funny lady, I wouldn't move across the street without you. He said, he was going over to Alan and Mary's after dinner to give them two weeks to find another foreman, and hoped I'd drive over with him. I said, I guess I can't avoid babies for the rest of my life. So, we finished the dishes and took off down the road a short way. When we got out of the car, I almost chickened out, but Clarence put his arm around me and held me close. I always felt safe in his arms. When we rang the doorbell, Mary answered and said how happy she was to see us. She said, come in and have something to eat with us. We are eating late because I had a check-up with the doctor this afternoon. Clarence said, thank you but we just finished dinner. When we went around into to living room area, Alan was sitting there holding the baby. He started to get up, but we sat down before he had a chance to. I think he was feeling funny about holding the baby in front of us. I said she was a beautiful baby. Alan seemed to relax just a little and said, thank you we think so but I guess we are a little on the partial side. Mary came in quickly and said, would you like me to put her in her room while we talk. I said don't be silly you two, you're both making things worse. I have to be around babies sometime and I'm glad it's yours, because she is so pretty in that little dress. Mary said, I have been meaning to come by and thank you for all the beautiful clothes and blankets and so many of everything, I can't believe it. We won't have to buy a thing for at least a year or more. That was so thoughtful of you Stella and Clarence. So many things it was overwhelming. I had been given a shower, but only got the generic things that can be worn by either, but this was simply amazing. I love every single outfit. I told her my friend had very good taste, and only shopped at the finest stores. Mary said, I can tell by the quality of everything. I asked, by the way, I don't even know her name. Mary said, because you are so beautiful and gave so much to make her beautiful, we named her Stella Marie. I started to cry and said, I feel so honored, I never thought my name sounded pretty, but the way you said it, made it sound very pretty. We think it's a beautiful name. I said, she makes it sound beautiful because she is so pretty. Such a tiny dainty face. Ronald was such a big boy and so chubby. As my eyes filled with tears, Clarence held me tight and made me feel stronger. Mary could tell how hard this was for me, so she tried to change the subject. Won't you come into the kitchen and let us be rude and eat in front of you. Clarence said that's not rude, that's just wanting to eat your dinner before it gets cold and I don't blame you a bit. Since we just finished ours, we are certainly not hungry, so we would be glad to have a chat while you eat. Mary said, I'll go put Little Stella down and be right back. I spoke up without even thinking and asked if I could hold her while they ate. Mary looked at Clarence quickly and saw he thought it was fine, so in my arms was this beautiful little girl, so pretty in pink and looking all girl. I said she feels like holding a feather. Clarence said, she is definitely a beauty, just like her namesake. Alan said, you seem to have an agenda Clarence, you forget how well I know you after four years in the same tiny room. Clarence said I wouldn't exactly call it an agenda, I just wanted to let you know we are moving to Southern California. They need engineers real bad at Northrop Aircraft and I can make really good money. Oh Alan said, so I'm not paying you enough. Clarence said, you are paying me too much for what I do, but I have an education in engineering and need to start using it before I lose it and now is the time they need me. Most of their young men have been drafted into the military to train for this war that is bound to happen. Anyway, I am not trying to dodge my reason for coming over. I wanted to give you two weeks notice, so you have time to choose which one of the guys you want to be your new foreman. Alan said, I really appreciate this Clarence, and I would like to know, who you think, just for my own peace of mind, to see if you pick the one I am thinking of. Clarence said, they are both very qualified, but Joe is the one that will give it his all. Alan smiled and said thank goodness, great minds think alike. Alan finished his plate and Mary cleared the table and during their whole conversation I just sat quietly admiring this beautiful little baby, who was so different from my own. As I blurted out that I would hold her, my next thought was what am I thinking, I can't hold her, but then it was too late, she was in my arms, and it felt so good. I knew she wasn't Ronald, but it still felt wonderful to have her in my arms. So very tiny and petite looking. Such perfect little features, just like Mary's. Mary asked if I was still okay with holding her. I said yes, I'm fine. Mary did the dishes real quick and then came and sat down on the chair next to me. She put both her arms around me tight and said, she knew there was nothing she could do or say, but she wanted me to know how much her and Alan both treasured mine and Clarence's friendship and she hoped we could remain close even though we would be a thousand mile apart. I told her I would like that.

The next two weeks flew by and when it was time to pack all of Ronald's beautiful crib and furniture in the trailer, I told the guys to put lots of blankets around everything so that there was no way a scratch could get on any of the baby furniture. Our furniture had already been well packed and all our beautiful bedding and things were boxed up safe and tight. Clarence walked through the house and asked if I was sure we had everything? I assured him there was not so much as a grain of salt left in any cabinet in this house. We found it clean and I am leaving it clean. So, the truck left and we were right behind it. We told the truck that we would probably get ahead of them soon and gave them the name of the motel where were would be staying about halfway. They said they knew the place and would see us there later tonight.

As we were leaving Oregon, I thought of the day we arrived, not all that long ago. We were filled with such happiness at starting our family. The first of many children we wanted and the excitement of being in a new place which was so much bigger and nicer than our first home in Pacific Grove. I loved our first home though. It had been so special being Clarence's wife and discovering each other in every way. Our love was so wonderful and so deep that I was sure it could withstand anything. Now we had been put to the test in the worst possible way and though we were both still grieving so much, we still had each other and that got us through the worst of times. It had to be the best of times soon.

CHAPTER 16

New start in California

Clarence had heard from Northrop Aircraft and the job they offered him would pay him three times what he had made working for Alan. But the house also came with the job, so that was a big amount more that he actually made. But still, I felt California was our home since we had started there. And we needed to be in a new place where Ronald had not been. Being in our home where we had loved him for just a little over four months and watched his every precious new discovery had made living there so hard for us both. We woke so many mornings, remembering Clarence going in and bringing him to me to nurse, while he fixed our breakfast. Then we would bathe him and watch him learn something new every day. He was such a joy to us and why God choose to take him I would never know. I only know I believed in my heart that no parents could have loved a baby more than we had, and taken any better care of him. I would never understand, and I knew that no matter how many more babies we had, no one could replace Ronald. Not that we wouldn't love another baby just as much and take just as good care of our future babies God gave us, through our love, but he or she could never take Ronald's place. That one place in my heart would always grieve him until the day I died. I just knew I wanted another baby to hold and to love and take care of. I felt that would be the only thing that would keep me from becoming old and dried up before I reached twenty years old. These silly thoughts wouldn't leave my head.

I knew more important than anything Clarence was still with me and would always love me more than anything and I felt the same about him. We were each other's rock and that rock together made our love so strong, that nothing could ever hurt that part of us. We may be both hurting about Ronald, but our love was still strong and would always be. I knew that with all my heart. All these thought went through my head as I laid with my head in Clarence's lap as he drove quietly, so as not to wake me. I don't think I really ever actually went into a deep sleep. I just dozed enough to make me have strange thoughts. They weren't really strange thoughts, after all, everything I was thinking, was true and always would be. But how is it that I can think of having another baby already when it had only been barely two months since our baby died. Was I getting too anxious to have another baby, thinking it would make me not think of Ronald. No. I knew I would never get over losing Ronald, I just needed a baby in my arm to keep from being so sad and trying so hard to keep a smile on my face for Clarence. When I knew he was doing the same for me. It was all so darn confusing. The only thing we weren't doing together was talking about Ronald to each other. It hurt so bad to think about it, yet talking about it always ended up with me crying my eyes out and Clarence trying so hard to help me, because he couldn't stand watching me in so much pain. He felt the same pain, he was just stronger and able to hold his tears because if we were both crying it seem too much to bare. We would just both fall apart. We were both smart enough to know that there was nothing we could do but go on and we also knew it would never be easy, but as they say, the living must go on. It's really easy for me to think all these things and then another to actually follow through with living it. I moved around where I was looking up at my handsome Husband's face. He smiled at me and I felt the love that I had felt since the first day of meeting this wonderful generous man. That first day I looked into his eyes, I knew from that moment that we would always be together, I just never dreamed that our beautiful life would have such dark times so very soon after our marriage. In just one year and six days, we were given a precious gift, only to have him taken from us just four months later. Why, I kept asking, over and over in my prayers at night and in the morning or any other moment I thought of Ronald. I kept waiting for God to give me a reason, but it never happened. I would always know there was God and I would always trust him, like my Mama had taught me, but I would always wonder, what I did for this to happen.

We reached the motel and Clarence went in and paid for two rooms, he told them that the two men would be a bit later and gave him their names. He explained that they were driving our moving truck, which wouldn't go as fast as our car. After carrying in our bag and various things that I needed, Clarence asked what kind of food I wanted to eat. He looked around and said there seems to be signs for about any kind of food you could possibly think of. I said, just a big juicy hamburger sounds good to me. He went in and asked the man in the office who served up the best hamburger in town. The man told him the little diner on Main St. was great. So, that's where we headed. It was pretty crowded, so we considered going somewhere else, but the hostess was with us in less than a minute and asked if the back booth was okay. We told her anywhere was fine. We ordered a couple of burgers loaded with everything and one order of fries. Clarence ordered coffee and I had a coke. I had become addicted to them. I would have one for breakfast once in a while lately. It was so much better than coffee to wake up, or to go to sleep with. I don't think I've seen Clarence have a coke more than twice since I had known him. Funny how a person could become addicted to something so fast. I remembered that one I had bought just hours before getting to Carmel, it had tasted so good and I knew right then, I would always love them. Our burgers came and they looked delicious, and they were. We stopped at the office before going to our room and thanked the man for leading us to the right place to eat. He said they have great breakfast also. Again, Clarence thanked him and said our room looked really nice and clean too. Now the man thanked Clarence. We went to our room and took our usual shower, together. It had become a habit that I loved. The baths were even better, but we did our best with what we had. We were clean and felt refreshed as we started our usual foreplay. Our lovemaking was something always so satisfying. I wondered if my poor Mama had ever been able to enjoy sex. I couldn't imagine that horrible old man ever taking time to satisfy her. Strange thinking of my parents making love with six to seven kids in the same room with them on pallets all around the room and usually a baby in bed with them until the next one came along. How could she ever have enjoyed anything with that beast who called himself a man. He beat her one minute and had his way with her when he decided to come to bed. It made me sick, but Clarence and I were just the so different. We loved exploring each other's bodies and seeing how much better we could make each other feel and we always talked and asked if something felt good or if we like it another way better. But no matter which way we made love, we were both completely satisfied before we were finished. Clarence never quit worrying that he would climax before I did, but most every time we made love more often than not, we climaxed together. It was like we were just fine tuned to each other. No matter what else happened in our lives, we always promised to talk every night and we always made love before going to sleep and quite often again during the night. It never got old for us. It was our way of letting each other know that together, we could face anything the world through at us.

The next day we arrived at Los Angeles by mid-afternoon. We had told the guys to sleep in as long as they wanted, because once we got to the Los Angeles area, we had to get a newspaper and find a place to put the furniture in. We had saved the biggest part of Clarence's pay, because all we had to pay for was our groceries and utilities on the house, which were very low. Even after Ronald had come along we had everything we could possibly ever need until he was at least two years old. Annie, Kathleen, and Tony had seen to that. But now some other lucky little baby boy was getting to enjoy all his things. Clarence had insisted that I had to do this in order to get a grip on reality. I had protested, but he put his foot down when he found me sleeping on floor with Ronald's favorite blanket and holding his fuzzy toys he loved to play with. He was very gentle with me, but also firm. He said he loved me too much to let me go off the deep end. And I was heading there fast. Clarence got back in the car and I changed my thoughts back to looking for places to live. Sleeping in the car didn't appeal to me. I had done it the backseat of old cars huddled up together with five or six brother's and sister's way too many times and it didn't sound fun even with the love of my life.

We found several places that sounded pretty good, but looking good were two different things, we found that out after looking at the first two. I couldn't see how people described a place as clean and spotless and then we got there it they looked worse than some of the dirt floor places I had lived in as a child. We had two more to look at and when we drove up at the next one, we both looked at each other and said Thank You, Lord. We hadn't seen the inside yet, but the neighborhood was so clean and everyone's yards were mowed and it looked like an advertisement for a model home. While we waited for the people to show up that were supposed to meet us there at 2:00 o'clock, we got out of the car and looked over the fence to see the backyard. It was also perfectly manicured. In just another minute, the lady drove up and said she was there to meet the Rader's. We said, that's us. So, she opened the front door and said, you two look around, I don't want to be in your way. Clarence and I walked all around and every room was perfectly clean. There were hardwood floors in every room except the kitchen and bathroom and they both had tile floors which looked practically new. We asked again the price to be sure we hadn't read the ad wrong, but she said it was $55.00 per month and a $25.00 deposit. We told her we would take it, providing we could move in that afternoon when our moving truck arrives here from Oregon. She said that sounded great and we filled out and signed the rental agreement she had with her. We paid her in cash, which I think surprised her. We explained that we moved in a bit of a hurry because Clarence had been offered a good job at Northrop Aircraft, and he didn't want to lose the job. She said that was very close, so he wouldn't have much of a drive. She gave us two sets of keys and said that she always had an extra set in case of an emergency and we couldn't be located. We said that was fine, but I was usually home during the day. She told me there was lots of grocery stores close by, if I liked to walk and also a nice park if we had any children. I guess she could tell how quiet I got, all of a sudden and Clarence told her we had just lost our little baby boy a few months ago, but hopefully we would have more before too terribly long. She said how very sorry she was and she shouldn't have said anything since we didn't have any children with us. She patted me on the arm and said her heart was breaking for me, just to think of it and again how sorry she was she had spoken out of turn. We both told her she had no way of knowing and not to worry. When she left, we went back in and couldn't believe our good luck in finding this place. It was too good to be true, but here we stood in our new home with 3 bedrooms and a small garage behind the house. You had to open the gates to drive back in, but that made it very safe. Clarence said, we had better get to the corner where we had told the truck we would meet them at 5:00 o'clock. We were an hour early, but there they sat waiting for us. We told them to follow us and we would be ready to help unload in just a few blocks. I carried in boxes that I knew weren't too heavy and put them in the rooms where they went and before I knew it the three guys has it all in the house. But when Clarence saw me looking at Ronald's furniture, he told the guys he thought it would be best if we put all that baby furniture in the garage for now. I didn't argue because I knew it would do me no good. Clarence was only trying his best to make things as easy as possible for me. So, in a couple of minute they had his crib and dresser in the garage. I told them to cover it really well with lots of blankets. Clarence said he made sure it was well covered and he said even the garage had concrete floors and the door was well fitted so that not any bad weather could ever get in. I felt better knowing that. We paid the men and Clarence followed them to where they had to drop off the truck, and then he took them where to the bus station and bought their tickets back to Oregon. When he returned home, I had most of the kitchen boxes unpacked. He said I had been quite busy. Then I took him by the hand and led him into the largest bedroom where they had set up our bed. I had it all made up with my favorite sheets on. He said, wow you have been busy. I told him I thought we should christen our new room as soon as he got home. He got that gleam in his eyes and said, I guess you have the towels in the bathroom already, as I am a bit sweaty. I told him the bath awaits us. And so, there we were in just as few hours from finding our new home and we were already making ourselves at home. And after working up quite an appetite, we got dressed and went looking for a nice restaurant to have dinner at. There was the cutest little café not far from the house and we weren't disappointed we had tried it. The food tasted just like home cooking. So with our bellies full we went back to setting up our kitchen. We wanted to have the whole weekend to get acquainted with our new area. Clarence first found his way to Northrop. She wasn't kidding when she said it was not far. Clarence said, after he taught me how to drive a little better in heavier traffic than where we had practiced in Oregon, that if I wanted to keep the car for anything he could even walk to work. I told him not to be silly, that if I did need it, I could certainly drive him to work and pick him up.

About a month after we moved into out nice little house, during the late afternoon while I was starting dinner, I heard a knock on the front door. I dried my hands and rushed to see who it could be. I wasn't expecting anything or anyone, for that matter. I open the door, and there stood my little brother who had grown up to be bigger than I was. W.K. what in the world, I mean where did you come from and how did you get here? Are mama and daddy working here in California again? I had so many questions and I hadn't given him a chance to answer any of them. I grabbed him and squeezed him so hard he almost couldn't breathe. He said, I ran away, and Mama and that sticking old man of ours are still in Texas. I said, how did you get here? He told me he was so sick of being beat on for doing nothing and he just couldn't take it anymore, he said, he not only couldn't take it anymore, he couldn't stand to see how daddy treated mama and Velma and it was sure to be Garner before too long. I said, you still didn't say how you got here. He said, I crept out of the house as soon as he knew the old man was snoring and out from his latest drunk and he hitch hiked for the past four days. He said, he got pretty lucky and was picked up a couple of times from people who were going a long ways towards California, so I rode for a full long day with a couple of people and they even had some food they shared with me. I don't think I could have made it without them. I asked him if he remembered all the times Mama read to us from the Bible and how she told us God would always take care of us when we really needed him. W.K. was pretty bitter, so he was in no mood to listen to this right now. He said, I took care of myself, no one got me here, but me. I hugged him again and said however he got here I was so happy to see him. I said you are the first I've seen of my family since I was 16. He said, we all missed you so much when you left, especially Maxine, I think she was about to run away too, but she said, she didn't have anywhere to go. She went to Lamesa, and lived with Aunt Willie Mae for a while as soon as she could get away. She got a job doing something there, I'm not sure what, but she met a man named J.P. Derington and they got married just a little while ago. I don't think she had your address when she left or I'm sure she would have written you by now. She probably will, since she is free to go and do whatever she wants to now. She'll probably go to Lola's and get it. I asked if he was going to stay here with Clarence and I for a while and he said, he came to us to ask a big favor. I said, whatever we can do, I'm sure we will. He said, he really wanted to join the Navy, but since he was so small, he didn't think they would believe he was eighteen. He said, I know J.E. and Preston joined when they were younger than me, but they weren't small like me. I told him he wasn't so small anymore. He said, for a guy, you know I am. I said, what can we do, and he said, he asked around, while he was hitching rides and some guy told him if you have someone older that says they are your guardian, and they are willing to sign that your eighteen, they accept that. I told him Clarence would be here any minute from work. Come on in to the kitchen with me while I fix dinner. Are you hungry? He said, I am starving, it had been almost a day since I ate. I told him we were having meatloaf and it would be about 45 minutes before it was ready, but I could make him a peanut butter sandwich to tide him over. He said, that sounded good even if he hadn't had one. I laughed and said, yes there's a lot we never had at home. Daddy never thought anything other than beans and potatoes were important for us. He looked around and said it looks like you and Clarence are doing really well. I said yes, Clarence is a very smart man. He was only picking cotton for a while, until he decided where to go next. He graduated from college as an Engineer a long time before we met, he just decided to travel around and see the country while times were tough with the beginning of this war. He is now working at his profession at Northrop Aircraft. He makes pretty good money considering how bad off we are, trying to help with this war. W.K. said if it wasn't so bad, he probably wouldn't get accepted into the Navy. He had finished the sandwich in about three bites and I asked if he wanted another? He said, yes please Stella if you're sure you don't mind. I said, of course I don't mind, I'm glad you liked it, although, I'm not sure you chewed enough to taste it. I asked if would like a coke? Another, what is that? I told him it was a drink that I had come quite addicted to, but you can also have a glass of milk which would probably go better with your peanut butter sandwich. He said, oh thanks, Sis, milk sounds great. I'll try a coke some other time. He got real quiet for a minute and then he said, how sorry he was about Clarence and I losing out little baby. I told him thank you for saying so, and it was the hardest thing I've ever had to go through. I'd take a thousand beatings from daddy, if it would bring back Ronald. He said, wow, you must really be sad. I told him he just had no idea how hard it was to love something more than life itself. It was very hard for Clarence and I. We are still grieving, but we love each other so much or we would never have been able to get through it. Clarence had been so patient with me, because I thought I would die of a broken heart. It is still very hard and we haven't been able to get pregnant again yet, so I keep hoping every month. He said, Kenneth was sure a cute little stinker. His hair is white, just like Velma's. I asked how daddy and Velma were getting along. He said not good at all, she is just like you were, if not worse. She tries to get him to leave Mama alone, and all he does is beat on Mama worse and then beats the hell out of her. I just couldn't stay around there anymore, Stella. I think daddy would kill me one of these day if I hadn't left. He just seems to hate me an extra lot for some reason. Always telling me how worthless I am. I was crying by now, and I went over to him and told him just to never think of that worthless old man ever again. He didn't ever have to see him again if he didn't want to. He said, you don't have to bet on my answer, do you? I told him the only reason I would ever see him again is that I wanted to see my mama again and I don't think he'd let her come here, that for sure. I heard Clarence drive up and I went to the door to greet him. I kissed him and then told him, we had company. He said, who is it? My little brother W.K. He couldn't stand daddy's abuse anymore and has been hitch hiking for four days. Actually he got here faster than I did on the bus, but he had to do a lot of walking part of the time between rides. He got lucky with a couple of rides with people coming pretty close towards our direction, or he may never have made it. He left without a penny to his name and just a change of clothes. We went into the kitchen and Clarence shook his hand then hugged him and said how much he had grown up since he last saw him. W.K. said I wish I could grow some more, but as long as I can get in the Navy, that all I care about now. I told him that he needed us to sign for him saying he is eighteen. Clarence said, will they believe he's your son. I laughed and said no, we just have to say we have been his legal guardians and verify he is eighteen years old. Clarence said he had no problem trying it out. I can't see how it could hurt. W. K. said how much he appreciated it. So he stayed with us for a few days and we got him a new set of clothes that made him look a little older and also we had to feed him enough so he didn't look like he hadn't ate much in four days. Like he hadn't. W.K. just couldn't get over being able to eat all he wanted to and how much food we had. He really went nuts when we took him to our favorite little café and he saw the amount of food they gave us and he ate three pieces of pie. The poor kid had never been able to eat all he should have been able to or he may have grown better, but I didn't say that to him. On Saturday afternoon, we took him down to Long beach to the Navel Headquarters. We went in and filled out all the papers and signed that he had been living with us and he was my brother and was eighteen years old. He had already decided on his birthdate to put down. He got signed up with no problems. They were so badly in need of young people it took no time at all for filling out the paperwork. He signed his name and they said you're in the Navy now, Son. W.K. looked so proud and said when do I start, and they said you just did. So, we hugged him and made sure he had our address and I told him he better write to us regular. He promised he would and I believed he meant it. I told him I would write to Lola right away, so she could let Mama know he was fine. I told him I loved him and he thanked us so much and said he loved me too. I tried not to cry, but he was just a baby, still fifteen years old. He said not to cry, nothing could happen to him nearly as bad as his whole life had been. He had a point there. We said our last good-byes as a jeep pulled up and said hop in kid.

The next few months seemed to fly by, and Clarence loved his new job and everything about it. He said he was finally using his head for something other than being gorgeous. I laughed and told him he sure had that right. Each month that passed I got more and more concerned because I had not become pregnant yet. Clarence said not to worry, it was probably because we wanted it so much that maybe I was too tense to conceive. I told him I was going to ask the nice lady next door to recommend a good doctor. He said that was fine and told me not to forget to put my new insurance cards in my purse. I had my first driver's license, so when I called the doctor that Sally recommended, I took the first appointment available. I took Clarence to work and we sat and kissed for at least three minutes before he got out of the car. A couple of the guys he worked with walked by and whistled. He thought he better get going. I told him I would be there at 4:30 on the dot. I went right to the doctor's office, even though I was an hour early. They gave me a few papers to fill out and looked at my insurance card to make sure all the numbers were correct on my papers. I only had to wait a few more minutes and the doctor was ready for me. After a complete examination, he told me to get dressed and come into his office. It reminded me of when I had been to the doctor's, in Oregon that first time, but the office was a lot newer and much nicer. And I wasn't nearly as frightened. But also, I wasn't getting the same wonderful news that I had already known then. He told me that he could see no possible reason why I could not conceive another child. I was young and very healthy and not to worry. It would happen when I quit worrying about it. Pretty much, what Clarence had already told me. I had such a smart husband, but knowing how to not to worry was the hard part. I was glad to hear there was nothing wrong with me though. That did put my mind at ease a little.

When I picked up Clarence from work, I told him the news from the doctor and told him he was just as smart as the doctor. He smiled and said, I know that, now tell me that you are fine. I told him the doctor said that there was no reason that I could not conceive and I am very healthy, I just need to quit worrying about it and it will happen. Clarence smiled and said, uh I think that's exactly what I told you. I told him that's why I said he was as smart as the doctor. He told me that he would have no idea how to do the exam that tells you are okay to conceive. He said he just knew that he loved all my parts and that they were all in perfect working order, of that I am sure. As he started putting his hand under my dress and playing around as only he knew how to do best. I told him if he didn't stop we weren't going to make it into the house. I had just turned on to our street and I said, honey, I don't think the neighbors would appreciate us making love here in the car in broad daylight. So, we headed for the house and straight to the bathroom. As I leaned over to turn the tub on, he had his hand roaming all over me and I couldn't get my clothes off quick enough. He was already stripped naked and we were in the tub and he started soaping me all over and kissing and nibbling on my nipples. I laid down and let the water cover me and he straddled me and within a few seconds he entered me and we started our own beautiful movements that brought us both to a climax in minutes. He laid over to my side and said Stella Rader, I love you more every minute and I told him I felt the same. I said the days are so long with you gone and I just miss you so much. He said, Sweetheart I have to work to support you and they won't pay me if I stay home with you as much as I would love spending every minute with you. We got out of the tub and dried each other off and stood there with our naked bodies touching. He said if we don't move away from each other quickly, I can't be responsible for what might happen. I laughed and grabbed my panties and threw my dress over my head. He put his clothes on and we went into the kitchen and quickly fixed up a meal to eat. I don't think it mattered what we were eating, as long as we did it together. All we had was a salad and Clarence made the pork chops and then made some gravy to go over the fried potatoes I had cooked. When we were fixing dinner together it all seemed to come so easy. We sat there eating and then we washed the dishes together. When he was home he was my whole world, but while he was at work and I was alone, that's when the days seemed so long and I would sit in the living room and think of Ronald and my heart would just break all over again. I missed him so much. I knew Clarence did too, but he was used to being away for several hours twice a day and I spent every minute with him all day and watched his new discoveries and was so excited to tell Clarence about everything he learned to do when he came home. It was just hard to fill the days. I told Clarence that sometimes on nice days I would take long walks and many times ended up in a park somewhere around here and I would sit for a while and watch all the mothers with their babies, and I couldn't help but think, Ronald would be walking and probably chattering away by now and it hurt so much. He said, sweetheart you know that I have never wanted you to work outside our home, but with this war getting so bad over in Germany and so many men being drafted, more each day it seemed. They have been talking a lot at work about how many women were learning to do the jobs that men had been doing. They had one bunch of girls that they called the bomb girls, but I would want you anywhere near that job. Do you think you would like to work at Northrop doing some assembly work? I said I had no idea, but I was willing to try if it would not only help me fill the days, but help with the war also. I asked him how I would go about getting a job since I had never had one really, except cleaning Lola's neighbor's house for the few weeks and Lola had got me that job without me having to open my mouth. He said I would just go into the front office and say I was here to apply for a job.

The next morning I took Clarence to work again, and then came home and did the breakfast dishes and made the bed. Then I got myself all dressed in one of my nicer dresses and put on a little make up and fixed my hair to look nice. I was very nervous about this as I was driving back to Northrop. I parked the car and as I was walking into the office, all of a sudden I remembered walking into the police station that night and how frightened I had been, but pretended like I was very sure of myself. I thought as scared as I had been that night, I could surely do this. When I walked up to the front office, a lady asked if she could help me. I told her I was there to apply for a job. She said, hold on and I'll go get you the application you need to fill out. She brought me two papers and said to fill out both sides of each and sign the bottom, and bring them back here when you are finished. I went into the little room she had motioned to where there was a table and chairs. The first part was easy, just my name, address, marital status and then came the hard part. There were several spaces to put your previous employees. I put nothing, except for the fact that I had worked hard all my life doing hard labor, like picking cotton, fruit or whatever work my parents could find. I signed it and took it back to the front desk. She told me to have a seat in the lobby and someone would call me in a while. It seemed like forever, but it was only about ten minutes. A nice looking man called me and said to follow him. I did so and we ended up in a small room with a desk and a couple of chairs. The man sat there quietly looking over my application. Finally, he asked why I wanted to work here. I said I thought they needed help because so many men were fighting in the war and I wanted to do what I could do to do my part in helping with the war. He said, are you sure you are willing to work forty hours a week and still take care of your home and husband? I told him I was one of the lucky women who had a husband that loved helping out in the kitchen and anything else that needed to be done at home. He then got very serious and said I don't mean to sound so negative, but I just want you to know that it takes a lot of time and money to train each employee and we don't do so unless we feel sure that the person is really ready to take on a full time job. I told him I was here to do my part for this war and they would be lucky to have me. I was not a quitter and if they gave me the chance they wound not be sorry.

CHAPTER 17

I am a working woman

The man said well, you sound very motivated and that's what we are looking for. I stood there feeling very frightened inside, but trying to maintain my cool on the outside. After what seemed like a minute that lasted forever, he asked if I could start tomorrow. I smiled and said yes, I could. He then told me what my starting pay would be and said they held back the first week. He asked if I understood what that meant. I said I did. I asked what time I should be there and what should I wear. He told me just to wear pants and a shirt and when I arrived they would give me a pair of overalls that would cover my clothes. I was to take them off after each shift. The company was responsible for their cleaning. He told me what my hours would be and where to go when I got here in the morning. I said I would be there and he wouldn't be sorry he had given me this chance.

When I got in the car and the door was closed I let out a scream of happiness. I was a working woman. I went home and changed back into everyday clothes and straightened up the house. I sat down and wrote my mama a letter to catch her up on my life and give her my new address. I told her to tell all my brothers and sisters to write to me because I missed them so much. I told mama how unhappy I was at not getting pregnant by now. It only took three months the first time and now it had been almost a year since Ronald had been born. I told her all about going to the doctor and he said I am very healthy and there is no reason for me to not be able to conceive another baby. I said that I was sending this letter to Lola because I didn't want daddy making fun at my expense again, like he had when I had sent the picture of Ronald. Lola had told me, after Maxine told her what daddy had said. How a man could be so heartless about his own grandson is something I just can't understand. I love you so much mama and I pray that your life might be better. I wrote a short letter to Lola and told her the letter was for her also, just to read it and make sure daddy doesn't get a chance to read it. I love you Lola and will always be so thankful for your help in getting Clarence and I together. Without you, I don't know how I would got away form that monster. If only mama and the rest of them could get away from him somehow. Love you lots, Stella

It was time to pick up Clarence from work soon so I got the letter in an envelope and dropped it in the mailbox on my way to pick up him up. When he got in the car, I told him I didn't think they liked me. He said how could they not like me. He then asked what they said that made me think that. I said I don't get to start until tomorrow. He reached across the seat and gave me a punch. Not hard, of course, just playing because I had been playing with him. I said it was so great that I had the exact same hours he had, so we could drive to work together every day. I told him there was one big problem though. He said, I'm not falling for this again. I said really there is a problem. He asked what the problem. I said I have to wear pants and blouses and I only have dresses. He said that's not a problem, we will just go to J.C. Penney's and buy you some. So, we went straight to the store and asked for the women's department. When we got upstairs, the lady took us straight to the section with working clothes. She looked at me and said I would say you will need a size eight pants and at least a medium blouse because you are rather large breasted. Clarence whispered to me, and that's a bad thing? I laughed and swatted him. I took several different styles of pants and picked out a few blouses that I liked. I ask Clarence if he liked them. He said I like you best in nothing, but the blouses are very pretty. I was so glad the clerk was not paying attention to us, because he was being very seductive and it turned me on. I wanted to take him in the dressing room with me. Men not allowed in women's dressing rooms was written in very plain sight on a sign just outside the dressing room. So, that thought went right out of my head. I told Clarence to be good and quit trying to get me in a mood that wasn't going to go anywhere right now. I needed to try these clothes on to see if they fit. A couple of the pants fit me perfect and all the blouses fit perfectly. Clarence said to get another color of the pants that fit the best and he was sure I had picked out the best blouses they had. I told him all this was going to cost as much as I would make in a week. He said, well if you weren't working then we wouldn't be buying them silly. So, don't worry your pretty head about such small things. We have plenty of money saved in the bank and it will be just fine. With both of us working, we will be able to save lots of money. I said, I am not being paid nearly what you are. He said, anything is more than nothing. I had to stop and think about that. Then I laughed and said, okay let's pay for this stuff and get some dinner made. I am hungry, because I was too nervous to eat all day. He said we would just go to that little café by the house we liked so much. I said, what the heck, we are spending money like it's paper tonight. Clarence was laughed and said nothing was too good for his bride. I hugged him tight and told him I was the luckiest girl in the world to have stepped out of that miserable tent and look into the handsomest face in the whole world and not only was he the most handsome, he was the most loving understanding man ever. He said I must be delirious from hunger because I was talking crazy. I kissed him and told him I would love him until the day I died. He said you better because you promised me that on our wedding day. I said I meant every word and it only gets better and better. He said, yes it certainly does my darling wife.

We ate a delicious meal at our little café and even had a piece of pie for dessert, and it tasted like home made. I knew W.K. had said how good they were, but then I knew it was the first he had ever had so without anything to compare it to, he would say that. The waitress said she had made them herself. She said the café belonged to her husband's parents and she had worked here since before she met her husband. One day when he walked in to talk to his mother, she said we took one look at each other and knew we would always be together. I said that sound just like us, except much different places. Her name was Suzie and her husband's name was John. She said now that his parents were older, she pretty much runs this place. So, at that moment, we became friends. I liked her and so did Clarence. I told her I was starting work in the morning at Northrop, but once I got used to working we would love to have her and her husband over some weekend. I asked her if they played cards, and she said they loved to play all different card games. So, we had made some friends, sort of. Anyway, it felt good to invite someone to our house. We got home after a long drive to calm me down, Clarence said. I told him I was fine, just very tired and I needed to get to bed and get some sleep, after we make love, of course. The thought of going to sleep in his arms made me feel like everything would be fine tomorrow and always.

The next morning when the alarm went off, I jumped out of bed and got dressed so fast, you'd have thought the house was on fire. Clarence said, hey sweetheart, slow down and take a breath. We have an hour before work starts. I said I had to get breakfast started and get the dishes done and we have to drive to work. He said it will all be okay. If you're not ready for this, then you don't have to go to work today or ever if that's what you want. I only mentioned it because

I thought it might help you pass some time before we have another baby. That will happen, I know it will. Listening to his soothing voice made me calm down and take a breath. I sat down and Clarence put his big arms around me and I knew it would be okay. We went into the kitchen and he put a couple sausage patties in the skillet and I cracked four eggs into a bowl. As soon as the sausage was about done I poured the eggs into a hot skillet with butter and pushed the toast down. We ate and put the dishes in the sink with soapy water. I went to the bathroom and brushed my teeth, put on a little makeup and brushed my hair until it shined. Clarence said, Northrop had never seen such a beauty before. I smiled and gave him a kiss. I looked at the clock and said I have plenty of time to get the dishes washed, they can dry in the rack. He knew better than to argue with me. When the dishes were done, I dried my hands and put lotion on them. It was time to leave. I asked Clarence to tell me the truth. Do I look okay in these pants? He said Sweetheart, if you looked any sexier, I wouldn't be able to go to work right now. You look gorgeous and amazing in those pants. I guarantee you that not another woman in the plant could hold a candle to you. I put my arms around his neck and he held me tight. He said, are you sure? I said let's go or you're going to make me late on my first day.

When I entered the door where I was told to go, they asked my name and then found my badge that had already been printed. They gave me my overalls and said, keep your badge on your overalls in a place where it can be read easily. She was very stern and I wondered if she ever smiled, so I said I would be sure it was in a good place and smiled at her. She smiled back to my surprise. This wasn't going to be bad. She said it's up to you, but if you wear one of these scarfs around your hair it will be much cooler and your hair won't get so dirty. Sometimes the machine's make some dusty soot. Keep a handkerchief in your pocket if you have one. If not, I can loan you one of mine. They come in handy sometimes. I thanked her and told her I would return it clean and pressed. She said thanks, I don't get a chance to iron much with four kids at home. I said, wow how do you handle taking care of four children and working too. She said her Mother had moved in with her since her husband had been drafted and she needed to go to worked to make enough to cover all their bills. I said that's rough, I am sorry, I do wish I had the kids though. She seemed surprised at my remark, and I told her my husband and I wanted a large family and we had lost our first baby almost a year ago, and I hadn't been able to conceive again so far. A loud buzzer sounded and she said that means get your butts to work and laughed. She took me over to an assembly line and said just watch these parts go by and inspect each one to make sure the pins are in correctly. Then she showed me one that was in right and one that wasn't. It seemed like an easy job to me. About that time the line started moving and I watched very carefully to make sure each one was right. After an hour or so my eyes began to seem blurry. I quickly wiped them and kept close watch on the parts. Before too long a bell rang, and everything stopped and all the ladies walked over to a room with long tables and chairs on both sides. I noticed a few of the women went out the door. For the first time the lady that showed me everything introduced herself. Her name was Lucy, and I said I was Stella. We both had name tags on but who wanted to look at someone's shoulder to see their name. She said the ones going out that door were smokers and they weren't allowed to smoke inside the plant. She saw the relief on my face and she said I agree, Thank The Lord they can't smoke in here, I couldn't stand it. I said I couldn't either. My husband smokes, but never inside or even around me.

So, we got along very well considering she was my foreman. I asked her if it was normal for my eyes to start getting blurry after a while. She said it was and that's why we change around every break, so things don't get overlooked which would be easy if you had to sit and stare at the same things all day. After break she showed me another job to do until lunch time. She said I noticed you didn't bring a lunch. Are you going to leave at lunch break? I told her my husband was an engineer in another plant and we had planned to meet at the car and eat, if that was allowed? Lucy said it is as long as you get back in the door before the buzzer rings because the doors automatically lock from the inside after that. I told her I would watch the time closely. At lunch Clarence and I ate our sandwiches quickly as I told him what Lucy said. He said we probably shouldn't make a habit of doing this. I don't want you to have to eat so fast and worry about being locked out. I agreed that it was rather stressful thinking of it. So, we decided we would pack our lunches in separate bags and get another thermos, so I would have something cold to drink. I told him I would ask Lucy if there was somewhere that kept things cold, so I could take a coke in with my lunch. He laughed and said you and your cokes. I said what can I say, I admit I am addicted, just like you are to your coffee. He said, touche. I looked at my watch and said I timed it to see how long it took me to get to the car from the door I go in and it took three minutes and I was rushing. It is now six minutes before the door will close, so I need a one good kiss and I'm gone till the end of the day. Our kiss lasted a little too long and I cut it close. I got in and I told Lucy that we had already decided this was going to take too long and we couldn't even take the time to chew our food good.

I asked her if there was a cold place to keep my lunch. She said there was an icebox in the break room, but you better mark your stuff really good and still I'd make a bee line to get my lunch quick. I'm not sure who, but things have disappeared. If I ever catch whoever, they are history. We shouldn't have to worry about our fellow workers, but I guess some people are just born bad. When the buzzer went off we went into another room and I was shown how to polish some of the engine parts. I really enjoyed doing this and Lucy said she watched as they came through and mine almost sparkled. I was very glad to get a compliment on my first day. After the next break, the rest of the day seemed to fly by. I was so anxious to tell Clarence about my good day. I told Lucy I'd see her first thing in the morning. I was glad Clarence had two lunch pails, because I thought a sandwich would get so squished in a paper bag. I took an apple for my afternoon break. And a Coke with my name written with in ink pen that wouldn't wash off. It was there at lunch and I was very glad. Lucy introduced me to a couple of the ladies that sat around us. Some of the girls just plain didn't want to be friendly, so why try. But that wasn't my nature, so I tried to say hello when I went to the bathroom and had to walk right past them. They just turned their heads like it would hurt them to say hello back. So, I didn't try again. The ball was in their hands now. There was only 3 days to my week this week since I had started mid-week, but it seemed like things got easier each day. I told Clarence that I thought I would survive and the days were so busy I didn't have time to think about anything except what was in front of me at that moment. On Friday when we got to the car, Clarence said let's go to our café and celebrate you first week. Sounded great to me and the meals were so good and their prices so reasonable that it was almost as cheap as eating at home. Especially, since I was working and couldn't make meals that took a lot of preparation which were cheaper to cook. Things like meatloaf or a roast which lasted us two meals. But we would see how it went. Clarence and I both watched for good sales on meat, but they were getting harder and harder to find. A lot of things were starting to be rationed. They sent out ration books and when you ran out of your coupons for that item, there was no more until the next month.

We got a letter in the mail from Clarence's brother and he was coming to visit us, unless it wasn't okay. He said if he didn't hear back in a week, he would start out. Orce was his name and I could tell right away that he and Clarence were very close growing up. They were the closest in age and therefore had done the most together. I was so anxious to meet someone in his Family that I was cleaning everything in sight. I wanted to make a good impression on him. Clarence assured me he would love me. Work kept going fine and I felt sure it was because I had made friends with Lucy from the start. She put me on the polishing engine parts a lot because she said I did it better than anyone else and the parts were very important to our soldiers flying these planes. They had to be done just right and Stella had a knack for polishing them perfect. So at least half of everyday I spent doing this which I really enjoyed doing. It was fun to watch them sparkle when I sat each one down. Before I knew, it the next week was over and I received my first paycheck. It was only for the three days this time, but it still felt like I was helping out, in these times which seemed to get tougher all the time. In a few days I figured Orce would be here and I was so excited. Clarence told me he was just an ordinary guy like he was, and I said oh no, two perfect men. Clarence said, well maybe he's not quite as perfect as I am. He laughed and I knew he was just joking with me. I asked him why some of the others didn't come along with him, so he didn't have that long drive alone and he said they were still in school or college, Orce and Oscar were the only two of his siblings that didn't want to go to college. Oscar was a deaf-mute so I needed to have Clarence teach me sign language so I could talk with him when he came out. And he said that Orce had always been sort of a quiet guy. He was well liked and had a great personality, but he was still rather withdrawn is the only word that comes to mind, when describing him. I love him dearly and I know you will too. You'll see, he is just different. I asked if he had ever been married and Clarence said no, and I don't think he ever will. He is just a loner in many ways. He said his sister, Ellen was a school teacher and very smart. His sister Dora was also smart, but right now I think she is just interested in dating guys and looking for Mr. Right. And I'm not sure what Cindy is up to. I've written my dad and mom several letters and kept them informed of where we are and what has happened in our lives, but they aren't much for writing, so I don't really know what's going on in their lives right now, until Orce gets here and he will fills us in on all of my family's updates. I told him it just seemed so strange to me not know much about his life, sense he knew my life story practically, and it wasn't a pretty story. But at least he had met all my siblings, except my older brothers and Lola, but he had written her back and forth many times, so I felt like he knew her. I could hardly wait for him to meet Al and Preston and J.E., they were all such great guys and I hadn't seen them since I was ten or eleven, I couldn't remember for sure. I just knew how good they were to me and how they protected me so many times when they were still at home. Life changed so much after they left, but I didn't like thinking of all those years now that I was so happy with you and our life was so completely different now than how I was raised. Thank The Lord.

Things were going great at my job and I had met lots of friends that Clarence and I would go out to dances and things once in a while. It was nice. In another month or so there was going to be a big dance at Northrop with some movie stars there to raise money and awareness for war bonds. I have heard that one of my favorite stars, Ronald Reagan was going to be there and I was thrilled about that. Clarence still loved his job also and our life couldn't be better, except I wanted to get pregnant so badly. I tried to keep our life so busy that I didn't have time to think about it, but it was always on my mind no matter what was going on. Clarence and I were so in love and our sex life couldn't be better, some people would think we were addicts or some crazy thing like that, but we just loved each other so much and couldn't keep out hands off each other when we were alone. We made love every night, and quite often when we would get home from work and I took a bath. I always felt dusty and dirty form the plant machines, but Clarence didn't work in any area like that. He wore dress shirts and ties to work every day. But if I ran a bath, all he had to do was see me bending over to check the water, before stepping in, it wasn't too long before he was in the the bath and within seconds, we were helping each other scrub our backs or my front and one thing always led us to that wonderful perfect part of our life. My love for this man was just deeper than I could ever put into words.

CHAPTER 18

Clarence's brother comes to visit

Late in the next week, Orce just showed up and knocked on the front door. I went to answer it and I knew immediately who he was. My instincts took over and I hugged him as I was telling him who I was, he laughed and said it was the best introduction he had ever had. I called for Clarence who was in the kitchen trying to balance the check book. If I wrote checks at the grocery store or somewhere I often forgot to write it down and he would warn me to start writing it in the book so it wasn't so hard to balance it. I yelled for him to get in here and see our company. He walked around the corner and saw Orce and ran into his arms and picked him up and swung him around a couple of times and said how much he had missed him. They both had tears rolling down their cheeks. It was so obvious how much they loved each other. Clarence turned to introduce me and Orce said she has already done a great job of that. I told Clarence that I had hugged him the second I saw his face I knew who he was. I was so excited to meet him. I asked if he was hungry, we had planned to just have some leftovers, but now this was a special occasion. Clarence said, let's take Orce out to our favorite little café. Orce said, can I wash up first? I said of course, the bathroom is right in there and Clarence is carrying your bags into your room. It's all ready for you. My heart was racing, because I was so excited. We had bought a new mattress and a nice dresser and headboard for the guest room. I wanted it to be very comfortable for any family that could come and visit. I told Clarence that Orce was so nice just like he had said, and I was so happy he was here. It was only a short while before he came out all fresh with a different shirt on and said, am I presentable? We said you are fine, it's just our favorite little café that we are going to. If we had known when you would be here for sure, Stella would have been cooking up a great dinner for you, but you will love this café. We almost feel like we are home when we are there. As soon as we walked in, Suzie said, you must be Orce, I've heard all about you. So glad to meet you. He said, likewise. We looked at the menu and Suzie said, let me bring you dinner tonight. I have a special thing in mind for you three. So we sat there drinking coffee and me coke, talking and catching up. Shortly out came tree big salads, after eating our salad, Suzie came out with a large tray with three plates filled with huge steaks and a large hot baked potato filled with butter and she had a large bowl of sour cream in case we wanted it on our potato. She sat down a platter of hot corn on the cob with little trays to set them in and soak up the butter. Then she sat a bowl of yeast rolls down and made me think of Kathleen. We started eating and felt like we were royalty being fed like this. Suzie said that she had been waiting to meet Clarence's brother and wanted to have a grand meal when you came in. I said you out did yourself

Suzie, Thank you so much. This is delicious. My steak is so tender I hardly need the knife. Clarence and Orce said the same thing. We were all very impressed. She said wait until you have dessert. I asked, where are we supposed to fit dessert after all this? She said you'll manage. We all laughed and kept eating because everything was so good. I don't think any of us left a crumb. Then out came Suzie with the busboy to clear the table. She then brought out the most delicious looking coconut crème pie I had ever seen. I said if we ate like this, every night I would weigh five hundred pounds in no time. Suzie said, it doesn't hurt once in a while to spurge on a special occasion. Clarence said where in the world did you find such great steaks these days. She said she had some pull with the butcher. I do favors for him and he does the same for me. She sat down with us and had a piece of pie. It was so good I think I could have eaten half of it, but as full as I was just eating one large piece was all I could get down. I told her she had to teach me how to make a pie like this. Clarence said, don't do it. We will get fat and won't be able to fit in our clothes. I laughed and said only on very special occasions I would make one if Suzie is nice enough to come over and show me the tricks. She promised to one day when we both had time. I thought to myself, when would that be. Our lives seemed so full these days with both of us working full time. After finishing our meal and dessert I wasn't sure we were going to be able to get up. Orce said just roll me home. Then after thanking Suzie and paying her for our meal, which she tried to say it was on the house, Clarence just insisted she take some money which he tried to be generous, but not overboard, so Suzie felt like she treated us a little.

Then Clarence said, sweetheart, do you mind if Orce and I walk home so we can catch up and walk off this huge meal. I told him I understood and I would drive home and get all our things ready for tomorrow. I was so glad that tomorrow was Friday, so we would have the weekend to enjoy and spoil Orce.

I drove home and went in and made sure the kitchen was spotless and that there was plenty for Orce to eat the next day while we were at work. Then I placed a couple of clean fluffy towels and washcloths out for him on the dresser in his room. I looked in the closet and made sure he had plenty of hangers to hang anything he had that needed hanging. About the time I was all finished, they walked in. I asked if they wanted me to fix a pot of coffee? Orce said not for me, but thank you. He said if you don't mind, I would love to take a quick shower and go to bed. I drove a long day today. I said help yourself, I put clean towels in your room and there are hangers in the closet for anything you want to hang. He looked at Clarence and said, I think she's a keeper. Clarence put his arms around me and said he had known that from the minute he saw me. We said good night and help yourself to anything in the icebox you want to eat tomorrow while we are at work. Make yourself at home and get some rest. We will be home at about four-forty.

Clarence and I went into the kitchen and he quickly finished the checkbook. I promised to remember to write it down in the registry when I wrote a check from now on. I would make it a habit and do it. He kissed me and said I know you will or I might have to spank you. I said oh that might be fun. He said, quiet we have company in the house you know. I giggled and said let's go to bed too. I am pooped and want to have time for a little romance before going to sleep. He said that sounds like the best idea all night. The next morning when we got up Orce was already in the kitchen drinking a cup of coffee. I said, I see you saw the coffee was ready to be started. He said yes, I'm pretty used to using kitchens. I've been a bachelor for many years. I said, you are so handsome, I'm surprised a beautiful woman hasn't swept you off your feet. He said, I'm too quick for that. I started cooking some breakfast and asked if there was something he preferred for breakfast. He said I am not picky, whatever you fix will be fine. I decided to make sausage gravy and biscuits and some scrambled eggs. He was very pleased with breakfast and said he wouldn't want another bite till dinner time. Clarence had made our lunches while I was making breakfast. That was our usual practice, whichever of us made breakfast, the other got our lunches ready. Before we left, I reminded Orce to help himself to whatever he could find in the ice box and the bread was in there also. He said he would be just fine. On the way to work, Clarence said what should we have for dinner tonight? I told him he knew his brother's likes best, what did he think? So after a minute or two of thinking, we decided to fry up a chicken. That sounds good, we haven't done that in weeks.

We came in from work to find Orce outside pulling a few feeds along the side of the house. I told Clarence, this is very embarrassing, I should have done that. He said He just likes to stay active sweetheart, don't let that bother you all. Clarence yelled to him that he hadn't mowed the lawn yet. They both laughed and Orce followed us in the house and washed his hand on the service porch. I told him he didn't need to be pulling the weeds and he said exactly what Clarence had just said, he likes to keep busy if there's something he can find to do. Clarence and I fixed dinner and he sat there reading a paper we had brought in with us. After dinner, we all just sat in the living room and they laughed and told stories of antics they had got in trouble doing as kids. It sounded like they had a very happy childhood. I was enjoying watching how much they seemed to love each other and how they could almost finish each other's stories I asked if they would like me to go get some dessert from one of the stores around us. They both said they were full and didn't need anything at all. I said that I thought I would go take a bath and wash my hair so it had time to dry before going to bed. Clarence got up and gave me a kiss and said to hurry back. I really didn't think he meant it because I'm sure they had lots to talk about. He said they would miss me and I laughed and said, sure you will. I laid there in the tub thinking it wasn't near as much fun as when Clarence was in here with me. After I got out and had to actually dry my own back, the thought made me laugh to myself as I toweled dried my hair just as much as I could. Then I put on a gown and my long robe and went back in where the guys were having a big laugh about something. I didn't ask what. We all just chit-chatted about various thing of no importance the rest of the evening and then we all went to bed. Clarence said he was going to wash up and would be in shortly. We lay there thinking how different it was having someone in the house with us. For almost three years now, it had always been just us and Ronald of course, for not long enough. He told me that they had talked a little about Ronald a little while I was in the tub and he said he just didn't know what to say to you, but he could not feel any worse for us and wanted me to let you know that.

Orce stayed for a couple of weeks and started to get comfortable and would even go to the store and get some groceries and start dinner for us on several occasions. He was really a pleasure to have around. Clarence was right when he said they were a lot alike in many ways. The main difference was that he never married or wanted children. He was just too much of a wanderer he said, and he didn't think there was a woman on this earth that would put up with that. Not a wanderer as in cheating, just like to come and go as he pleased, and one morning we woke up and he was gone. No note, no goodbye or anything, just gone. Clarence said not to worry myself about thinking I had done something wrong, that's just the way he's always been. He only came to visit once when I was married before, he didn't like her one bit and I could tell. He never said a word, just stayed a couple of nights and he was gone. We never talked about it, but when I got divorced and went back to Wagoner, he said I had really lucked out not having kids with her. He said he couldn't imagine her being loving to a baby. I said, I wished I'd have noticed that years ago instead of wasting nine years with her. You'd think after that long I would have been smarter. Just got into a rut and stayed unhappy for six or seven years. But it's all in the cards that God deals us.

Had I not stayed so long I might not have got depressed and went on the road and then I never would have met you, and I can tell you sweetheart, you are the best thing that ever happened to me in my whole life. I told Orce that and he said he could sure see why I fell so hard for you and he also told me one night that if there was another one out there like you, he might have changed his whole outlook on marriage. So, I didn't want to bring up my first marriage to you ever again, but I just wanted you to know that Orce adored you and it was very obvious to me. I don't mean flirty, just that he thought you were so good for me and he could tell how very happy we are.

Before we knew it, it was time the company started planning for the big dance where Hollywood stars were coming. I was so excited and was hoping to at least get a good glance at that handsome Ronald Reagan, he was just so darn cute and all the women were worried about how to fix their hair and what to wear, so he might notice them. I just want to get a good look at him to see if it was lots of Hollywood make-up or was he really that good looking. I already had the best man in the world, not only the handsomest, but the sweetest most loving man and every woman we ever became acquainted with thought the same. I lost track of the amount of ladies that told me how lucky I was. And I let them know I knew it and he was mine. The next week came and Saturday night was the big dance. Clarence asked if I wanted to buy a new dress, I told him I still had nice dresses that Mrs. Peterson had bought me that I hadn't worn. He said are you saying I don't take you places to wear your dresses? I said, of course not honey, I was pregnant for our first year, then I haven't wanted to go anywhere. Seeing babies is just too hard for me even now. I want to get pregnant and just don't understand why I am not conceiving. I went to work and we stayed busy and had lots of fun with our friends, so it's not like I dwell on it all the time. I just don't understand. I got pregnant the third month after we got married and now it been close to two years. He put his strong arms around me and said he was doing all he could do. Then he asked if maybe he should go to the doctor, and see if maybe it was because he was getting older. I told him I knew he was fine. And I also know God would not take my baby and not let me have another one. Mama always told me that God was good and if he took my baby there was a reason and someday we will all know all his reasons. I need to believe this or I would just lose my mind. Not really, because I just couldn't do that to you. I know how hard I made it for you the first three or four months after losing Ronald. I just couldn't leave his room or his things. It was good that you decided we move here. I love California and I love our friends here and our neighbors are all so nice. There is a new couple that moved in across the street I met for just a little while when I went for a walk last Saturday. I think I'm really going to like her. Her name is Ruby Lee Hinds. She has a little boy and a little girl. They were both so cute. It is not so hard seeing little children now, just babies. Anyway, back to the dance, I don't need a thing. I have shoes and a pretty dress that I fell in love with it and just never ended up wearing it, so now I can.

CHAPTER 19

My claim to fame

Saturday came and I got more excited than I thought I would, but when I saw Clarence in his best suit and a beautiful tie that matched my dress, I thought, who need's Ronald Reagan? We got to the dance and it was so crowded that I figured I would never even see him, except maybe up on stage. Clarence and I went to get something to drink and they even had a few appetizers. They were really good, but I didn't want to eat much, so my dress didn't look too tight. I was a little larger than when I had got the dress, since then I had a baby and then I had put on a little weight since I had been working. Maybe it was because I ate three meals and I was used to just eating very little during the day after I had Ronald. I was nursing all the time and that's keeps weight off or at least it helps. Clarence and I danced several dances and we were just standing over to the side resting for a while, when to my amazement, Ronald Reagan walked up to me and asked Clarence if he minded him dancing with his wife. Clarence just waived his hand like, go for it buddy. I couldn't believe I was dancing with this famous movie star. I starred closely and he no make-up on and he was just absolutely gorgeous. I mean I adored my husband and thought he was just the handsomest man for me, but Ronald Reagan was just so Pretty Handsome, one of those men that just get better with age. We danced for several minutes, and he asked how long I had worked at Northrop? I told him it had been close to a year now. I told him I had a baby we named Ronald, he said that's very nice, then I told him we lost him when he was only four months old and it was very hard. He said how very sorry he was and I told him I had to learn to live with it even though I would never get over it. I told him we were trying to get pregnant again, but it just wasn't happening. He said, don't give up and he told me I was a beautiful woman and my husband was a lucky man. I told him I was lucky also because my husband was the best man ever. When we got back around to Clarence and he stopped and thanked me, then thanked Clarence and told him he was a lucky man. Clarence squeezed me tight and said, don't I know it.

Before we knew it, it was Christmas and then 1942. I couldn't believe we would be married three years before we knew it, the months just flew by. And I was becoming such good friends with Ruby Lee. She had just found out she was pregnant and she said she hated to tell me for fear it would hurt me. I told her I was very happy for her and it would be fun watching her grow. I remembered loving to watch my belly move around. Being pregnant was just the best. She agreed. After just a few months she was growing so fast we couldn't believe it. She said her doctor wanted to X-ray her to see if the baby was okay, but she refused. She said it would not be good for the baby, so by Christmas the next year she and her doctor both was sure she was having twins. Her stomach got so big, the only way she could sit was to put her legs apart and pull up another chair to lay her belly on. Clarence thought it was the funniest thing. We would sit and watch her belly. There were arms and elbows and knees and everything else that could move was moving. it was so entertaining to watch. We couldn't believe she could go for almost two more months. But she did and when the twins were born, between the two of the little boys, they weighed a little over seventeen pounds. I had so much fun helping her watch them on the weekends. All four of her children were just beautiful and such sweet kids.

About the time they started crawling around, I started feeling sick to my stomach and Ruby Lee said Stella, you are pregnant. I hadn't been thinking about it so much, but know that she said it, I counted back and I had missed one period. I tried not to get excited, but I almost ran home to tell Clarence. He was mowing the lawn, and I ran up and hugged him tight. He said sweetheart, I am so sweaty. I told him I didn't care and he had to come inside with me. So, he followed me into the house and I said I think I am pregnant. He picked me up and swung me around and that sent me to the toilet again. Throwing up again, I never threw up. I had to be pregnant. It couldn't be anything else. I raised my head and said Thank You God. Clarence said, please sweetheart, don't get your hopes up too high until we are sure. I told him in my heart I knew, I just knew. He said he prayed I was right. He also said, as soon as we find out for sure, I want you to give notice at work. I don't want you in that factory with all that dirt and soot. I agreed the minute the doctor told me for sure that I was pregnant I would tell them I was only working for two more weeks, I made an appointment the first available I could get, which was a whole week away. Clarence laughed at me and said to calm down or I would drive myself crazy by next week. I went to work every day except the day of my appointment. I had given them all the notice I had about going to the doctor. Just not the reason I was going. The doctor first introduced himself, He said, I am Dr. Grey and I'm very glad you chose me. I told him he had been my friend's doctor, the one who had seventeen pounds of twin last year. He said, oh that must be Mrs. Hinds? I said yes, she lives across the street from my husband and I.

CHAPTER 20

Finally pregnant!

Then, he examined me and said as far as he could tell by the size of my uterus, I was about three months. I said I didn't think I had missed that many periods. He said it wasn't unusual to have a small period and not notice it. Many women did. So when I picked up Clarence I told him we were expecting a baby about the first of June. He said how could we not have known? I told him what the doctor said, and he was just so happy. He said at least this way the wait won't be so long. He also said he wanted me to give notice immediately. And I promised I would go into the office just before work in the morning and give my notice. To my surprise, they said that since I was that far along, they would rather I just quit now. I told them I didn't feel right about doing that to them and they assured me it was fine, and they would not want something to happen to hurt my baby with all the chemicals we work with. I said, you don't suppose something could already have happened? He said I doubt it very seriously, as we have just started working with some of these things. I told him I didn't have any key to our car and my husband wouldn't be off until four. He said he could run me home and I could leave a note taped to our car window. So, that's what we did.

When Clarence rushed in as soon as work was over, he was so concerned that there was some problem. I said, no honey, I told you in the note, all was fine, and I would be at home when you got off and I would explain everything. He took a deep breath and said, Thank The Lord. Then I told him about the chemicals they were just starting to use for something and my boss said, he appreciated the fact that I was going to give them notice, but with me being three months, he thought it best I just went home now and he told me while he was driving me home that I had been a model worker and he wished he had more like me. That made me feel really good and also that he was so concerned that he wanted to drive me right home, so there was no chance the baby would ever be in any contact with the chemicals. Clarence said he sounded like an okay man. I assured him he had always been nothing but nice to me. And best of all I will still get a paycheck this week, because of them holding back that first week. All of a sudden it hit us both like a ton of bricks. This was really happening and we only had six months to get ready. I said I hoped all of Ronald's furniture was still okay. I had checked it during the summer, but with being over at Ruby Lee's so much and with all the holidays, I hadn't been out there. Clarence said, everything is fine and dry as a bone, I just checked it two weeks ago, when you said you thought you were pregnant. I didn't want to show it, but I was just as excited as you, so I wanted to make sure everything was going to be okay.

The next week we received a letter form Clarence's Sister's, Dora and Ellen. They wanted to come and visit us if it was okay. Clarence asked me what I thought? I told him it was more than fine with me. I would be thrilled to meet them finally. So, he went over to Ruby Lee's and asked if he could pay her and use their phone to make a quick call to his Sister's in Oklahoma. He would call information and find out how much a minute the call would cost. Ruby Lee said, don't be silly, I don't know how I would have got thru the last year without Stella, she has held one of the twins for me so many times when I was going crazy trying to get something done with the two older kids. What a lifesaver she has been. You make your call and think nothing of it. So Clarence called his parent's house and first talked a few seconds with his mom. She cried just hearing his voice. He always wrote every week and kept them up on our lives. But hearing his voice for the first time in so many years made her so happy. He told her he was on someone else's phone so he didn't want to run up their bill, but he had received Dora's letter say she and Ellen wanted to come and visit if it was okay. He said, tell them, Stella and I can't wait to see them and he quickly told her about the baby and how happy they were and promised as soon as the baby was old enough to travel, he and Stella would come and visit them. He said he had three week's vacation time coming. So, that was it, he said how much he loved her and his dad and tell the girls to start packing.

Before Ellen and Dora could get there, we had a big surprise. Early one evening, a knock on the door came, we both immediately thought Ellen and Dora had got there quickly. I ran and opened the door and to my happy surprise, there stood Maxine with who I presumed was her new husband that W.K. had told us about. I grabbed Maxine by the arm and almost dragged her into the living room hugging and kissing her a million times. I was so happy to see my very closest sister, with whom I had so many shared memories and so many shared tears and heartbreak over the way we were raised. Being the closest girls in age, we had done so much together and loved each other so much. I had naturally missed her the most. After just a moment passed, I realized I was being rude, I hadn't even given her a chance to introduce her husband. She said Clarence and I are a lot alike, which puzzled me. She said, this is my husband, J.P. Derington. He was a very handsome young man with blond hair. Maxine turned and said she was a little older than her husband and I was a bit younger than my husband. So now we all laughed and I got the meaning of her previous statement. Then she looked at me and said, you are pregnant again, aren't you? I said, my goodness, how did you know? She said seeing mama pregnant so many times, it just shows in your waist which was always so tiny and now I can see a bit of fullness you never had. And you also have such a happy glow.

I told her I was a little over three months and we couldn't be happier. I asked if they were hungry and she said no, they had stopper to eat dinner an hour or so ago and were still stuffed. Clarence, who had been standing to my side was surprised when Maxine grabbed him and squeezed him tight. She said, it is so good to see you again, I should be mad at you for taking my sister away from me, but in truth, I am thrilled for both of you and I thank you for taking her away from that monster we had to call daddy. J.P. come over here and meet this wonderful man my sister married. He was the nicest man we ever had to work in the camps with. He always bought all of kids candy and things we had never had before. But what he stole from us was my best friend and sister. I said, And I couldn't be happier if I tried. Clarence is the best husband any girl could ever ask for. Maxine said, well I'm pretty happy with my mine also. Maxine and I said we were going in the kitchen for just a little while to catch up if that's okay with you two gentlemen. Clarence said that he thought he and J.P. would do just fine for a while. They stepped outside to have a cigarette. I was so thrilled that Clarence rarely smoked around me, and never when I was pregnant. He always went outside to smoke. He stepped back in and said, he and J.P. we're going to drive around a bit, then I am going to go to our little café and we can drink coffee there, so you girls have time to catch up. I said Thank you, honey, I appreciate that.

Maxine and I hugged so tight like we had been separated since birth. We talked about how hard it was for her after I had run away. She said, daddy accused me of knowing all about your plans. I promised him I hadn't known anything about it. He was about to raise his fist to me when I just started crying and pleaded with him not to hurt me because I didn't have any idea where you were. I became a pretty good liar to keep from being daddy's new punching bag. He asked each one of us kids if we had any idea where you had gone and we all told him over and over, that we had no idea where you ran to. He said, over and over, I bet she went to meet that Clarence guy, that was sniffing around her when we were at that cotton farm. W.K. and I both said we hardly ever saw you talk with him and then I said you told me he was way too old for you. Finally, he calmed down and just went back to being his mean self. I just worry about how Velma is doing now that she is the oldest one left at home. I think she hates him worse than any of us ever did and she tries to help mama, just like you always did, so that means he gives it to her twice as bad. I worry about her. I told her that I would give anything if we could get mama to leave him. I told her I had asked mama, so many times to leave him. But she was just convinced that when you marry someone it for better or worse. She said, that what she said when she married him. And then I just think she felt stuck, after having so many kids.

She keeps quiet when he beat her, just to spare us. Daddy got to where he drinks more than ever, and he always comes in late, after we are all sleeping. He makes mama get up and make him some dinner no matter what the time, then he makes her sit across the table from him while he is eating, so he can curse her the whole time his is eating. I have seen him get up and walk over to her and hit her across the forehead with his fist. She never says a word, just sits there and cries. But one night he just was so loud with his cursing that it woke all us kids up, and we saw that he just kept getting up after every bite and going over to Mama and hitting her harder and harder, then say to her, "there, damn you, take that" and then he would spit on the floor next to her. After he had done this so many times, He would say, you don't like that, do you? He said, I'm going to kill you, I have a gun in the car. W.K. ran out when he wasn't looking our way to see if he really had a gun in the car. He didn't, but when he came back in he saw the hammer that was in the house and picked it up. I got up and went to where they were and said, daddy why don't you please leave mama alone? He got up like a bolt of lightning, and grabbed me by my gown and threw me into the corner. I hit my head and it hurt so bad, I just remembered all the time he had done so much worse to you. I said, I try not to think of those days, now that I am so happy and with Clarence. Anyway Stella, let me finish. After throwing me to the corner, Mama jumped up and Daddy hit her in the nose. and broke it really bad, and threw her to the side of the room. We were all jumping up and down, yelling leave our mama alone. He grabbed a butcher knife from the table and went to Mama, and stood there, with the knife drew back like he was going to stab her. W.K. had the hammer and tried to get to mama, but daddy grabbed at him and he got away and went to the other room.

Then he came back in, and hit Daddy hard over the head with the hammer, Daddy passed out and Mama was crying so hard and told W.K. not to say he did this. She wasn't worried about daddy, just that W.K. might get into trouble with the law, if daddy said who had done it. He was passed out on the floor till morning and then when Mama got up, she rolled him onto the bed. He fainted a couple of times over the next few days and then daddy's head got infected and he went to the Doctor for some medicine to heal it, but poor Mama's nose was swollen twice its size, and all red and purple, but Daddy refused to let her go to a doctor. He thought she was the one who had hit him with the hammer, and said he figured she got what she deserved. We left that place soon after, because there wasn't any work for us or daddy, where we were anymore. We moved to Lamesa, Texas, daddy got a job driving a tractor and tending to some stock. I told Mama I was going to live with Aunt Willie Mae, and get a job. I was almost 18 anyway so Daddy figured he couldn't stop me. So, that's where I met J.P. and started dating him and soon after he proposed and we got married. So now, here we are. She said, that J.P. is just a few months younger than I and he is joining the Navy next week, after turning eighteen, so he can learn some kind of trade while fighting for our Country. He said he knew he would be drafted anyway, so he might as well enlist and get in the Navy and maybe we could see the country. I asked her if she really loved him and she said, Certainly, I love him, or I would not have married him. She asked me if it was okay if they stayed and visited with Clarence and I, before he enlisted. I told her sure that would be fine. I told her about Clarence's sisters coming to visit from Oklahoma and that I hadn't ever met them yet, so I was really excited about meeting more of his family. I told her about Orce's visit and how much I liked him. She said, we will leave if they get here so you can visit with just them. I said, we'll worry about that when the time comes.

CHAPTER 21

A lot of Family

Clarence and J.P. returned in about an hour and said they had got acquainted and had a real nice visit. He came over and gave me a big hug and kissed me like he always did if he had been gone a while. He said Sally was happy to meet more family. I told her I was sure you would be bringing Maxine by for her to meet. That made her happy. It was getting late and we showed them where their room was and then I took out a couple of nice big towels and washcloths and gave them to them and showed them where the bathroom was. Maxine couldn't believe what a nice house we had and so many beautiful things. I told her I would tell her all about our wedding and reception one of these days, maybe tomorrow if we get a chance. Clarence had to get up early for work, so we will try to be quiet and not wake you honeymooners. I said Clarence would take his bath first so he could get to bed. They went into their room to unpack and Clarence and I headed for the bath. We were very quiet, but we had our fun in the tub. Then as we were both ready for bed, I knocked on their door and quickly said, we are both finished with the bathroom, it's all yours now. We are going to bed. Help yourself to anything in the kitchen if you get hungry. They yelled good night.

After a couple of days of them staying with us, and me running around with them, showing them all the sights I could think of. J.P. announced he was ready to join the Navy. So, he and Maxine went to Long Beach and he enlisted. He had six weeks of boot camp training, before knowing where he was going to be stationed. When he left, Maxine came back over to the house and said, she had enough money to rent a place, but if we didn't mind, she would rather stay with us while he was gone, because if she got moved in somewhere she wouldn't have any furniture and it would be pretty expensive to stay in a decent hotel for six weeks. I told her we didn't mind as long as Ellen and Dora didn't mind sharing a room. Clarence said, he was sure that wouldn't be a problem, since they had shared a room all their lives. When we went to bed that night I told Clarence, this is going to be interesting for you, having four women yacking their head off for a while, He said he had been raised with them, so he thought he could handle it fine, as long as they all got along.

Maxine and I enjoyed our days together catching up on each other's life. She told me she could have just threw a rock and hit him right in the head when he pulled that bad tasting joke about Ronald. Not letting us see the picture you had enclosed with your letter. She said we were all so upset and sad for you. I think mama wrote you a letter, didn't she? I said, yes she did and she told me how sad all you kids were for us. It was such a hard time and it's still very hard to talk about, even though I'm expecting another baby, finally. But one baby can never replace Ronald. I will love this baby and any future babies we have just as much as I loved Ronald, it is just not the same as having him back. He was such a precious little guy and so happy all the time. He was just beautiful, did you kids even get to see the two pictures I sent, or did the old man destroy them. She said, yes, they all got to see them. She said Daddy just tossed them on the ground with your letter and said, he would hate Clarence till the day he died, because he ran off with his girl who was almost half his age. We all said we liked Clarence and he treated all us kids so nice. Daddy then said, he didn't want to hear his name again, ever. Maxine said she was awfully worried about Velma. Daddy had been so mean to her and she just acted like she wanted to die. I told Maxine that I was going to write to Lola and see if she can get a letter to Velma without daddy knowing about it. So, that was all I could do. I asked Maxine, if J.P. had been given any idea as to where he might be going, and she was going to be able to go with him. She said, she had no idea and she didn't think they told him anything either, or he would have told me when he came out and kissed me goodbye. So, we just filled our next couple of days seeing a few things around town that I thought might interest her. She loved the ocean, so we spent several hours a couple of different times just walking and picking up sea shells. We always got home in plenty of time for me to have a nice dinner for us when Clarence got home.

Janet Lee

On Friday afternoon, we had just got home with a load of groceries and barely had got them put away, when we had knock on the door. I went to see who it was and just as I had guessed, it was Dora and Ellen. I introduced myself and then introduced them both to Maxine. We all sat there in the living room just chatting away, like we had all known each other for all our lives. The girls were so anxious to see Clarence. They said they hadn't seen him since he had left Oklahoma in late 1938. I said that I had met Clarence in around February of 1939, wasn't it, Maxine? She said she thought that was probably about right. Again, the girls brought up how sorry they were about us losing Ronald. I thanked them for their sympathy, but said it was awfully hard to talk about still. They asked if we were ever going to try to have another child. I told them we had never stopped trying, but for some reason, it just took longer this time than it did that first year we were married. They finally got the meaning of what I had just said, they both got up and came over and hugged me. How far along are you? I told them I was almost 4 months now and we were thrilled about it. They seemed so happy, you'd have thought it was them expecting. I looked at my watch and saw the time. I jumped and said sorry girls, but my husband will be hungry when he gets home and I need to get dinner ready. I asked if they all liked chicken. I got a trio of yes, we do. Maxine came in and asked what she could do. I told her to peel enough potatoes for the five of us. I told her not to skimp, because I didn't know how big of eaters his sisters are. About that time, Dora came in and asked what they could do? I told her there wasn't much more to be done, I had a large chicken all cut up and Maxine was peeling the potatoes. I told them they could put their things in that bedroom with the yellow bedspread on the bed. They said they would get their things all put away, so that the house wasn't a mess, because they could already tell, by the way everything looked that I was a perfect housekeeper. I said I try to be. I gave the chicken a good shake in the flour and started frying it in our largest frying pan. Thank goodness for our wonderful wedding presents. We had hardly had to buy anything. I was trying to decide what kind of vegetables to fix. I had made a large salad, so that everyone was not starving and one chicken would go far enough. Maxine said, quit worrying about it, when its gone, its gone. I wished I had bought some rolls at the store. Maxine asked if I wanted her to run get some. I said, sure if you don't mind.

She was out the door in seconds and Dora and Ellen came in and asked again what they could do? I said I was just watching the chicken, so that I turned it over at the right time. They said they would keep an eye on the potatoes so they didn't boil over. I asked what kind on vegetables they liked and they both said everything. So, I opened a couple of cans of creamed corn, one of Clarence's favorites. Maxine got back in record time with some delicious looking rolls. She said she got them in the bakery section and they said they made them fresh every day, so I thought they must be good. I thanked her and asked her how much I owed her. She looked insulted, and said for pete's sake Stella, I am living here, you know. Did you think I was going to stay here and not contribute enough for at least my food and some of the utilities? I said I really hadn't given it any thought, I am just so happy to see someone in my family and now I've also got to meet a couple of Clarence's sisters. I told them how much we enjoyed Orce's visit. They both said, isn't he just a doll? We are so lucky to have such wonderful brothers and sisters. I said, there is only one more girl, right? They said yes, there's Cindy. She is going to college, her first year. Ellen said she had finished college and took some extra classes to become a teacher. That's what I've always wanted to do. I love children and hope to meet the right man soon, so I can get started on a family of my own. Dora said she wasn't sure what she was going to do, but she wasn't in any hurry to get married and be told what to do. I said, Clarence never tells me what to do, we discuss everything and decide things together. She said, she guessed that was probably part of her problem, she had such sweet brother's and it was going to be hard to find anyone to measure up. I asked if their dad told their mom what to do and they said, dad just runs the house and does everything, and mom has always been pretty quiet. She just keeps the house clean and cooks and thinks that is all there is. When we told her we were coming to visit Clarence and Stella for a while, she said, you girls be careful, and have a good time. I mean, Really, how can you do both? We all laughed.

Clarence came in quietly and surprised them both with big hugs and kisses. They told him he looked younger than when he left home. He said it all the love this woman gives me, as he kissed me a nice long happy to see you kiss. They said how happy they had been to hear about our upcoming baby. He said, not half as happy as we are, as he had his arms around me from behind. He rubbed my belly and said it was actually becoming a bit of a tummy there. He said I can't wait to see all the movement soon. We had enjoyed that with Ronald so much. I changed the subject and asked Clarence if he wanted to make the gravy, or did he trust me. He said he trusted me completely, but since I was used to just making it for two, he had better make it since he was used to making it for large numbers too. I used to cook a lot when I was home, to give Mom a break. She always worked so hard around the house, and never did anything for herself. It had to have been a lot of work having 7 kids all close in age. Of course, I knew Clarence was the oldest and had a different Mother than the rest of them, but I had never thought to ask if the kids all knew. I told them my Mama had 12 children, but I think there was only 6 at home at home at a time, because the older ones ran off and joined the service, except my older brother, Al worked hard on a farm near where he had run off to, and Lola had got married as soon as she turned 18. She had already left home and was working in Dallas, when she met her husband. We weren't raised like your family was. In all truthfulness, I feel like we were just born to work for daddy so he had drinking money. We all had a very terrible life. Maxine, who had been quiet, letting Clarence catch up with his sisters, heard this and spoke up and said she that exactly right. We were just bred to be workers. They said, what about your mother, didn't she do anything about this? We both said, to save us and herself more beatings, she just stayed quiet most of the time. They both said how awful that sounded, and we assured them it was much worse than it sounded. We couldn't begin to tell you what a miserable worthless man our daddy was.

At that, Clarence said, dinner is ready. I had sat the table while we were talking and everything had been put into nice serving things and the table looked so pretty, like a picture out of a magazine. Ellen said your china is gorgeous, and you two have so many beautiful things. You have done quite well my dear brother. We explained that we had a wonderful wedding and reception and received many nice gifts. It's a very long story for some other time, let's eat. We bowed our heads to say the blessing and Dora and Ellen were surprised at this, but they bowed their heads and listened as Clarence said how thankful his sisters arrived safely and how nice it was having Maxine here also and he blessed the food to the nourishment of our bodies and said, In Jesus Name, Amen. We also echoed Amen. We had a great dinner with a full table of family. It can't be better than this. I love having all of you here so much. We are going to be such great friends, Dora said to me. I thanked her and said I felt sure of this also. Everyone loved the dinner and said what an excellent cook I was. I laughed and told them Clarence had taught me everything I know, For real. They said, well you're a fast learner. I said I try hard to remember what I have been taught. Well, Clarence said, she was a quick learner and it took no time at all, before she had the hang of it, and I wouldn't trade her for all the chef's in the world. She is all mine and I love her more every single day. Maxine said she would take care of the dishes and she would hear no argument about it. So, we all went into the living room and Clarence had about a million questions and they answered back as soon as he asked the next questions. Maxine said, I have to run out to my car really quick. Back in she came with a huge Chocolate Cake she had bought at the bakery while getting the rolls. We all said it looked like a winner to us. We went back into the kitchen and had cake and it was amazingly good. Not as good as Kathleen's or even Lola's, but for a store bought, it was delicious. We all ate till our bellies hurt.

For the next few weeks all the girls seemed to have a great time. They went out to dances and night clubs and every fun place they could fine. There was never a shortage of servicemen to meet and take them to all these place. There were several nights that Clarence really got on to his sisters for coming in too late. They always came back with the fact that they were grown women and had been dating and coming home when they wanted for a long time. He said, Yes, but you are living with us now and I feel responsible for you, as your older brother. Life is much different here in Los Angeles and Long Beach, where all these horny servicemen are just looking for one thing. It's a lot different than Oklahoma where you might be looking for Mr. Right. Dora said, Clarence, I love and adore you, but we have both been away to college and been around all kinds of men. We know how to take care of ourselves and each other. Clarence came back with the fact that now, you two are living at my house and as long as you are, I expect you to be in by at least two a.m. and I don't think that is too much to ask. They went into their room and slammed the door.

I looked ahead into the future, when we might have a grown daughter and I had to laugh, but also be proud that he cared what she was doing. He loved his sisters and just wanted to know they were safe. Maxine had gone out with them several times and she assured me that, all that went on was having a little fun dancing, and having these guys buy our drinks. No one ever separated and left with any guy alone. When I was with them we all made it a point to know where each of us were. I assume it's the same when it is just the two of them. I told Maxine that she was married, and I hoped J.P. wouldn't mind her out dancing with other men, but Dora and Ellen are both single and may have different agendas than you, being married and all. Maxine said, well, all I know is that I have nothing to hide from J.P. and he is not the jealous type, and would not mind me having some good clean fun. So, that is all I have to say about it about the subject. All I could do is hope that she was right. It was a little less than 2 weeks until J.P. had a short leave, so time would tell. But as far as Dora and Ellen went, I had no idea how long they planned to stay. It had never been brought up in any conservation. They may get tired of Clarence's curfews since they were grown. I could see both sides, but I just knew I would never go out without Clarence. We still had plenty of our private time, we made sure of that. I was sure glad the house was well built and very well insulated. When doors were closed to any of the rooms, you couldn't hear a sound going on inside that room. This was great for us, but I was already thinking ahead to when our baby was in the room closest to us and thinking, I will always leave our doors open so we hear our precious little baby's every sound. I was determined to be the best mother ever. I would not lose another baby. I knew I could not live through that again. I had to quit thinking about this. Ronald was loved well and he was always watched and kept safe until that one night. If only I had chose to call Dr. Brody and be told to take him to the hospital he was born in, rather that that little hospital which had been closer. They should have been sued, but that would not have brought him back. But thinking back, we should have sued them to help any future things like that happening. They should have been held accountable. It's amazing how much you learn as you get older. I just knew that no one would ever take my baby from be again, whether he or she was sick or not. I would be with them every minute. I wish with all my heart I could get all these thoughts to stay out of my head, but it seemed the further along I got, the more I think of my baby. This one I'm carrying, and the one I lost almost four years ago. I prayed so many times a day that God give me the strength to leave my precious Ronald in the past and dwell on this one that I am going to have in just a few months. I knew when the baby was in my arms, I would let Ronald stay in the back of my mind and heart, where that special place for him would always be until the day I died.

When J.P. returned, he looked so much older in just a few weeks, he had gained so much muscle and his body just looked more like a man, than a boy. After all, he had just turned eighteen, He said he was going to be on a submarine for quite a while, depending on the war and he thought the best thing for her to do was go back to Texas and live with his Sister, he said they would be great company for each other while both their husbands were serving in this crazy war. Maxine said, she agreed since her and Mary Lou had got along so well, and she loved the little town she lived in. So, within a few days J.P. was out to Sea and Maxine was on a train back to Texas. Clarence said, I love my family dearly, but the girls are quite a handful and he couldn't help being the older brother that had watched them grow up. He finally said, out loud for the first time since the girls had arrived one night at dinner, very tactfully, he asked, how long do you two sisters of mine plan to stay in California? They said we figured we had worn out our welcome, and we want to be able to be welcomed back for another visit again someday, so we have been talking about leaving next week, if that's okay? Clarence had tears in his eyes and said anything he had said to them had only been out of love and worry for them. They both got up and hugged him and said how sorry they were for causing him so much worry, especially when you and Stella have been so good to us and put up with our partying so much. And you two are having another baby and that's all that should be on your minds right now. Instead you have had three women coming and going constantly for over 6 weeks now. Clarence said, all is forgotten and never forget how much I love my little sisters. They both said, their feelings were mutual and always would be. You were always our protector when we were little, how could we expect less now? So, all was fine with everyone.

The next week we drove Dora and Ellen to the train and saw them take off. We had our house to ourselves now for the first time in such a long time and it felt so good. As soon as we got home, we ran a tub full of hot water and some of my special bubble bath. We lay there together, with the door open and laughed and talked about the day we talked about wanting lots of family to visit. I said, you can't say we didn't get our wish. We forgot all that as I could feel Clarence behind me, growing quickly. He took the bar of soap and reached around me and started soaping up my breasts and my big growing belly. Then splashing water over me to rinse the soap off, he then started taking his hands lower and lower until he reached my special zone that only he knew and he would always be the only one that knew. After just a little of his fingers doing their magic, I couldn't stand it any longer and I turned around and let him gently enter me and we wanted this to last forever because it felt so good, but our rocking and moving up and down made both of us reach our best ever, wonderful deep inside and all over feel good climax. Clarence said to me, is it just me, or was that absolutely magic. I said I think I've died and went to Heaven and what a way to go. We lay there in each other's arms and both agreed life could not be any better than this. I patted my belly and said this little one will only make our love grow and things will be better, I just know we will be such good parents again. Clarence said, that's one thing I am positive about.

Ruby Lee's twins were getting so big and I had missed spending time with them while we had a house full. They hadn't forgot me though. When I went into where they sat in their playpen. They both pulled their selves up and held their little arms up, wanting me to pick them up. I said what do I do, I can't pick them both up with this belly, So Ruby

Lee reached in and picked both of them up and then I too first one, then the other. I gave them both big kisses up their chin which made them giggle out loud. What a beautiful sound. She said they had been doing that a lot the past few weeks. Once they learned what a response they got, they decided it was great fun. They are both starting to try and walk. And I think I might go crazy when this happens. With Larry and Ila Jean being so young, they will be all over. Running after four at a time will be fun. I said, oh you're getting a little carried away. It not like the older two don't stop when you call them. They are such sweet little kids that mind so well, you have done an excellent job with them. She said, I know and really, they have been such a big help to me already. If I need clean diapers, or anything else I need them. They already do or bring whatever, whenever I asked them. And lucky for me, one of them is always around, since I have a very secure fenced back yard. She said, I just can't wait to see what you have in there. You better hope it's a boy because you'll have a ton of little boy cloths. I am sure not saving them as I know I am finished. They cut and tied my tubes after the twins were born. Thank the Lord, I was awake to tell them to do it. Four kids are enough for anyone to take care of. I can't imagine having twelve like your mama did. The poor sweet dear women. Yes, your right, twelve kids were way too many babies for one body to have to carry. And I never once heard her complain about having all of us, nor did I ever heard her say a thing about how my daddy beat her every day. I can't remember a single day if he was home and not, or in jail, that he didn't at least slap her around. More often than not, it was usually being hit with his fists. I don't understand how she could stay with a horrible monster like him. And not only mama, but his own children were his punching bags. Some of us worse than others. I just can't talk about this anymore. It's a happy time for us and I can't have these feelings coming out all the time. It's over, and I have a wonderful husband who adores me. I am the luckiest woman in the world as far as I am concerned. I just keep feeling guilty because I got away, and the poor little ones left to take it day after day. If my poor mama get pregnant again, I think I'll go cut his penis off myself. Enough about this.

That night I fixed Clarence one of his favorite meals, He loved a big pot of pinto beans and a pan of hot cornbread. And of course, some buttermilk to go with it. We were so happy to be in our house with the peace and quiet of all our loved ones gone. We enjoyed their visit very much, but it was just a little too long this time. I needed these next couple of months of peace and quiet and just the love of my precious Clarence. The next couple of months went by so fast, I could hardly believe that my time was close. Clarence rushed home from work every night and asked as soon as he came in the door, how do you feel, Sweetheart? I always answered the same way. Just feeling fatter by the day and all I want to do is eat. Clarence said, you remember what the doctor told you our last appointment, he said you have not gained as much as normal pregnant does, so quit worrying about your beautiful body. I happen to think to think it is perfect. You just say that because you love me, he said that I do, but I love every inch of you.

That night I woke Clarence up when my water broke and the bed was soaking wet. I told him I was barely having little pains once in a while, so I didn't give it any thought and now here I have soaked the bed. I hope it didn't go through on our beautiful mattress. I do have a thick mattress pad on. Will you help me change the bed really quick, Honey? He said, are you kidding me? We have to get to the hospital. I told him we had plenty of time, before my contractions start getting harder. I don't believe you, I can do this after the baby is born. I told him, lets at least get these wet ones off and maybe it won't go through to the mattress. Finally, he said I can see I'm not going to win this one, so we stripped the bed and I was so relieved that nothing had gone through the pad. I told him I hated to put clean sheets on without the good mattress pad. He told me he would see to it that the mattress pad got washed and put back on, and he would just put the same sheets back on after they've been washed. Then he said, I can't believe this, I said, what Honey? He said, you're in labor with our baby and your obsessed with the mattress. I told him I just knew how expensive this mattress was and I want it to stay nice and I'm not even having contractions close together yet, almost before the words were out of my mouth, I almost doubled over with a pain that lasted a good minute. Clarence said, I've already called your doctor and we are on our way to the hospital, now Stella, do you hear me? I said I am definitely ready to leave now. That was a big and long contraction. Wow, it came on so fast. So we were off to the hospital to have our baby. That hard pain really hit me hard and now I was really sure this was happening now. I had just remembered that when I started having pains with Ronald, they had started out so mild and it was all very slow for hours before I really felt like I was in labor. It just hadn't dawned on me it might be different this time. I wasn't due for several days yet and with Ronald I was about a week late. I guess you just never know. Babies come when they are ready. I told Clarence I was so glad the he and a friend had got the mattress for the middle guest room all taken to the garage and all Ronald's beautiful furniture was in the middle room closest to us. I had polished the furniture and crib till it looked like new. Clarence very tactfully said, Sweetheart, you know you have to quit calling this Ronald's furniture. I said, I know as soon as I have this baby it will be his or hers and I will get that out of my head. It's just hard, seeing it again and looking so new just like it had when Annie and Mike sent it to us. Anyway, that was over a week ago and I had got all the bedding washed and put on the bed and I just got so excited as my stomach did a few flip flops. I said, hold on little one, you'll be in your beautiful bed soon. When I told Clarence about that, he felt much better. When we arrived at the hospital, before I could get out of the car, my stomach got hard as a rock and this contraction was twice as hard as the last one had been five or six minutes. They brought the wheel chair out to me and as soon as they got my name and our insurance information all taken of, I was in a room and having another contraction. About the time Dr. Richards was there and examined me. He said I was getting pretty close to having a baby, so he hoped I was ready for some pushing. I told him I was more than ready for having this baby. I felt like I'd been waiting ten years at least. It had been just under four years ago that I had given birth to Ronald, so I sure hadn't forgot the pushing. It was just all happening so much faster this time. He said, I've never heard a mother complaining about things happening to quick. I said, that's not what I meant, really.

CHAPTER 22

The arrival of David

So, about two and a half hours later, on June 7th, 1944 at 8:32 P.M. I delivered a healthy beautiful baby boy, at the Inglewood Hospital. I had secretly been hoping for a boy, even though I would have been just as happy with a little girl, had it been one. Clarence and I were both so excited as they handed him to me. We both were amazed at how chubby his little cheeks were. He had weighed 8 pounds and 5 ounces. And was 20 inches long. We were thinking of what to name him and I told Clarence that I loved the name David. He said he liked that really well also, now for a middle name. He said, what about Alan? I said that's a wonderful idea and David Alan Rader sounds like an important name, so it is settled. We told the nurse and she said she would tell them in records, so his official birth certificate would be recorded with the state and we would have a Hospital Birth Certificate when we left in a couple of days. As soon as she walked out of the room, Clarence had to unwrap him and make sure everything was there and all his beautiful little toes and fingers were all there. I said, so does he pass inspection. Clarence said, oh yes he is perfect. We do great work, my dear wife. I had to agree. David was just perfect, I didn't want to compare babies, but I couldn't help seeing the big difference between our two new born babies. David was so light and the little fuzz on his head was almost white. He was so much chubbier. But he was also so beautiful, and took right to my breast like he was a pro. I already fell in love with this sweet happy baby. He slept right after he ate and was changed. So far that all he did, which was very normal. The other ladies in my room all had their babies in at the same time. There was four of us in the room. Different from the hospital in Oregon. It had been a much smaller hospital and the rooms were tiny, so each patient had their own private room. The two visiting times were for only one hour in the late morning, after we all had time for our shower, and then another hour after our dinner time. So having three other women in the room made the time go by faster. We all would have our babies brought to us at the same time for their feeding time and we got to change them and spend precious time with them. Two of the girls were very young and this was the first baby for each of them. Both of their babies would not take hold of the breast and cried almost the whole time we had them. David had not cried at all. He was very alert and happy and when I had changed him and just let him lie there quietly, so that I could watch him looking all around the room like he was taking it all in. When I picked him up and held him to my cheek to feel the softness of him and his smell it was almost magic. After having him brought to me only twice to feed, he was already a pro at it. I lowered his little head to my breast and immediately he latched on like a snapping turtle.

After just a minute or two of his feeding those terrible sharp pains came into my stomach that I remembered from the first time. I was told it helped tighten my stomach muscles so it was easy to ignore them, I had this beautiful little baby to enjoy looking at. I felt so sorry for the two young girls that were trying so hard to get their babies to latch on with no success. I very nicely called their names and told them both to try very hard to relax. I told them that the baby could feel their tenseness and that what was making them fussy. I told them this was my second baby and I remembered seeing other young mothers feel this same fear. I felt like an old mother hen, but I could see how afraid they both were. I assured them that they couldn't hurt the baby, just hold them tight and be soothing when you talk to them. They will feel it when you become calm. They both tried it and within minutes both babies had taken hold and were nursing. They said, why in the world would the nurse not tell us these things? I said, very quietly that the nurse that had brought in the babies just seemed to not really care, just do your job and pick up a paycheck at the end of the week. It was very obvious to me as soon as they walked in. Couldn't you see the difference in the night nurses, when they brought in the babies to us? They both said they were very nice and stood and talked with us for a little bit. I said, yes, that was their way of calming you, therefore calming your babies. They both thanked me and said it was so nice to see their little ones eating and feeling so content. I felt like an old woman, when in fact I was all of twenty-two years old. I just felt so much older having had all the life experiences I had gone through. And watching my mama so many times with new born babies. I didn't have to be told what to do even with Ronald. I guess babies are smarter than some people give them credit. I knew mine was for sure. I could already tell what a good baby David was going to be. He was going to be something special, I just knew it. After about an hour they came in and took the babies back to the nursery. Now it was time to rest or get up and fix your hair, or just whatever you wanted to do till it was time to bring back in the babies. I for one, was not tired, so I walked down to the nursey and just watched all the baby. All beautiful to their own mother's and father's, but for me one stood out far above the rest. My precious little David Alan Rader. My love for him was swelling my heart up so big, I thought I would burst with pride watching him lie there sleeping like an angel. Nothing bad would ever happen to him. I would protect him with my life, if necessary.

Clarence came in that night with a big bunch of beautiful roses. I told him how much I loved them but he didn't need to spend that much for me to know how much he loved me, because I could feel it with his every glance. He said, and don't you ever forget it, because I will until the day I die. I've told you this before, I just want to make sure you never forget it for a minute. He said he got to the hospital almost an hour ago, but he just stood and watched David, until he could come into the room. Clarence whispered to me, is it just me, or is our baby the most beautiful little perfect baby in this hospital? I said, you just a little off, I think he is the most beautiful perfect baby in the Country. We laughed and snuggled together like a couple of teenagers. He said quietly in my ear, do we really have to wait six weeks before we can make love? I said, it is supposed to be, but as I remembered before, we didn't wait nearly that long and the way I feel now, it won't be three weeks. Maybe two, and I'm not sure I can wait that long, and I giggled. At least our doctor this time didn't say to not make love the last six weeks of my pregnancy, he said just take it easy and if it doesn't hurt, it should be fine. So, we made sure it didn't hurt.

When I was dressing David in his very cute, very soft, little outfit to go home in, I made sure he was wrapped up tightly so he wouldn't be afraid. I had heard that since they had been used to being in such a small area for so long, that it helped them feel secure to be bundled up tight. Clarence was right on time to pick us up and we drove right home. I held David so close and Clarence drove like he was just learning. He made sure he made complete stops and stopped at every yellow light for fear of someone else trying to push the green light coming from the other way. He said his family was going to get home safe and sound and he would see to it that we always stayed that way. We arrived home all in one piece were just about the happiest two people or I should say three now, in the world. We sat down on the sofa with David lying between Clarence and I. He lay there sleeping with the most beautiful pleasant look on his face. Like he knew one day he would be the best at whatever he chose to do. Clarence took a week off work, so he could help me, and to bond with David. Every little sound he made was music to us. We just stared at him and still could believe he was really ours. In about an hour, it was time for him to eat and I could sure tell, because it was the third day and my milk came in like a waterfall. I was so full of milk, I think I could have fed three or four babies, but just this one for right now. He wasn't waking and I was actually hurting so Clarence and I both wiggled around and then I decided to change his diaper. He started waking as I washed him little bottom. As soon as I got a diaper back on him and wrapped him up a bit, he was ready to start nursing and I was certainly ready. He grabbed hold and started eating like he was starving. I gladly felt the strong pains pulling on my stomach. David nursed for about 15 minutes on both sides and he had a full tummy and my breasts felt much better. I took him in his room and laid him in his fresh clean crib. He looked so peaceful. It was warm enough that he need nothing for covers except his pretty blue receiving blanket which was a gift from Ruby Lee. He had many gift from her and after washing each piece, they all looked brand new. I was a lucky mommy. We hadn't need to buy anything except a few dozen diapers. The ladies from my work and went together and sent us, a one hundred dollar gift certificate to JC Penney's. So we had plenty of credit left of our account there. I can't imagine how we will ever use it all with constant hand me downs from the twins.

David was growing so fast. We had so much fun just laying him in bed with us on the weekends when Clarence didn't have to go to work and we could both enjoy him learning new things all the time. He was happy and content and hardly ever cried unless he happened to get hungry when I was in the middle of fixing dinner for Clarence and I.

Usually, I would stop and feed him as soon as he woke up and was changed, but every once in a while, I would be in the middle of something, like my hands all messy mixing a meatloaf or peeling potatoes. I would hear him immediately, but I decided it wasn't going to hurt him to fuss for a few minutes. It was never really crying, just kind of, hey I'm awake, don't forget me. I would go into his room and he would see me and stop as soon as his eye saw me he stopped. I would tell, listen little precious one, I was busy fixing your daddy's dinner. You know he has to eat also. As I was changing him he would smile and squirm like a worm. I kept telling to be still, but he began to think it was all a game. In the afternoons before his nap, I would take him on long walks to the park and just sit there on a bench and let him watch the birds in the many trees. He loved that. He just loved being outside. I went over to visit Ruby Lee quite often, he loved watching her four kids playing. The twins were running all over the place and with the two older playing with them, there was constant laughter and they all loved David, but lately, it seemed one of the four kids or more would have a cold and I would leave as soon as I heard a sneeze or a cough for fear of my precious little guy catching something. I knew I couldn't keep him in a bubble his whole life, but I could do my best to see that he didn't catch a cold. The fear of it turning into something worse just terrified me. I just wasn't able to cope with the chance of losing David.

The months passed and David grew and everything he did just seemed to be early. He was walking good at ten months. I had been writing back and forth to mama and sending her pictures, but a few times the letters came back. In one letter that I received she said, they had been moving so much, it was hard to keep up with receiving mail. She also told me in one letter that daddy was getting meaner by the day and every one of the kids seemed to hate him so much, and he was extra hard on Velma. Her hate for him worries me, Stella. I just didn't know what to do. I don't think she will run away like all of the rest of you did, because she tries so hard to protect me. That's what gets her into trouble so much. I try to tell her to just ignore him and he will quit hitting me as much if he doesn't think it stirs her up so much. She just wants to protect me. Joyce is still the same, she just stays quiet and stays out of his way as much as possible. She is so different from Velma, who just seems to thrive on keeping everything in an uproar. The boys, Garner and Kenneth are growing up so fast and your daddy expects so much from them and they are really still so young. Garner is only nine and Kenneth is only six, but he thinks they should be able to work like men sometimes.

When Clarence came home from work, I read her last letter to him. Then I asked if he would mind if I went for a visit to see mama and the kids and David meet his grandma and his aunts and uncles. I said David was just over a year old, and should be fine to travel on a train. He said, I think that sound like a fine idea. I have three weeks vacation time built up, so we will just buy you a one way ticket and I can drive back there to pick you up, and then we can go to Oklahoma and you can meet my daddy and mom. I got so excited about all this, I could hardly stand it. So, we started making the plans and writing to all our relatives and told them we would be there to visit and would give them a closer date when we were sure of exact travel dates. I found out where Mama was and told her what day I would be there. And as I packed I was so excited, and also frightened at the thought of having to see my daddy again. I knew from other times when family came to visit, that daddy was usually on his best behavior so no one would ever believe what a complete monster he really was and always had been. But I was different, I had been one of his favorite punching bags, so he couldn't and maybe wouldn't be on good behavior for me. I guess time would tell. I had no doubt of him hurting me or David, because I was a married adult and was capable of, and would call the law if he tried anything while I was there. And I would also be sure he knew Clarence was on his way to pick me up very soon.

CHAPTER 23

Taking David to see Mama

Clarence put in for his vacation days and said they had been okayed, so he put David and I on the train, and said how much he would miss us the next week or so. He said the next week as soon as his vacation was due to start, he would leave next Friday when he got off work. The night before we left, as we had just made love and were lying in each other's arms, we discussed how hard this trip was going to be on us, because since being married, we had never been apart except for the couple of night spent in the hospital and even then, we saw each other a couple of times each day. And when home there was never a day when we didn't make love, unless, of course we couldn't because of just having the babies or when I was on my period, which thank goodness, they were almost always very irregular and short when I did have one. I told Clarence I would miss him so much and our alone time like this. And he agreed it was going to be so hard without David and I there this next week. While David and I rode on the train for the first time. We just loved watching how fast things went by and all the beautiful scenery that was in our Country. I was so excited about seeing Joyce and Velma and of course the boys. Garner was so little when I left home that he would not remember me, and little Kenneth I had never met. David was just so happy sitting here in my lap watching people walking around and looking out the window as we sped by everything so fast. I would get up to go get us both something to eat and then come back to our seats and feed him. He had weined from breast feeding about the time he decided it was more run to run around and play. So, I would find things to feed him that were soft and easy to chew. He loved bananas and peanut butter and applesause and so there were quite a few things that I had brought on the train with me that I knew would not go bad. Soon we will be there little guy, so Mommy wants you to be the angel that you always are. I always seemed to talk to him in full sentences, so that when he talked, he never talked baby talk. He was saying lots of words already and was quite concerned that daddy wasn't home from work. I tried to explain he wouldn't see daddy for a while but of course he was way too young to understand this.

We should be pulling into the station where I had to change trains to get to to a train the that went to Lubbuck, Tx. My family were in some town call Abernathy and someone would have to drive us there after we got off the train. Thank goodness the train didn't stop right in town, so we were closer to Abernathy according to what mama had said. I asked if there was anyone willing to drive us to Abernathy if I paid them. A man very clean and neat looking said he did that all the time for people who got off here. He said that was his business, the only source of money he had. So, we loaded up in his car and off we went. He said he knew exactly where Abernathy was and it would cost me about twenty-five dollars. I said that sounded fine. When we got there about two hours later, I paid him and off he went. I had no idea how I was going to find out where Mama was from here. I asked a few people if they knew where the Attebery's were working and the second man I asked knew and said it was only a mile in that direction. I said I could walk with a baby and two suitcases, plus my purse. Finally, a woman who had been out back said she would drive me over to the place where they were working. When we drove up, at first all I saw was this little tow-headed boy. who I was sure must be Kenneth. I tried to pay the woman five dollars, but she refused saying it had only taken five minutes to get there and it was no big deal. I told her thank you so much, it's really nice to see there are still some nice people in this country. She smiled and drove off.

A minute later I saw Garner, he looked the same, just twice as tall as when I'd last seen him. I walked over to the house and put my finger up to my lips telling the boys to be quiet and let me surprise mama. Then I got to the front door and there was my mama sweeping the floor, she looked up and saw me and let the broom drop. I let David get down and I ran to hug my mama for the first time in over six years. We were both crying and she said, stand back and let me look at you, then she said, how beautiful I had grown up to be and how fancy I was dressed. I was only wearing a tan colored suit with brown colored trim on the collar and pockets.

She said it was fancier than she had ever had since she got married. I told her I was going to buy her something real nice while I was here. She said that wouldn't be necessary because she wouldn't have anywhere to ever where it. I said, don't you ever go to church and she said, now Stella, you know your daddy would let me go off and do something that would make me happy. He hasn't change one bit. I hugged her again and said how much I had missed her, then I picked up David and said this is your Grandson, David. She said what a handsome little guy he was. white hair, just like Kenneth. Then she called Garner and Kenneth and told them to come in and meet their big sister. They both came in the door immediately when called and looked at me like I was a foreigner. Mama said this is Stella, do you remember her at all Garner? He shook his head no, then she told Kenneth that I was Stella, his big sister and this little guy is David, he is your nephew. They said you mean we are uncles? Mama told them that they had both been uncles since before they were born. They looked pretty confused and she explained that their oldest sister, Lola, had two daughters who were almost grown now. They asked why they never met them and she said because she lives far from us and Lola would never bring them out to most of the places they had lived. They are very refined little ladies and are probably going to college by now. Garner said he remember Lola coming out to some old place we lived a couple of times. Mama said yes, she did, she brought me letters to let me know how Stella was and W.K. and Maxine and everyone who wrote to her to have her let me know they were fine and not to worry about them. And you have an older brother Al, who works on a farm somewhere here in Texas and he married a woman named Mae, you have two more older brothers J.E. and Preston and they are in the Army off fighting in this terrible war. As soon as she finished telling them all that information, Joyce and Velma came running in and hugged me till I thought we were all going to end up on the ground.

I was so happy seeing them, then I noticed David had gone over and sat down right in a little puddle of mud. I ran and started to pick him up, but realized then I too would be covered in mud. Velma went and picked him up and said, Hi David, I am your Aunt Velma and this pretty lady with the red hair is your Aunt Joyce. And this wonderful lady is your Grandmother. He was very happy to be all dirty. I couldn't believe how fast he had got in this mess, this was the very first time he has been dirty. Mama and Joyce both said, my goodness, where do you keep him that he stays so clean? I said we just have nice grass in the front and back yard and when I take him to the park, he plays in the sand or on the grass. Velma said, I'll bet you this isn't the last time around here. He held up his hand to Velma with a fist full of mud and very proud of it, when he said, here. Velma said, we are going to have to show you how to make mud pies. I hadn't even thought of all this when I was packing his clothes. I had brought so many cute outfits, but he didn't even have a pair of jeans. Mama said I am sure I have some of Kenneth's old jeans that I can cut down to fit him in just a bit. He'll be a regular cowboy in no time. David let Velma carry him all over the place showing him different things. He had been around strangers so seldom that I couldn't believe how he took to her. And everyone for that matter, it was as if he just knew they were all family. It was so wonderful to be here, dirt and all. Mama looked the same, just all the kids had grown up. I also hadn't thought of where we would sleep. Mama said we have a couple extra rolled up mattress's and I have clean blankets to put over them. Don't worry so much, sweetie, that little boy is having a ball and you survived being raised this way and it sure won't hurt him for a while. I knew mama was right, she was always right, except when it came to staying with daddy. I asked if he was gone, hoping to hear a yes, but I got a no in unison from Joyce and Velma. And neither one of them looked happy about it either. Mama said, I wish I had something special to feed you, but we just have beans and cornbread for tonight. I said that sounded just fine. Thank goodness, David wasn't a picky eater.

In about an hour Daddy rode up on a horse and this, really excited David, who was still playing outside with Velma and the boys. Daddy said, who's kid is that? Velma picked him up, really quick and said, this is David, he is your grandson. That's not what I asked, now is it? Velma started to say something and before she could open her mouth, I was standing there and said, David is mine and Clarence's son. He said how the hell did you get here? I told him I took a train to Lubbock and then I paid a nice young man to drive us to Abernathy? Is that alright with you? He didn't even answer, just walked in and said, how long till dinner. Mama told him she didn't know what time he would be there, so she had been waiting to start the cornbread. He then said, in a more hateful voice, can't a man get an answer around here? Mama said in about twenty-five minutes, Was that so hard? Mama just said no. Oh I hated that man, after more than six years being gone, and not even a hello. I wanted to pick up David and go back to safety. But as far as being safe, I was not worried about that. He didn't dare to touch a hair on mine or David's head and I think he knew it, that's why he was showing off. Just thinking it would frighten me. Well, he didn't frighten me anymore. Those days were gone as soon as I was with Clarence, I knew I would always be protected. We ate dinner in pretty much silence. As soon as I had finished mashing up beans until they were, pretty smooth and took as many hulls out as I could, I started feeding David. He seemed to like them just fine. I guess he is definitely his father's son. I gave him tiny bites of cornbread soaked with a little juice. He liked that too. I had several containers of applesauce in his diaper bag that I had brought along. So, after he had his fill of beans and cornbread, I fed him a container of applesauce. Now he was ready for a bath and time for bed, with a bottle. I hadn't thought about milk. So I asked mama if she had any milk for David's bottle. Before mama could answer, Daddy said what, your milk dryed up already. I told him nothing about my body is any of your business.

He gave me a dirty look and headed for an old barn out back. mama said, I guess he's going out because that where he keeps the car. I thought to myself, Thank You Lord. Mama said they usually had plenty of milk because there were so many cows running around, the boys could catch one and milk it and bring in the milk for me to keep cold in the ice box over there. I asked if They had someone bringing ice by regular. Mama said that they only came one in a while, but Daddy would bring a block home from town if we got low. It hasn't got low, so the milk is nice and cold. Mama was pretty smart she saw the wheels in my head turning, she said, I could tell you was worrying about the milk being bad. I told her I knew all my worrying about everything must seem so silly to them, but I just couldn't take losing another baby. Mama said, I understand, and I believed she did. It was about five days before Clarence arrived, and he was so happy to see us. David was so happy to see his daddy too. He recognized the car when it pulled up and he started saying daddy here, daddy here. Mama said, he a smart little guy, isn't he? I said, yes, he really is considering he is only one year and two months. He has been saying so many words since he was eight or nine months. Mama said I think they learn so much faster when you have time to spend with them. I never had any spare time to sit and play with any of you when you were babies. There was always so much to do. I know mama and all of us kids know that you did the best you could with that worthless husband of yours. She said, now Stella, he is you daddy. I said, Mama the last thing I want to do is hurt you, but that man had never been a daddy to any of us any more than he's been a husband to you. He is just someone to control and use everything around him and if he can't, then he will beat you until he can. Being a daddy is what Clarence is, He loves and nurtures his son with all that's in him. He is so full of love, we could have twenty children and he would love them all. But I'm not going to have that many for sure. Mama, actually laughed at that. I told her it was so good to hear her laugh. I couldn't remember the last time I had heard her laugh out loud like she just had. She just lowered her head and quietly said there's not much to laugh at around here. I patted her hand and said, I'd give anything to be able to help you out of this situation.

Clarence had stopped the car, and I jumped up to run meet him. We stood there kissing and hugging like we had been apart for a year instead of a little over a week. All the kids came running to see him. All except Kenneth, had met him, but Garner probably remembers nothing. But then, Garner was the first to say candy. I guess Clarence made quite an impression on them all. He brought with him a big bag with all different kinds of candy bars and he had a cooler full of cold cokes. I couldn't wait to open one. I took it over to Mama and said have a drink of this. She took the bottle and turned it up and drank until it was half gone. I laughed till I cried. Mama looked at me and said, that is some good stuff. I said I know. I am literally addicted to them. I said you can drink that and I'll open one for me. The kids were all in seventh heaven, going through the bag and picking out which one they wanted. Clarence told them to keep the bag in the cooler or a cool place, so if they had one or they wouldn't melt. They said, mama can we put them in with the milk? She said sure, now what do you say to Clarence. They all said Thank you Clarence and the two boys ran over and hugged his leg. It really was cute.

He had another cooler in the back of the car, which he got out and handed Mama a huge delicious looking ham and a couple of big chicken fryers. Then it was Mama's turn to hug him. She said Thank you Clarence. I don't remember how long it's been since I fried up a chicken, but I sure haven't forgot. He said if you need anything else, it's not that far to the store where I bought all this. Mama's eyes were full of tears and she hugged me and said how happy she was that I found such a good man. I told her she had a lot to do with it. If she hadn't had us taken to that cotton farmer when the old man was in jail, I would never have met him, so thank you, mama. We all sat there drinking our cokes, Joyce and Velma had been given one too. I would have them all addicted and then I would have to leave. Didn't seem quite fair to them, but at least they had the pleasure for a few days. I asked Mama if she had any cooking oil for the chicken and she said, let me go look and came back with just enough in a bottle to fry up the chicken. Clarence said, do you have potatoes I can start peeling for you? Mama told him where the potatoes were and we all started fixing dinner. Clarence went back to the back of the car and brought out another bag he had forgot. It was a big bag of yeast rolls that were homemade by some lady in town and a big bag of home canned corn. The lady said she cut it off the cobb herself and canned it immediately, so it should taste like fresh corn if you have butter and I didn't know if you did, so I bought a few pounds.

Mama said she felt like she was a kid again back home when they all fixed big meals together. When everything was done, we didn't have to call the kids twice. Clarence had mashed the potatoes up with butter and milk and made them so fluffy. David just love mashed potatoes and I pulled off tiny pieces of chicken breast for him and he gobbled it up. The little guy was really learning to eat. Clarence just cracked up when he saw his little homemade jeans and how dirty he was. He said that's my country boy. David just seemed twice as happy as usual because of all the attention he was getting from his aunts and uncles and also his daddy was here too. We all seated starting to fill our plate when we heard the horse coming. All of a sudden the room got real quiet. They all knew what daddy had said about Clarence, but Clarence didn't give a hoot, he wasn't afraid of that louse. When daddy walked in the door he didn't say a word to anyone. He just walked over to the sink and washed the dirt off his hands, then took his seat at the table. It's like we were all holding our breath waiting to see what was going to happen. He just started filling up his plate and as he started to eat, I said, wait daddy, Clarence was just going to say the blessing. I knew I was pushing my luck, but I didn't care, he couldn't hurt me anymore. Daddy stopped eating and said let's get it done then. Clarence bowed his head and said a very nice short blessing over our dinner with family who we hadn't seen in so long. He said and bless the wonderful woman who has cooked our meal. In Jesus name, Amen. Everyone repeated Amen except daddy. I'm sorry Lord, I said under my breath that I couldn't help it, I hated that man. We all began eating in silence, what we had hoped would be a festive meal, but no, daddy had to show up early. Someone had probably told him there was a new car at his house. And he had to come and see. We were all closed to being finished, when Daddy spoke up and said why don't you ever cook meals like this for me woman? Mama didn't hesitate. She said, I cook what you bring in and that's all I can do. You could just see daddy fuming and it took all he had to control himself. But he had to see what she had said was the truth. She had neither any money or any way to go buy something if she did, and he knew it. She had put him in his place for the first time I could ever remember, but then it was the first time Clarence was sitting at our table. I only hoped she didn't pay for it after we were gone, in a couple of days. I would ask the girls to make sure and let me know if it got bad for any of them after we left.

Clarence and I slept on a mattress with David between us. The girls Mattresses were touching ours. Before we laid down with David, Clarence had given me a big hug and kissed me long and gentle. He whispered in my ear, I'm not liking this arrangement one bit. I said back to him just as quiet that it couldn't be helped. So, we slept a night that neither of us slept really well. I think the only ones sleeping were the girls and David. When we got up in the early morning, daddy had already left and I Thanked God for that. Mama was up and peeling potatoes for breakfast. I asked what I could do to help. She said you can slice up enough of that ham for our breakfast. She said Garner and Kenneth had caught one of the milk cow and got a full gallon today. I told them Little David would be needing plenty and I would make some biscuits and gravy for breakfast. They were thrilled and even went and found some eggs from the chickens who didn't lay lots of them, probably because they didn't have much to eat themselves. Anyway, we had a wonderful happy breakfast all laughing and talking while we were eating. Velma told us how she had been promoted from the sixth grade. She wasn't sure how since she had gone to school so seldom, but she said she passed all the tests so, if she got to go back to school she would be a seventh grader. I asked Joyce what grade she was in and she said, she stayed home to help Mama with her chores. Mama said she had tried to get her to go, but she said she wouldn't know anyone and they would make fun of her clothes anyway. Clarence and I asked Joyce and Velma if they minded watching David for a little while so we could go stock up our coolers for our trip to Oklahoma. They were thrilled. Clarence and I went into town and first of all went to the little dept. store and bought Mama A couple of pretty new dresses and then we went to the young ladies dept. and picked out two really nice outfits for Joyce and Velma. We went to the young men's dept. and bought each of the boys a new pair of jeans and a couple of nice shirts. I had really looked the kids over last night and was sure everything would fit everyone. We then went over to the grocery store and bought a couple dozen eggs and a big bag of stew meat and several bunches of carrots and a bag of onions and a stalk of celery. And of course, a few more packs of cokes and this time Clarence went over to a bakery store and bought a big Chocolate Cake. They were all going to be in such a state of shock after seeing all of this. We waited until we unloaded the groceries and Clarence started a stew for dinner. He was so thrilled to be able to do this for Mama and the kids. You could just see the pride written all over him that they loved him, and not for the presents, they really loved him.

After the stew was on to cook, Clarence called all the kids over to the house. He had secretly unloaded everything when they were playing with David. He said, it's Christmas in July. He handed each one their box which we had marked and then handed Mama hers. They all began opening and yelling and laughing and holding their things up to themselves. I told them to go into their rooms and put something on and come model for us. The boys just dropped their drawers and started putting on the new things. Everything fit perfect. Mama sat there with big tears in her eyes and said, how can I ever thank you? At that moment, all I could think of was Mrs. Peterson and me saying those exact same things to her. Now I knew what she meant when she told me how happy it made her to do it. Mama went around the corner where her and Daddy slept and put on the prettiest dress and I had never in my life seen her look so happy. She had big tears rolling down her face and when Joyce and Velma came out and saw her, they cried too. They said Mama, you are beautiful. The girl's outfits looked wonderful on them too. Everyone looked so happy and we really felt like we had our first Christmas together. They tried on everything and were thrilled. Joyce said, maybe I'll go to school next fall. I'll save these things so they are still new. We understood completely, where or why would they wear them around all this dirt. Velma agreed she was going to save hers for school also. Mama said she didn't have anything to save hers for and she was wearing it. What a happy woman she looked right now. I wish I could save this moment forever. The boys had changed back to their old clothes and put their things back in the boxed all folded neatly. They all came and hugged us and thanked us for their new things.

Then they all said thank you for Our First Christmas ever. They looked so happy, but I could see the hurt Mama tried to hide. When the kids left and it was just the three of us sitting there, I took her hand and told her we all under stood that she had done all she could and all of us loved her with all our hearts. Daddy is nothing but a mean old vulgar man and only The Lord knows what made him that way, but it is no fault of yours. And we all know that.

Clarence started peeling potatoes and Mama started to get up to help. He told her to sit herself down, this was her day off. He got all the vegetables peeled and ready to put in the stew. Mama sit there rocking David and singing old hymns to him. I could hear her back when I was little singing the same beautiful hymns to all of us. I don't know what made it happen, but something made daddy a worthless old drunk and at this point I just didn't see him changing. About the time dinner was ready a car pulled up, and I recognized Al, even though I was pretty young when he left. He introduced us all to her pretty new bride, Mae. She was a very likeable woman that was as funny as I remembered Al being when daddy wasn't around. I asked Al how he knew we were here, and he said word gets spread pretty quick for farm to farm when someone new was in town. I heard it was a new car with California tags, so I figured it had to be you. I try real hard to keep track of where all my Family is, except that old man. I hope to never see him again. I get over to see mama when I get a day off once in a while when I'm sure he's not going to be around. I usually asked some of the other hands, when he's going to be working a long day. Mama said Clarence had made a big stew and even bought a cake, so stay and eat. Its early and I don't think your pa will be home early today. I said, the only reason he was letting the kids not work this past week was to put on a show for me and then mostly for Clarence, so we didn't think he was so bad. The stew was finished and Clarence got the package of rolls out along with a block of butter. He sat the table with bowls and small plates for the rolls and then got the spoons out and had everything ready. He called for the boys to get cleaned up and then called Joyce and Velma and told them that dinner was ready. Everyone was sitting at the table and I said a short blessing to Thank God for this last meal here with my family who I loved so much and to please keep them safe from harm. In Jesus name, Amen. Everyone said Amen and we started passing our bowls to Clarence to fill, since the pot of stew was so large and so hot it couldn't be passed around. The kids all said what a delicious stew this was and so did mama, she said it had been so long since she had any beef, she couldn't remember a stew tasting so good. She thanked Clarence for all his work fixing it and both of us for all the presents they had bought for her and her brothers and sisters. It was such a wonderful happy meal and we were all so thankful for letting us finish up and get the dishes washed before Daddy got home. I wanted to get a Family picture of all of us, we all got as close together as we could and just about the time we had taken a picture daddy rode up and said he wanted to be in a family picture. After all, it was his family. Al and Mae gave us a quick kiss goodbye and said thanks for a great dinner. He kissed Mama and said he'd get over to see her when he could. Daddy was obviously drunk and asking for his dinner. Mama started to get up and Clarence got up and said he would get it. He asked what the hell was wrong with his woman that she couldn't get his meal. Clarence said I made dinner and I gave her the day off to rest. Everyone needs some rest, once in a while. He looked over at mama rocking David, and asked if she was wanting another baby. She said no, she was just enjoying this beautiful grandchild before he left tomorrow. He asked her where she got the new dress and she told him Clarence and Stella bought is for her and they also bought the kids some new clothes for school. He said why didn't he get any presents? No one answered him. He ate and then went in and passed out on the bed. Another Thank You Lord.

The next morning, we ate breakfast and then Clarence loaded up the car while I was giving David a good bath to get all the dirt off before dressing him in a cute little outfit. Joyce and Velma both came over and said they wish we didn't have to go, I hugged them both and told them to try and stay out of daddy's way and stay safe. I told them I wish I could take them with me, but daddy would throw a fit. Velma said she was sorry she let daddy teach her to drive that tractor. Now he expects me to work like a man. That's what he's trying to make out of me, till the boys are old enough to make them work harder. At least there is not much for us to do around here. Daddy just, has to keeps the cattle rounded up. We are surprised he hasn't figured out a way for us to do that. But I guess he knows the boss would not like him not doing his job and it was supposed to be a lot better pay than picking things like cotton and fruit, but we never see any extra money. He brings in a box of groceries consisting of s big bag of beans and some flour and cornmeal. And maybe a piece a salt pork to flavor the beans and that was our food. Joyce said it was sure nice having some good food and even a cake, which was a big hit. Daddy didn't even know about it. He had passed out before he was offered a piece, if it had been offered. Maybe we can finish it off before he comes back tonight. Garner and Kenneth said they would sure give it a try. They all thanked us over and over for all the presents and the real food. Kenneth said, can't you guys stay another week? Clarence told them he had three weeks off from his job, and we still had to visit Lola and get to Oklahoma and see his daddy and mom, who he hadn't seen in over six years and that's just not right. So, after a few more rounds of hugs and kisses, we finally, drove off watching them all stand there crying. Even my poor mama was crying, which I hadn't seen her do in years.

CHAPTER 24

Clarence finally meets Lola

When we got to Lola's, she was ready for us. Clarence had called her from a phone while we were in town and told her we would be leaving Mama's right after breakfast and heading her way, if that was okay. He was anxious to meet her after all their letters back and forth years ago, while I was waiting for Clarence to be found. They had formed a sort of bond you might say. Whatever, I just knew how very worried they both had been, and for good reason. But as my Mama always told me the Good Lord would take care of me and I believed in that and all could not have turned out better. Well, I would like for Mrs. Peterson to have lived a much longer life. She always seemed so full of life in everything she did. I told Lola all about her in more detail than I had ever put in letters. And Lola just adored Clarence, it was very obvious. They got along so well and talked all about the weeks and weeks that they had worried about me. And then Clarence said you should see the mansion she was holding up in. I punched Clarence for even saying such a thing. I said, it just didn't matter how much I had there, it was nothing if I hadn't had the faith that Officer Joe would find Clarence. And Mrs. Peterson was always telling me she knew he wouldn't stop until he found him. So, I just worked there making things for the soldiers and taking meals to the train stations for soldiers on quick lay-overs and to families who were having a hard time making it on the small amount of money they received. The families were so happy to get the extra food. Okay, that's enough talk about me, how are you and the girls and Henry? Lola said the girls weren't girls anymore. They are young women and out in the dating world. I wish mothers could choose their daughter's boyfriends, or better yet, their husbands but I just have to accept that they have the right to make their own choices and just hope it's the right choice. She said Henry was still away a lot driving cattle trucks, so it's just me here alone most of the time. Clarence told her she was sure a great cook that evening after dinner. We just sit and talked a lot catching up on each other's life. She thought David was about the best little guy she'd ever seen. I said, thank you, we think so. She said he was so good sitting at the table while we were eating. I told her we were so lucky that he wasn't a picky eater and almost anything we are eating I can mash up or cut in to small enough pieces that he eats it fine. She finally, said something about Ronald. Even though she had said how sorry she was back when it happened, we hadn't mentioned it all day. So, I guess now that I had put David down to sleep, she decided we could talk about it. She said again, how sorry she was and how terrible it must have been for me being so young and so far from any family. I told her I had Clarence and he was all I needed and he spoke up and said it was very difficult for us both. Ronald had been such a beautiful smart and healthy baby one day and then, just like that, he was gone. We both had so much to deal with and if our love hadn't been so strong, I don't think either one of us could have survived it. It is so hard for Stella to talk about it, still. It's just something you never get over, and we thank "The Lord" every day that he finally gave us another baby. And believe me, one baby never takes the place of the one we lost, it just gives us a family that we so badly wanted. David is a blessing and we love him just as we loved Ronald. He is not taking Ronald's place, he is his own precious little self. So, with that, I think Clarence got the point across that it was just too hard to talk about. The pain just goes so deep that there are no words that help. He is in my heart, always. When it got a little later, Lola said, we would be sharing the room with David, because she never knew if the girls were in town or not. Since starting college, they come and go quite often. Clarence and I said that was fine, we had been sleeping practically on the ground at Mama's. David was between us and Joyce and Velma's mattress was almost touching ours. Lola said, oh don't remind me, I remember those days all too well. She said it had been quite a while since she had seen mama or the kids, but it's such a long drive and I just can't stand the thought of seeing Daddy. I hate him so much for the way our poor mama and brothers and sisters have always had to live and be mistreated. I said, I know all too well how horrible he was to us, I was his favorite punching bag for quite a while before you helped me run away to marry Clarence. Even when I was here, I never told you how bad it got for me. I guess that why I was so frightened that night he came to the house drunk. I so worried he would find me before my bus took off. She said, my sweet little Stella, you should never have had to put up with him and none of the other kids should have to either. I just can't see why Mama lets him get away with treating the children the way he does. I said mama feels trapped and she doesn't know what else to do. Daddy was his usual hateful self while I was there, but he didn't dare hit anyone. And when Clarence got there, he pretty much stayed away except to eat. I told her about Al and Mae coming over to see us and have dinner with us. Then I told her about us buying the kids and Mama all a couple of new outfits. Clarence made a big stew and wouldn't let Mama do a thing, he told her it was her day off. I imagine that it was the only day she's ever had off since she married that worthless drunk. He came home just as we were taking some family pictures and he and Al didn't speak, as soon as the pictures were taken, Al and Mae drove off and daddy demanded his dinner. Clarence got up and got him a bowl of the soup and daddy was not happy, but he kept quiet, Clarence told him he had given mama, a much needed day of rest. Daddy as usual, passed out on the bed as soon as he ate. He left early before the rest of us got up, so thankfully we didn't have to see him again. I just hope mama doesn't have to pay for our taking charge while we were there. Joyce and Velma promised to write us, so I hope we don't hear bad news. Velma says she is daddy's new punching bag now. She said Joyce is so quiet that he leaves her alone, but she said he is trying to make a boy out of her. He makes her do all the tractor work and you should see her. She has the muscles of a man, and she is so strong. It would be great if she could beat the crap out of him, but she is not that big. Just strong, but she is so afraid of him. Joyce just says she hates him. What a horrible life we have had to live through. Lola says, she thought she was the lucky one. She married as soon as I found a man I loved. It's kind of like, I just closed my eye to how he was becoming. I hated him so much I can't stand the thought of having to see him. That's why I never go there anymore now that they live so far away. It was easy when they lived close, I could run over there and drop off your letters and hug mama and the kids and be gone before he got home. I told her I didn't blame her one bit, I got out as soon as I found the love of my life also. And now Velma is getting what I did. I just hate that there is nothing we can do. So enough is enough, I can't talk about this anymore. Children should not have to hate their father. Clarence was the best father a kid could ask for. We will do everything possible for our Children. At least we hope to have more. I guess the good Lord works in his own time.

Clarence had gone in and took a shower and let us have this sister time together. When I went into the bedroom, he was sound asleep all curled up with Ronald in the middle. I showered and then went in and got in bed on the other side. David was way too little to have him on the side where he might fall off. This is the longest we had ever gone without making love and it was so hard. I reached over and put my hand on his arm lightly so as not to wake him. Just touching him made me feel better a little. We were leaving the first thing in the morning for Oklahoma, or we weren't going to have enough time to really visit all Clarence's brothers and sisters and his dad and mom. I was looking forward to meet all of them. I had only met Orce and Dora and Ellen. There was Alvin and Oscar and Cindy and Pearl, but most important, his dad and mom. I was so anxious that they like me. Clarence said that he had no doubts that they will love me. I sure hope so.

We were on the road immediately after Lola fixed us a great breakfast, it was only, a four hour drive. Clarence called his dad and said we would be there by two o'clock. We were both so excited to see everyone.

CHAPTER 25

Meeting all the Raders

When we arrived, the whole family was there. I was introduced to everyone and we all hugged and they all went crazy over David. It's a good thing David was such a happy little guy, because the girls were passing him from one to the other. They kept making him giggle by kissing his neck, he loved that, and it was amazing to me that they had discovered it so quickly. They kept telling him that they were his aunts and how happy they were to meet him. He started to get a look on his face, like where's my mommy? I said I think he needs changing, I said as I reached for him. They gave him up unwillingly, but said they would see him in a little bit. Clarence asked his mom which room he should put our bags in. She said put them in your old room, but a couple of the girls are in there too. All the kids live several miles out of town, so were going to be bunked up a bit while you're here. Everyone wants to visit with you and Stella. I was already in the room changing David when Clarence came in with the news. I said, I guess we'll survive another few days. We don't have much choice, do we? He took me in his arms and kissed me and my whole body was just wanting to strip right here, but my head knew that was not possible. So, we settled for kisses and hugs when we could steal a moment.

The house wasn't that large and we had Orce, Oscar, Alvin and the four girls, Dora, Ellen and Cindy and Pearl. Plus, Mom and Dad. That's eleven of us in a small three bedroom house. There was a screened porch with a cot like thing, which someone would sleep on. The house was just buzzing with people. I thought this was going to be an interesting few days. I got David all changed and took him into the kitchen to feed him some applesauce I still had in his bag. He was hungry, because he ate it up without breathing almost. I asked his Mother if she had any soft food I could feed David. She said, there is a big roast in the oven with potatoes and carrots, but I don't think it's quite done yet. She looked in the ice box and said, does he like jello? I said that would be great, he loves jello. So, she dished up a big bowl and David really did like it. He almost finished the bowl and then turned his head when I put the spoon to his mouth. That had been his little game for a couple of months now. I said, hey big boy, now you're not going to eat any vegetables. Mom had sat down at the table and said it will be a while, he'll work up an appetite by then. She said, he is so beautiful. Such a perfect little boy. I said, we think so, but we are his parents. She said, well, I'm his grandma and I know he perfect like his daddy and mommy. I thanked her for the compliments. She said, you are just about the most beautiful woman I've ever seen. No wonder Clarence fell so hard for you. I told her I fell just as hard for him and I think he is the most handsome man in the world. And believe me, there will never be another man for me. I meant it when I said till death do us part. He did too. We are so much in love you would think we just met. It just gets better and better. She hugged me tight and said I know you mean that. I said, I certainly do.

Dinner was delicious and mom was right, David was hungry again. He ate carrots, potatoes and even the roast was so tender, he was able to eat a pretty good size piece of it. Now he just wanted to run around and visit with everyone. What a little ham he was. He was just eating up all of this attention. Clarence was so proud of him and I could tell he was proud of me also. He kept looking at me with so much love. And I loved him and his family were all just as sweet and natural as Clarence had always been. I could tell he was raised with love and it made him the man I fell in love with. We stayed there for five days and then Clarence said that he had to be back at work in a week and we had to stop and spend the nights at a couple of Stella's family's places in Texas and in New Mexico. They are expecting us. We wrote to them and told them our schedule. And as much as we would love to stay longer, we just can't. His dad and his mom came and put their arms around him and said, how very proud of him and his family they were. He said thank you as he hugged them back and then he told them it was their turn to come to California next. They said they would, one of these years. It was over an hour, before we finally got out of there, with all the hugs and kisses. David was so tired and he slept better if I wasn't holding him. His mom brought out a couple of blankets to fill the floor space.

Then we put another blanket all across the back seat and it looked just like a square bed and he just cuddled himself up back there as soon as I laid him down. It was getting late, but we decided it was easier to drive at night because it was so much cooler. We had a long drive to get to My aunt Nita and uncle Hoyt's place, so we figured we would get there by early morning. Clarence had taken a long nap so he would be able to drive all night. I told him I could drive for a while as long as it was early before I got sleepy. He said he would be fine. After a couple hours, I moved over to sit close to him. I just want to feel our bodies touching. It had been so long and this just was not something we were used to. As I got myself just as close to Clarence, my hand on his leg moving up to his thigh, I wanted to move over to his penis, but I knew it was important that he keep his mind on driving. He said, sweetheart, your killing me. I said oh I'm sorry, I just miss being close to you so much. He said, believe me, I know what you're talking about. We were quiet for just a minute or so, and up ahead Clarence saw a street he could turn off on safely. Up about a half mile there was a huge tree and it had a bit of a clearing next to it, like it had been parked there many times. I said, are you thinking what I'm thinking? He said very quietly, David is sleeping like a rock and I don't think he would notice a bit if we got out of the car, do you? No I agree completely. I reached back and picked up other blanket that Mom had given us just in case he might need it. Little did she know it was us who needed it. Clarence opened his car door quietly so as not to wake David and then I slid out. We spread the blanket out and looked around and made sure no one else was around. Then, within seconds we were both stripped of our clothes and laying there kissing and touching each other all over as we always did, we loved touching and teasing each other. It only added to our excitement, but this time we couldn't take the usual time, we were both just wanting each other so much, Clarence reached down and put his fingers into me and I almost lost it, I put my leg over him and he pulled me up and I reached down and stroked his hard penis and guided it into me. We felt like we could be like this forever, the ground was so soft with grass and with the blanket we were very comfortable to move up and down and enjoy this wonderful feeling that we so much enjoyed and had missed so much for almost three weeks, and because of that we just couldn't last as long as usual. Within a few more seconds, Clarence said, I can't hold on much longer and I told him I was ready also, and we climaxed so strong that it felt like the feeling would be with us forever. In a few minutes of just lying there and feeling like one, I slid over off of him and we just laid there enjoying this wonderful feeling that we had missed so much, for it felt like a year, when in fact it had only been three weeks. In the far distance we heard fireworks and then we realized it was the fourth of July. Someone was starting the day early with fireworks. We had been right there with them having our own fireworks. Like heaven it felt. After a few more minutes, we both decided we better get back on the road before David woke up. He would be a little grouch tomorrow, if he didn't get to sleep all night like he was used to. It was about two in the morning and we had started the day off with our own fun. Now it was time to get on the road again. Clarence said it would be nice to find a few more places like that on our long drive home between visiting relatives, where were are in cramped quarters along with other family members. I second that for sure.

I fell asleep sitting close to Clarence and slept till we were almost to Midland, Texas where my Aunt Nita and Uncle Hoyt lived. I had always loved seeing them, because when they came to visit, daddy would be on his best behavior since he didn't want mama's brother to know how bad he was. They never stayed more than a day or so, depending on where we lived. So many times, we just had a one room shack or a tent. On those times, they would only come for the day, because Aunt Nita had been in a wheelchair all her life from polio, I think. It's been so many years since anyone has talked about it, but I think that was why. Anyway, if we were in a house with more than a couple of rooms, sometimes they would stay overnight, but those were the only times in my life that daddy didn't drink or hit on mama and one or more of us. I was so excited to see them now that I was a grown woman and I couldn't wait until they met Clarence and David. I was so proud of my family. For good reason in opinion. We were almost there so I brushed my hair until it shined and put a little blush on my cheeks and a little pink lipstick. I had worn my favorite dress that was so pretty with tiny pink and purple flowers all over and it never wrinkled, which was good because I was curled up asleep next to Clarence when I woke up. I told him to turn up at the next corner to the right, I had only been to their house one time but I was pretty sure this looked very familiar. I had probably been ten or eleven, but it was such an exciting time for me, it was hard to forget any of it. We had eaten a full delicious meal with dessert and everything. I remember how much I had liked sweet tea. That was the only time I had it, until I went to Lola's just before running away to Clarence. Yes, I am sure that was the correct street. Their house is on the right after you turn one more time to the left. There it is. Just as Clarence pulled up to their house, David woke up and that was his happiest part of the day, and had been since he was born. I pulled him into the front seat and changed his diaper really quick, and he squirmed and laughed the whole time thinking it was a big joke. I ask Clarence if he was exhausted after driving all night? He said, he actually felt like he was getting a second wind. I was glad so he could enjoy meeting my aunt and uncle. Clarence picked up David and gave him his million morning kisses that made him giggle with happiness. I could listen to these sounds forever. Nothing could ever sound better. It was seven-thirty and I was pretty sure they would be up by now. We went to the front door and knocked pretty quiet just in case they were still sleeping. But within a few seconds, Uncle Hoyt answered the door and grabbed me and swung me around and said what a pretty sight I was first thing in the morning. When he put me down, I introduced him to Clarence and David our Son. Uncle Hoyt shook Clarence's hand and then held out his arms out to David, who went right to him. This really made Uncle Hoyt very happy. He said, well get in here, we've been expecting you anytime now for the past half hour or so. Nita just started frying some potatoes and put some bacon in the pan to start cooking slow. He yelled, turn the bacon up, they are here. We all went into the kitchen and I introduced Aunt Nita to Clarence, He leaned down and took her hand, then gave her a hug. Aunt Nita said, now that's how to start a morning. I was so happy they really like Clarence, I could tell right away. And he liked them also. As we were eating breakfast, Aunt Nita announced that she was pregnant, after waiting all these years. I said I knew that feeling well, and I was so happy for her. She said, what do you mean, you know that feeling? I said after losing Ronald, it took so long to get pregnant again with David. They both looked at me like I was they had no idea what I was talking about. Clarence, knowing how hard it was for me to talk about it, told them we had lost our first baby when he was four months old and it was very hard. I fought to keep the tears away, but they always came when it came up for more than a passing comment. Aunt Nita leaned over and hugged me tight and said how very sorry she was to have said that, but no one told had told them. Eunice never said a word in her letters. I told them mama didn't know for a while after his death and then daddy took my letter and never even showed any of them the only two picture I had of him. It was so very awfully hard, and it took a long time for me to feel sain again. Poor Clarence thought I was going crazy, and so did I for quite some time. It was three full years before I got pregnant again, and I was beginning to feel it would never happen. We had only been married three months when I got pregnant with Ronald, so I thought it would happen again that fast. I was never trying to replace him, that's not possible, but I just wanted another baby so badly. My arms felt so empty and there's not a day that I don't grieve for Ronald, but there's also not a day that I don't love David with all my heart and it's just as much as I loved Ronald, it just that there is a little place in my heart, that will always be just for Ronald. I could have ten more babies and it still wouldn't take that spot away. Clarence said, bite your tongue. I looked at him strange and he said, ten more babies? I said it was just a figure of speech. So now let's celebrate Aunt Nita's wonderful news. She said, they could not be happier about it, they had wanted a baby since they got married and it took twelve years. I had given up, she said. Uncle Hoyt, being the funny guy he was said, it's not for lack of trying, and just as I knew she would, Aunt Nita reached over and slapped his leg. We had the best time eating breakfast and telling funny stories. Breakfast was delicious, especially this cream cheese Danish she made. It was amazing. I told her about how good the ones Kathleen made every morning. But she never put any sweet cream cheese in them. Aunt Nita said she had learned how to make them from a lady that they used to have come in and clean for them, but she moved away and I sure miss her. I get most of it done okay, and the things I can't do, Hoyt does. After the dishes were cleaned up and everything put away, I went in to put David down for a nap, but I found him sound asleep on his Daddy's chest and he also, was sound asleep. Hoyt had gone outside to get a few things done in the yard. Aunt Nita said, I told him to get those things done before you got here, but he puts thing off till the last minute. He said yesterday, he'd get up early and do them before you guys got there. You see that happened. I said everything looked perfect to me. She said, thanks, but it's not up to his usual perfection, especially when he's expecting company. I said, we aren't company, just family.

We went back into the kitchen to chat. I decided there was no time like the present to ask her what I wanted to. I said, Aunt Nita, Does Uncle Hoyt or any of mama's other brothers and sisters know how terrible our life has always been? Aunt Nita said they all know you were awfully poor by the places you've lived and the terrible jobs your Daddy does. I looked at her and said, I'm sorry, I hope you believe me when I say that most of those terrible jobs were done by us kids as soon as we were old enough. I told her I had picked cotton until my hands bled so bad I could hardly stand the pain and would still get slapped around if he didn't think any of us had picked enough. Aunt Nita looked shocked. She said, I had no idea and neither does your uncles and aunts. She said, of course we always loved you and Uncle Hoyt so much, but we also looked forward to your visits every years or so. It would be the only time daddy wasn't drunk and beating on Mama. Aunt Nita opened her mouth and words just would not come out at first. Then finally, she said he hits your Mama. I told her he not only hits her, he literally beats her on a regular basis, for nothing other than maybe something wasn't done like he thought it should be. We have all tried to stop him and it only got us a beating, then he goes back and beats Mama again. I hadn't been back since I ran away at sixteen to marry Clarence. I think he really saved my life. I always had such a big mouth and just couldn't keep it to myself, when I saw him hurting mama so bad. He was pretty easy on Maxine and Joyce now, because they both kept to their selves so much because they were so darn afraid of him, but I just wouldn't let him frighten me even though I knew how bad it got for me. The last time he hurt me so bad that Mama was sure he was going to kill me and she picked up a hammer without even thinking and the claw part stuck in his head. Mama sent W.K. for a doctor and when he came he fixed me up and called the law on Daddy and he was in jail for quite a while that time. He didn't remember anything that happened because he was so darn drunk.

That's when Mama asked a man if he knew where we could get some work. Poor Mama had to feed us. At that time, I was the oldest at home and the man took us to this cotton farmer that always needed help. We all lived in a tent and that's when I met Clarence. He lived in the tent next to us and the first time we saw each other we knew we would be together for the rest of our lives and forever. All the kids loved Clarence because he was not only very nice and so polite, he would drive the kids into town and buy them candy and gum, which they had never had. When daddy got out of jail, way too soon, he came out to the cotton farm where were staying.

He immediately hated Clarence because he could tell we liked each other. Of course, he had to say vulgar things about Clarence. Clarence had already proposed to me and gave me this engagement ring, but I told him to keep it till we were able to be married or daddy might find it and not only beat me, he would sell my ring for whiskey money. Clarence said he was going to California because, he heard he could make much better money there, so our plan was that he would send Lola all the money he could until there was enough to buy a bus ticket to go meet him. Well, then everything changed, I told her about thinking he killed someone and then letting Maxine and I go stay with Lola for the weekend, just because we were close and we begged and said it had been so many years since we'd seen her. Then I told her all the rest up until we lost Ronald and moved back to California because it was not only hard being in the house where we had him, but also since the war was getting worse, Clarence got offered a job at Northrop Aircraft as an Engineer. I told her all about his education and why he was traveling around for a while. I also told her about why Al left so young and that J.E. and Preston left at thirteen and fifteen because Daddy had beat Preston so bad that the blood was dripping down to his pant and soaked them too. They told me after Daddy had passed out drunk that they had all they could take and, they left a note with me to give to Mama telling her they loved her so much, but couldn't take daddy anymore and they both looked old enough and they were going to join the army. I haven't seen them since or Al. W.K. got the worst of it after I was gone and he finally ran away and hitch hiked to California and asked Clarence and I to lie and say he was living with us and he was eighteen and he wanted to join the Navy. He was so short I was worried they wouldn't believe him, but he was so strong from all the work Daddy made him do that they took him right then and there and I haven't seen him since either. He did write to me and say he loved the Navy and he was going to see the world. I wish I had a way of finding Preston and J.E. but I wouldn't have any idea how to start.

I hadn't been paying much attention to Aunt Nita, I had my head down crying most of the time, while I was telling her the different stories, and when I looked up, I saw that she had been crying too. Her eyes were so red and her face covered on tears just rolling down her face. I said I'm sorry to be the one to tell you all this, I just think daddy's been getting away with it all for too long.

He was okay as far as not hitting mama or the kids while I was there for a week, before Clarence came and then when he got there you could see daddy's hate, but we wouldn't let him frighten us, we just took charge and Clarence brought a big ham and a few chickens and we ate like real people, and then Clarence and I left David with Joyce and Velma who had a ball playing with him. We went back into town and bought Mama a couple of real pretty dresses and all the kids a couple of new outfits. Joyce said she might even go to school in the fall if Daddy let her. He would hardly ever let us girls go to school, because he said we were good for nothing, but to work and having babies. When we came back from the store, Clarence had bought a ton more groceries and he put on a bunch of stew meat and when it was almost done, he got up to start peeling vegetables and Mama tried to help and he told her this was her day off and she was not doing a thing. So, mama got to play with David and rock him and sing her Christian hymns that she always sang if daddy wasn't around. Daddy came home drunk after we had all eaten and the dishes were all washed and we had huge pieces of a chocolate cake Clarence bought at a bakery in town. When daddy came in and asked mama where his dinner was, before she could move or say a word, Clarence jumped up and dished up a big bowl of the delicious stew which was still plenty hot. Daddy yelled, why can't that old woman get my dinner? Clarence simply said, because I cooked dinner and I gave her the day off. Daddy just made a growling sound and ate and then passed out on their bed. So, we almost had a whole pleasant day without him except long enough to eat a bowl of stew. Mama was so proud of her new dress and also the kids were just over the moon. Well, I guess that's all I have to say. I think I've told you as much, as possible without going over each day of our miserable lives. Aunt Nita just pulled me over to her and kept crying and she just stroked my hair and hugged me tight. About that time, Uncle Hoyt came in the back real quiet, so as not to wake Clarence and David.

He saw that we were both crying and sat down and said, Hey Ladies, whatever is wrong. Aunt Nita told him to just hush for now, that is was way too much for poor sweet Stella to have to tell again. She said she would tell him all of it later when they were alone. He didn't understand, but he usually listened to his wife. He was such a good sweet man. I told him how much I loved them both and I sure wish I could have met my Grandparents, because as sweet as my mama is and as sweet as you are, they must have been wonderful people. He said they were very loving parents, strict, but always with love and fairness. I asked him if they knew how unhappy mama was, and he said, they guessed by a lot of things that happened, but they were strong Christians and believed that when you got married, it was for life. I was little, but I can remember them telling Eunice when she said she was getting married, they told her, don't expect to come home if things don't go your way little lady. When you marry, it says in the Bible your wedding vows say for better or for worse. Well, I know that they knew things weren't perfect, but daddy did all he could do about it. I told Uncle Hoyt, I was young, but I heard the talk and knew about Daddy sleeping with Aunt Willie Mae and that he got her pregnant. And he had Daddy thrown in jail for statutory rape. I even knew about him paying some man in town to marry her, so she wouldn't have a bastard. Maxine and I were really happy, thinking he'd be in jail for a long time, but we didn't get that lucky. He said, do all the kids know. I told him as far as I could remember, it was just Maxine and I that heard them yelling. Mama was so mad, she changed Joyce's name, but I don' think Joyce knows why. She was real young, probably five or six, I'm not sure, but Maxine and I never talked about it anymore. He said, that's good, because I'm sure your cousin, doesn't know he also your brother. No sense stirring up a pot of worms, if you know what I mean. I told him that I never even talked about it with Mama, so she doesn't even know we know. I said, I just have one question, I always wondered why they never came to see any of us," Their Grandchildren" he said most of the time, they didn't even know where you all were, you moved from place to place so much. And then there was the previous mess we just talked about and your daddy moved you guys far away after that because he probably figured My dad wound have killed him. And then they both died fairly young within just months of each other. I was the only one still at home then. I'm sure they did think of all of you that they knew of. Daddy said someone he knew that had seen all of you somewhere, and said you were a bunch of beautiful children. I couldn't imagine who it could have been, because we went to town so seldom, except when Daddy was in jail and someone would take us in to buy groceries. That had to be when.

I told him Clarence and I were going to spend the night at Aunt Willie Mae's in New Mexico on our way back to California. I am anxious to see what my brother looks like, but I would never say anything or act different than with any of the other kids. Uncle Hoyt was very glad to hear that. You just don't realize how much kids hear. I said, especially in most of the shacks we lived in. you can hear someone blink in the next room, that if we had two rooms. I sure don't know how Mama got pregnant without any of us kids hearing anything. I guess she just kept her mouth shut for fear of waking one of us. Poor Mama. I wish I could get her to leave him. I've tried since I was fifteen years old. She pretty much repeats what her Daddy told her. I guess she took it to heart. I am just glad she didn't have more babies after Kenneth. There's only so much a body can take. Twelve babies, I can't even imagine. And working till the end and maybe two day's rest before she was back to work again after birth. I said, I think I hear my two big boys in there. Clarence came in and said I don't even remember going to sleep. One minute I was talking to Uncle Hoyt and then I woke up few minutes ago when David started squirming around. I laid there still, thinking he was just going to sleep. I told him they had been asleep for about three hours plus. Clarence said, I guess I was more tired than

I thought. He said I'll be wild eyed tonight when everyone else goes to sleep. Uncle Hoyt said, don't worry, we don't go to bed all that early. I'm used to being awake a lot at night being a fireman all these years. I asked Aunt Nita how she takes care of everything around here when Uncle Hoyt is on duty. She said, I can manage most everything pretty well. He said she is as strong as I am. Her upper body strength could probably out punch mine, but I'm sure not going to punch her to see. A man that punches a woman is just dirt as far as I'm concerned. Aunt Nita and I just shared a look and let that go. Aunt Nita asked if there was anything we wanted to do or see while here in the big old town of Midland. We both said just being lazy sounds good to me, I've been running my head off trying to keep David alive out there in all the dirt. He had never been dirty until we got there and Velma had him and before I knew it he was sitting in a pile of soft dirt just having a ball with the cutest little outfit that will probably never look the same. Mama made him the cutest pair of jeans out of a pair Kenneth had outgrown. I swear she must never throw anything away. Maybe she was still thinking she might get pregnant again. I said, bite your tongue. He said I meant when Kenneth was little. Even then, she had twelve babies. Aunt Nita said she is younger than I am by a year I think. I said oh my Lord, Please, spare my Mama. Let Aunt Nita have a couple and keep Mama safe form any more babies. She looks fifteen years older than you do, Aunt Nita. She has worked so hard all her life with Him. Poor Mama. I wish, oh well for all the good my wishes do. We sat around all afternoon and played with David. He was just loving having all this attention. I said, when we go home he is going to wonder where all his audiences have gone.

We had a wonderful visit with Uncle and Aunt Nita, but it was time to go. I told her to be sure and write to me and let me know how Uncle Hoyt took the news that I had given and also be sure and let us know when your baby is born and if you have boy or girl. She said, she just wanted a baby as healthy and Happy and David is. So we had another long day of driving to get to New Mexico. Clarence said he had slept great even if David was between. He said he thought driving during the day was so much safer. Even though he made it fine, he was so worn out all day the next day, even with the long nap he had holding David. He said somehow the sleep wasn't sound because he could feel David and in the back of his mind somewhere it was awake, saying don't you drop that baby. We laughed, but he said he really thought there was some truth to it. So, we decided to only drive during the day, or at least start out during the day. David was such a good little traveler. He liked his built up bed in the back. He thought that was great fun back there with all his toys. I kept a close watch on him back there anyway. I didn't want him falling down into the floor and the other side. So far, he was staying right up there on the built up area. We stopped and had lunch at a nice little diner and David ate a whole bowl of vegetable soup with crackers crumbled up in it. He was starting to want to feed himself, but I wasn't giving up the spoon yet. Especially not in a diner with people having to walk around the mess he would probably have on the floor. We would have to give that a try at home first. After we got in the car and changed his diaper, he wanted in the back again. It wasn't five minutes and he was sound asleep. I don't think I was far behind him. We both took a long nap and I asked Clarence if he wanted me to drive, but he said he had slept so well last night, that he was feeling fine so far and he also said we should be there in a couple of hours according to signs he had seen. I had never been there before, so we were supposed to call from a pay phone and let them know where we were and someone would drive there and we could follow them to the house. Aunt Willie Mae told me in her letter that when you're out in the boonies, it's hard to give directions. Like turn right at the second tree and then a left by the third big rock. I got the picture and told her we would call, and what day we would be leaving Aunt Nita's. I had to admit, I was nervous, I had not seen Aunt Willie Mae, since she got married and moved away. But we would be in town very shortly.

I did my ritual of combing my hair and putting on a little blush and some lipstick. We called and then, just sat there playing silly games with David to pass the time. They said it would take about twenty minutes to get to where we were. We said we'll be here. David thought all this jumping from the front to the back was real fun. After about half an hour, a man drove up and asked, if we were the Rader's, of course we said yes, and he introduced himself as Alonzo Brown, he said to follow him so that's what we did. It really was out in the middle of nowhere, Aunt Willie Mae knew what she was talking about when she said we would never find it without someone coming to meet us. When we got there, Willie Mae came running out to meet us and we all hugged and kissed each other as she introduced me to her husband, who we had just followed there, but didn't know who he was, and I introduced them to Clarence and my baby, David. Alonzo was Willie Mae's husband. She had divorced S.A. Cantrell, who was the father of James Maxie. I was sure that she didn't know that I knew about his real father, and mine, and I never breathed a word about it while we were there. When we all got into the house and she said, this is my oldest son, James Maxie, and this is Kenneth, then this is my baby girl, Geneva, who said, I'm not a baby. Aunt Willie Mae said, well your still my baby for a while longer. She then told me she was pregnant, which was quite obvious. We all sat and talked, and Geneva just took charge of David. She was three and made such a great caretaker of him. David just loved being around all the little kids. He had never been turned loose with so many kids to play with. At the park, when I walked him, sometimes I would take him out of his stroller and put him in the baby swing and that's all except for Ruby Lee's children and they didn't stay around the babies much. Her twins we only a year older than David, so they played together, but were all just babies. This was different, he had Geneva, Kenneth and James Maxie, all old enough to watch him. After just a short while Willie Mae jumped up and said you must be starving, it's dinner time. We agreed, it had been quite a while since we had stopped for lunch. She said she had a big pork roast that should be about done in the oven. And all she had to do was get potatoes peeled and the rest of dinner going. I said I would be glad to get the potatoes peeled and she yelled James Maxie to come and get the corn shucked. She said he liked doing it, because he got paid five cents for every ear he cleaned good. I couldn't help starring at him to see if there was any Attebery blood showing. He was a really good looking little guy, and I thought maybe there was a resemblance to W.K. or maybe even Preston. I hadn't seen either of them in so many years now. But anyway, whoever he looked like, he was very cute little boy almost 10 years old, Willie Mae said. She said, he is my only son from my first husband, S.E. Cantrell. I acted like I believed her completely. She said he has a darker complexion than the other two. Who knows what this one will be or look like, you never know till they get here, she said, as she patted her large belly. I got busy and peeled a huge pot of potatoes, she said her bunch were all big eaters. By the time I had the potatoes peeled, James Maxie came running in for the yard with fifteen ears of corn cleaned better that I could have done it, especially as quickly as he had done it. He put them in the sink and added fifteen on a sheet of paper in a small drawer. Aunt Willie Mae said, he makes sure he keeps track of how much he is owed at the end of each week. He then asked if that would be enough. She told him yes, and thanked him for getting all the silk off and doing such a good job, he smiled like he was so proud of himself. That smile was certainly a familiar one. I had to force myself not to stare at him anymore than I had the other children, who were all good looking kids.

Dinner was wonderful and we were all stuffed. I told her that was the best pork I had ever eaten and she said they raised their own so they fed them corn and all the thing necessary things to make the meat taste the best. Clarence said, I sure wish we could get pork that this in California.

I told him good luck, the stores only have pork from who knows where. Anyway, Clarence and I both told her again what a wonderful cook she was. She was very happy we like everything. I looked at James Maxie, who happened to be sitting right across the table from me, and told him the corn was especially good and so clean. He smiled that big smile again. Willie Mae said she had made a big cobbler this morning and the boys had churned some homemade ice cream. We said, well I guess we could force ourselves to have some. Oh my, I said this cobbler is really delicious, you are just amazing to get all this done and still take care of three little children. James Maxie, Kenneth and Geneva all spoke up at the same time and said, we aren't little. I said, excuse me, I'm so sorry but I had forgot how big you all are. Then they laughed, and said we help Mommy all the time. She said they really are a big help to me. I don't know what I would do without them. With me getting so big, things are harder to do than usual. Kenneth and Geneva went out and picked all these berries this morning for the cobbler. She really had them all trained well. Of course, they each got their allowance according, to what they had done to help. I told Aunt Willie Mae, I wish I had them at my house. She said, you haven't seen them fighting yet. They all frowned at her. She started clearing the table, and Kenneth said, it my turn to clear the table. I thought they were all just the sweetest bunch of kids. We were never allowed as kids to do anything but work for money that went to Daddy's whiskey money. Poor Mama had to do all the kitchen work for all of us kids and sometimes when there was lots of work to do, even Mama had to go out for the biggest part of the day and pick too. Her poor hands would be bleeding and she would

411

stand there at the sink and peel potatoes and wash them twice to get the blood off. I just cryed when I think of how bad Mama had it.

When the dishes were all done, we sat and talked a while again, until Alonzo got up and said, I'm to bed folks, it was real nice meeting more of Willie Mae's kinfolk, but I'll be up and working before all of you get up in the morning. We told him, good night and thanked him for coming to get us in town and told him how nice it was to meet him. He had been pretty quiet all evening, I guess with him not knowing us, he thought it better to just listen as we talked about our childhood. Willie Mae was not that much older than I. But she hadn't been in our lives since she married S.A. Cantrell. We didn't talk about why, just that she had married and moved away young. A little later we all were going to bed and Aunt Will Mae said we would have to share a room with Geneva if that was okay. We said, wherever you put us is where we'll sleep. So, another night crowded up with little ones. Clarence whispered to me he would sure be glad to get me home and in our bed. I poked him and said, me too, Honey. We all took turns using the bathroom to shower and it was an hour at least before we were all in bed. Geneva wanted David to sleep with her in her bed, but we told her he was too little and needed to sleep between his Daddy and Mommy. She finally agreed to that. We got up pretty early and had breakfast, delicious sausage and gravy and biscuits and eggs. I told Aunt Willie Mae that she was sure lucky to be able to raise their own pigs. That was so good. She thanked us, and I helped with the dishes, after Geneva very carefully carried most of the dishes to the kitchen sink. It was so obvious Aunt Willie Mae was proud of her kids, for good reason. We gathered up all our things and Clarence loaded up the car for the long ride home. We thanked Aunt Willie and told her how much we had enjoyed our visit and all her wonderful cooking. Then we loaded up David, which wasn't easy to get him away from Geneva. I told Aunt Willie Mae that she was going to have great helper on her hands. She said yes she is sure looking forward to have "our baby" get out as she put it. We kissed her and hugged all the kids and thanked them for helping feed us and Geneva for sharing her room with us. She just smiled.

So, we were headed for California and I was so glad. Getting home and back on our own schedule was going to be such a blessing, even though I had enjoyed every minute of my almost 4 weeks away, visiting with Mama and seeing my baby brother for the first time. The only bad part was having to see daddy, when he came home drunk, Clarence sure put him in his place quick. He knew better than to even think of trying anything with us there. And our visits with Aunt Nita and Uncle Hoyt had been great too, so all in all, it was a wonderful trip. Except for the fact, Clarence and I only had been able to make love that one wonderful evening we stopped and made love under that beautiful tree and heard the fireworks going off, like they were just for us. Even though we knew it was because it was the fourth of July. The rest of our over three weeks, we were either sharing rooms with someone else and, David had to sleep between us for safety reasons. This was very hard for us because of our normal making love every night being so much a part of our love and our marriage. It was a very long drive from

New Mexico back to Inglewood, Ca. and Clarence had figured it would take at least twelve hours, and that did not include the time so that we stopped just to walk around so that Clarence's legs didn't cramp up. I kept offering to drive, but he assured me it was more important that I keep David occupied and happy. This was not hard at all, David being such a good baby. He was such a joy to our lives and the most important thing to us both. We stopped at another little diner that looked busy. Clarence said, if they are busy, then the food is usually good. And it was, real good. We both ordered big hamburgers and fries and a bowl of chicken noodle soup for David. He ate all his soup plus some of our fries and even a few bites of hamburger that I crumbled up enough so that he didn't choke. He was beginning to really like all this big people food, which made it easier to order for him. We had left at eight o'clock that morning and after all our stops and lunch, Clarence said we should be home within an hour, which would be close to ten o'clock. Wow, 14 hours in a car with some children might be a nightmare, but with David's naps and all our stops kept him from ever getting cranky. What a good little boy you are, I said to him as he stood looking out the window at all the lights. We arrived in our driveway at ten minutes after ten, and I was never so happy to see a house. And very happy my poor wonderful husband, didn't have to drive again until Monday morning, two days from now.

Those two days just flew by and before we knew it, it was time to go back to our regular schedule. Making lunches and getting Clarence's breakfast before he left for work every morning. I missed him the minute he was out the door, just thinking of our lovemaking in the tub, and in our bed and basically anywhere we wanted to. It was our home and we had no company. But it was time to quit day dreaming and get David's bath done so he could go down for his morning nap and get him back on his regular schedule also. Life seemed so quiet and wonderful here in our home. I sat on the edge of the tub and watched David play, he loved his bath and love splashing me and seeing me jump. It made him giggle out loud and I loved that sound. I loved him so much. He quit splashing and his attention went back to his many tub toys. Ruby Lee had given us so many things, I probably wouldn't have to buy anything for years. Who knew, how long it might be if we kept living across the street and remained best friends. With the twins being a year older and her having to buy for two, she always had a huge box she was handing off to me. I was going to have to start buying the twins some outfits or I would never be able to accept all this stuff. I sat there thinking how easy my life was after being back there in mama's life again. I couldn't even imagine living like that again, and it broke my heart that mama and my brothers and sister's having to live like that. Joyce had told me while we had a rare moment alone, that she didn't know how much longer Velma was going to be able to take the way daddy treated her. She was only barely thirteen years old and daddy made her work like a man and beat her so badly a couple of times, it just made Joyce sick, but what could she do? She said she tried to just stay out of his way and speak only when she had to answer him about something. But Velma is more like you, Stella, she just can't keep quiet when he slaps Mama or hits her and it kills me too, I just watch and see how much worse it is for

Velma and for Mama when he's drunk and interfered with, so I keep to myself. I try to tell Velma she isn't helping, but she is even twice as stubborn as you ever were. I said that's pretty bad, but I just wish I had a way to help. But tell me if you can think of anything, What? Joyce just shrugged her shoulders and said I can't think of any way out. I wish Mama would leave him, but when I asked her to, she said she thought if she did, he would find a way to kill her and maybe even some of us kids. She feels so stuck and it makes me want to vomit at times. My mind had wandered off the most important thing in my life, beside Clarence, of course. I turned around to find David rolled over on his tummy splashing at some of his toys, like they should yell like I did. It frightened me to think that I let my attention leave him for a moment while he was in the tub. I had to watch my wandering mind, but it had all been so fresh still, after just being there again.

I told David to stand up, after I had pulled the plug. I had a big fluffy towel waiting for him and I picked him up and squeezed him so tight, like I could never let him go. He squirmed though, wanting down. I asked him if he had to go pee-pee? He ignored me, but I didn't want to push him, he was still too little, but I didn't think it hurt to make the words familiar. I dried him and put cream all over his cute little body. It seemed dry after playing in dirt for over a week. He really did have fun playing with Joyce and Velma and of course the boys played with him too some, but they were so busy off in their own little world. I dreaded them getting older and daddy treating them like he had Al and J.E. and Preston and then W.K. It had to stop sometime, but how, just how? I had to think of something. I was hoping that maybe Uncle Hoyt could talk to Mama, now that I had told Aunt Nita all I could think of to tell her, especially since I'd been gone for over six years. A couple of weeks passed and I finally received a letter from Aunt Nita. She said Uncle Hoyt had been beyond upset, when she told him the stories I had told her. She said it took all she could do, to get him not to bring it up at breakfast. She said she asked him what good he thought it would do? He had none, so he kept quiet while we were there, but he was on the warpath now. He was headed for Abernathy to have it out with that S.O.B. as your Uncle Hoyt put it. Before she had finished the letter, she said Hoyt had just returned after a long trip, only to turn around and come home. And he was madder than an old wet hen, when he got there and was told that your Daddy had collected his pay and left in the night, without a minute's notice. The farmer was not happier either, since he had left him without anyone to do the work he had been doing for almost a year now. I will let you know if we find out where they have gone or hear any news at all, and you do the same for us. I wrote right back to her and told her that I would keep them informed immediately if I received a letter from any one of them.

I felt very sick about all this, not knowing where that old man had taken my family and wondering if they would even be able to get any mail out from wherever they were. He just loved it when he had them all under his thumb, or I should say his fist, because that was more like it. All I could do was pray that Joyce or Velma wrote me a letter letting me know where they were. I actually, felt like I was going to throw up, and that wasn't something I did much. Thankfully, David was down for his nap, maybe I would feel better by the time he woke up. All I could think of was my family disappearing so, all of a sudden. Daddy must have felt I was going to tell someone about the things he had been doing for years. But, why would he be suspicious now of all times. Especially since he had been on his best behavior, which was still not good for a normal person, while I had been there, and then after Clarence arrived he really acted like a human being. Except for his coming home drunk the night before we left, but he had eaten and then passed out without much to say, except being obviously mad that mama hadn't fixed his dinner. He looked disgusted that my poor mama was just sitting there rocking David and singing to him. My mama had such a sweet voice and it amazed me that she remembered the words to so many old Hymns, after not being able to go to church all her married life. Daddy just wouldn't hear of it. She could not just leave when there were so many things that needed to be done. No matter where we had lived or how close we were to a church or little chapel, he refused to let her go, and she knew better than to cross him by going anyway. I just felt so helpless. I sat down and wrote Aunt Nita and to her to thank Uncle Hoyt for trying. And I told her that I had no way of knowing where Daddy might have taken them. I was so frightened for them all. Daddy could be so mean and vindictive. I also told her my feelings that he could somehow sense my feelings and the fact that I was going to tell someone about him. He may even have thought I would go to the police and tell them all the stories that I knew to be true. It was so bad that they would probably never believe me even if I did. I just wanted to know they were okay. Velma had voiced her hatred for him to me so many times the couple of weeks I had been there, I didn't think my fear was unwarranted. I just wish the knot I feeling in the pit of my stomach would go away. I will write again as soon as I hear from Joyce or Velma and maybe even Mama. Although she was usually too afraid to write anything for fear that he would come in and find her writing, especially since, he was trying to hide them. I just hope that I am worrying for nothing. My Love to all, Stella.

I could hear David awake and playing in his crib, so I quickly went to and change his diaper. I was always worried about a rash. He had never had one and I sure didn't ever to want him to have one, especially because my mind was on other things. He was my main priority always. My worry's, always went out of mind, when I saw his beautiful smiling face, which always lit up when I walked into his room. What a wonderful feeling it was to know you are some one's whole world. And I had that with my special husband also. I knew I was so blessed to have Clarence's love to fall back on when I was worrying about something. He always had a way to calm me with his great outlook on everything. David was all changed and clean clothes on waiting for his Daddy to come home. Somehow, he was getting old enough to sense that it was time. Which I realized it was also time for me to get dinner started. I figured David was getting hungry also. I put him in his high chair and gave him a banana cut up in small slices in a bowl. He was so good about entertaining himself while I fixed dinner. I couldn't think of what to fix. My mind just wasn't up to par, what with this sick feeling I had, which I'm sure is just my nerves about my other family. I had to put them out of my head. I knew there was nothing I could do, so I had to stop this crazy feeling. It wasn't long before Clarence came home and found me sitting at the table next to David, all hunched over with my head on my folded hands. He immediately knew something was wrong, because I never acted this way when David was so happy with his banana which was almost gone. Clarence came over and sat next to me after giving David a big kiss. He asked, what's wrong sweetheart? I told about aunt Nita's letter and how it had got me in such a frenzy and I just felt so sick about it all. He told me to go in and wash my face and maybe I would feel better. He said, let's go up to the diner and eat tonight, since you're not feeling well. I said okay that sound good, but are you sure we are okay with our money budget, what with just having a long trip and the cost of gas from all that driving? Clarence said, you let me do the worrying about those things, and we are fine.

When I got into the bathroom, I started feeling real sick and I leaned over the toilet and sort of dry heaved. I realized I had not eaten a bite since breakfast this morning. So, I chalked this up to that. I came out and said I'm ready if my guys are? Clarence said, are you sure you want to go? He said I can fix up something here, you look really pale and maybe we should stay in. I told him I would be fine as soon as I ate something, so let's go. When we got to the diner Clarence ordered their special plate, which was pork chops tonight, and I said I think I'll just have a bowl of your great vegetable soup and one for the little guy here too. They brought Clarence over a small salad which always came with their special. I started to order some fries too and remembered Clarence would have a big serving of mashed potatoes he could feed David some of. When they brought over two bowls of soup and a couple of rolls to go with it. I took a bite and said I need to go to the restroom honey. Can you feed David for a minute? As soon as I got to the toilet, up came the bite of soup I had just ate. What could be wrong with me? I splashed cold water on my face and dried it with a paper towel. When I went back out, Clarence said, you look like a ghost, You're as white a ghost. I told him I just couldn't shake this sick feeling. He got a big smile on his face and said, I bet you're pregnant. I said I wouldn't get sick this soon, we've only been home for a few weeks. He said, don't you remember that beautiful night under the tree, and you said you had just had your period the week before I came to Your Mama's. I thought back and said yes, and I think I should have had another one by now. That was almost two weeks before we got home and we have been home for three weeks, haven't we? Clarence said just about four weeks tomorrow. I said I guess it's certainly possible then, I will go to the doctor tomorrow and get checked. If it's a flu bug, I don't want to be spreading it

I called and they had an appointment available this morning at eleven, if I could make it that soon. I told them, that was perfect timing, I would get home just in time to feed David lunch and put him down for his afternoon lunch. Ruby Lee said she could watch him for a while. I don't know where she got all her energy, but she never seemed short of it. I dropped David off and went straight to my doctor's office. They said come on back, we are real slow this morning, we've had a couple of cancellations. Dr. Grey came into the room and I was laying down ready this time for my exam, I was getting to be a pro at this. Dr. Grey did him exam and said get dressed and come into my office, like I didn't know the drill by now. He asked when I'd had my last period and I told him it had been about the third week of June. He said that's just about what I thought. I told him about Clarence and I only having intercourse one time and that was on the fourth of July. and not again until we returned home, about eight or nine days later.

CHAPTER 26

Good news, Bad news

Dr. Grey said, well from my exam and what you've told me it, I am quite sure that you are going to be having a baby about the fourth of April. All things make this quite certain. I was so excited I actually, jumped up and hugged him. He said, I had nothing to do with it, and I told him that was just for confirming what I knew in my heart. He smiled and said your most welcome, young lady. I went and picked up David and, I didn't have to say a word to Ruby Lee, she said she could already tell, because I had that glow. I could hardly wait until time to pick up Clarence. When he came out and saw me sitting there, he knew also. I told him we were expecting a baby on April fourth. He said, I knew that night was magic. I told you we made our own fireworks that night, remember? I said yes, I do and I am so happy I'm about to bust. I don't care how many times I throw up, I know what the future holds and it worth every minute of morning sickness or afternoon, or whenever I feel bad, all I have to do, is remember what's waiting at the end. Well, the next month I had quite a few sickly moments, but now I was feeling fine and starting to show, the doctor said it was normal to show sooner, when it's been recent since your last pregnancy. He said, the uterus takes time to shrink back down to normal size. So, this time it stretches out faster. As the next few months passed, I felt wonderful and David, was the best little guy. I just hope this next little boy or girl is as good a baby, as Ronald had been, and as David has been since the day he was born. He was such a sweet loving baby and so easy to love. And also, so easy to care for. He was so good about taking his nap and such a good eater. I thank God, every day for blessing me with such a good baby.

Clarence came home from work one afternoon and said he had been laid off. He said, they said he would be the first called back, after this slow period. He said they told him how much they loved his work and it had nothing to do with him. They said with the war ending everything was at a standstill pretty much, what with not knowing what was going to happen next. So, we talked about what we were going to do. He said, he would call around in Oregon, He did, and he found a Dairy Farm that needed a Foreman with experience and Alan had given him an excellent reference. In a few days we were headed back to Oregon. Not that I didn't love Oregon, but I was getting used to my big a house and the thought of packing up everything didn't sound fun. And the worst part was leaving Ruby Lee. We had become such great friends. But we had to do, what we had to do. And Clarence would go crazy not working. We had some savings, but not enough to last very long with nothing coming in. And also, if Northrop was slowing down, then everything else would be too. Clarence was a big help with the packing.

He would bring boxes and packing materials to me and I would sit and wrap everything carefully. Then he would tape them up and mark exactly what was in each box. It really went fast with both us working all day. David just ran around playing and thinking we were having a big game and he was loving it. He would try and climb up on the boxes as Clarence stacked them. But when Clarence said no, he listened. He was real good with me also, but when Clarence said No, he knew he meant it. Clarence had never even so much as swatted him, but his voice just carried authority, I guess. Three days later, we were headed for Oregon and by the next day, we were moving into a little house for the foreman. It wasn't nearly as nice as the one we had at Alan's place, but the farm wasn't as large either. The people were extremely nice and they also had a few guys there ready to unload our truck. This time, we had a rented a big truck and a trailer to haul our car. So, we had been pretty comfortable in the truck driving. We had stayed one night in a little motel, because with David, it would have been impossible to drive all night. He was getting so big and needed to be able to lay down to go to sleep. There was no place to build up a bed for him, and also, with me as big as a house, I needed my rest too. So as Clarence helped the guys unload, he knew exactly where to tell them to put each box. Thank you Lord, for Clarence's great handwriting. And also, for getting us here safely. I told Clarence that I didn't want to seem unfriendly at all, but if they didn't push it, I would rather not become buddies with the owners. It makes it so hard to leave and I just knew Northrop would be calling Clarence before too long. He said, whatever I wanted, he didn't care, since most of the day he would be out in the barns with the workers anyway. He said they had given him a sort of walkie-talkie thing so I was able to buzz him, if I needed him right away. They sounded like they were being very thoughtful people. I felt bad suddenly, for not wanting to get to know them. I thought to myself, we'll see how it goes. I was sure if they were nice and tried to be friendly, it just wasn't my nature, not to be nice back. It just seemed so hard making friends and having to leave them. Time will tell as I always said.

It was starting to get warm early this year, of all years. I was just about due and this heat and the rain made it so muggy. I had felt so tired all day and the Foster's (the owners) came by and brought me a big fan. They said if I opened the windows on each side of the house, the air would feel so much cooler. They were an older couple and had done so much to try and make our move and new home nice for us. And the fan made a world of difference. I thanked them very much. Just as they were leaving, Mrs. Foster said, oh I almost forgot, the mailman put this in our box by accident. It was a letter from Joyce. I was so excited to read it and I'm sure they could tell as they said their good-byes quickly and were out the door. I had only heard from them a couple of months ago, finally. Joyce said, daddy had been moving them all over the place and he had been making Velma work so hard. She said she didn't understand why he ignored her so much of the time, and was just plain mean to Velma. She said, one day he came home so drunk and started yelling at Mama calling her a thick headed, Dutch-German and cursing at her like she could help what her nationality was. Anyway, she just ignored him and went towards the barn to feed the cows. That made daddy real mad because she wouldn't stand there and listen to him, so he went in and got the 22 rifle that had been left there to kill coyotes. I tried to grab the rifle from him and he slapped me down to the ground. He went to the barn and mama had a bundle of feed under each arm. He pointed the rifle at her and Mama just kept walking and tried to go around him. That made really made him mad, and he hit her hard with his fist and knocked her down to the ground. He stood over her with the gun pointed at her and kept cursing her. Then he turned and came back towards the house. Strutting like a rooster and grinning like he was so proud of himself. We were all standing outside, daddy handed the rifle to Garner, and said take this back in the house. Garner turned the gun on Daddy and said, "I ought to kill you "Daddy just screamed at him to take that gun back in the house. We all followed him and Velma checked the rifle to unload it, and it wasn't even loaded. No wonder he wasn't worried when Garner pointed it at him. The owner took the rifle back next time he came to the farm. I was so glad. I didn't trust myself or Velma not to use it if we had the chance. We both hated him more every day, but he was just so mean to Velma, I don't see how she takes it. I am leaving soon. Can I come and stay with you for a while until I can find work?

This letter had come to California and there no telling what Joyce was thinking when I didn't write back right away. In the time it took, for it to be forwarded to Oregon from California, almost a month had passed. I wrote back to the post office box she gave me and told her where we were and she was of course, welcome. Now this letter gets delivered to the wrong house. I sat down to read her letter. She said, 'Dear Clarence and Stella, I can't tell you how happy I was to finally receive your letter. She said that daddy had moved them five time in the past two months and she supposed it was because he was getting such a bad reputation that no one wanted to hire him anymore. They all knew he was just a big drunk. I kept forwarding my different post office box each time we moved. Mama suggested we go to California and try to find work, and we all couldn't believe he agreed. So, I will go to California with the family, then it should be cheaper to get a bus ticket from California to Oregon, where you are. I should be there by about the 28th of march. I just about fell off the chair. That was today. I got up and started cleaning everything in sight really good, I wanted everything to look it's best when she arrived. Clarence came home and found me on my hand and knees cleaning the kitchen floor. He said, sweetheart, are you trying to kill yourself, your poor belly is almost dragging on the ground? I told him about Joyce's letter, and he said the house is perfect and she will be so happy to get here and away from that ass. I looked around to see if David had come out of his room. He was like a little parrot lately. He repeated everything we said, and was so proud of himself. I sure didn't want him to hear that word. Clarence helped me up from the floor and gave me a big kiss and told me how beautiful I looked. I said okay, now I know you're not seeing well. I look like a whale. He said you have never looked any more beautiful to me than you do right this minute. I Love you and I love this beautiful belly here. This is our new baby. David came out of his room and said "new baby" He had been told over and over that he was going to get a new baby brother or sister and he was so proud of himself, because we had just gone and bought him a new big boy bed. Now he didn't have to scare me to death climbing in and out of his crib. It was getting time to start dinner and Clarence told me to sit still and he would fix dinner. We weren't sure if Joyce would show up soon or not.

CHAPTER 27

God Blesses Us with a Daughter

Well, she didn't get there till the next day around late afternoon, just as I had put David down for a nap. After all our screams and hugging, he came out of his room. I said, David, do you remember your Aunt Joyce? He just went over to my belly and said "new baby". We laughed at him and he looked quite proud of himself. I could see there was going to be no nap this afternoon. I asked her if she would like a coke and she said that sounded like it would just hit the spot. She said she didn't think it got this hot in Oregon this early in the year. I told her, it usually it doesn't, but at least it's better today than yesterday. I had the fan on, and it was pretty cool in here. David took Joyce's hand and said come see my big bed. I told her, he was very proud of his new big bed. I then told her we didn't want him to thinking the new baby would be taking his crib away, so we made sure he was excited way ahead of time to get him used to a regular bed. So, we took him to the store a couple of weeks back, and he picked out a new big boy bed. I told her she was going to have to share it with him, that why we went ahead and bought a full size bed. He is all potty trained, and hasn't wet the bed in over a month now. She said, are you kidding me, some of the shacks we lived in this past few months all our mattresses were touching in one room. It was disgusting to hear Daddy grunting and snoring or whatever. I tried to get to sleep and not think about him. I worry so much about Velma the worst, her hate for him is so deep, you can see it when she looks at him. He makes her work until dark almost every night. I went out to find her one evening just as it was starting to get dark. I saw daddy riding away from her and figured she was doing something he had told her to do. She didn't even see me coming, but after daddy was a bit away from her, I saw her stand up by the tractor, and say every curse word she'd always heard daddy say to her all the time. I could tell she was crying, but then, suddenly, she stopped crying and stood there and yelled as loud as she could saying, over and over, "I hate your guts, I'll kill you, I swear, I'll kill you". There was just so much hate and anger in the sound of her words. I think she really meant it. I said, can you blame her? Joyce said, well no, but she just sounded so angry it even frightened me, so I never let her know I heard her. I just waited a little while before I yelled, Velma, Mama is worried about you. When are you coming in to eat your dinner? She yelled back, she'd be in as soon as she finished fixing this stinking tractor.

Joyce and I were sitting on the couch talking when Clarence came in and first gave me a kiss and a hug, then hugged Joyce and told her how happy he was to see her here all in one piece. She said, she had really hated to leave Velma and the boys with that monster, but she just couldn't take it any longer. He is like a crazy man most of the time. He's always been mean, but now he is crazy and mean. I hate to think of what will happen to poor mama, when all of her kids leave as they are bound to. Kenneth is only nine and Garner just twelve, so they will be around to have to live with him for quite a while. And Velma, I don't know how she is still there, she said she wanted to leave so bad with me, but she just couldn't leave him there to beat on poor mama. She tries to be so protective of her, but so many times, like I'm sure you remember, Stella, that only get him madder and Mama gets it double bad, along with whoever tries to help gets it too. I said, oh it makes me cringe to think about the beatings I received trying to keep him off mama. What do you think he would do without someone to put on a show for? Maybe he'd stop. We looked at each other and said no, not likely. Joyce looked over at my belly and said you're getting pretty close, it looks like to me. I said yes, my due date is April fourth, so should be next week sometime. We all had our baths and decided we had nothing but time to talk, so let's get to bed, I am as pooped as I can be. Joyce said, she had a long day too. The next morning when I got up I found Joyce and David eating eggs and toast. She said, I hope this is okay, he seems to be getting it down just fine. I said, of course, he is getting to be my big boy now and can eat just about anything. He came running over to me and put his little head on my stomach and said new baby here. It's so cute that he is so excited about this baby. I said, yes, we've tried to keep him interested so there is no jealousy. After I ate a bowl of cereal, I asked Joyce what she would like to do today, since I would not have too many more free days, for a while anyway. She said, she hoped to find a job soon, so she wasn't free-loading. She didn't want to be a burden to us for long. I told her she would be a big help to me to be here with David while I was in the hospital. She said, I guess that will be okay then. So now what can we do? Joyce said she was enjoying doing nothing. She had never had many of those. I shouldn't complain, daddy works Velma like she's a muscle man and she's still just fifteen. He is just awful to her, Stella, I think maybe you had a few worse happenings, but hers just seems to be constant. She hates him so, and he knows it too and he better start watching his peas and que's. She then said, what are peas and que's anyway? Then giggled like a school girl. I said, beats me, just an expression from somewhere. We made a nice dinner for Clarence, but I kind of ached all over today. I couldn't seem to get out of my own tracks. After Clarence got home and found a delicious pot roast all ready, he was a happy man. Good dinners were kind of scarce lately, huh honey? He said, have you heard any complaints, my love? No, but you know it's usually better that this has been lately, he said, but usually you're not about to give me a new son or daughter. After we had eaten and I decided I really thought I would lay down a minute. Clarence said, this is not at all like you Sweetheart, do you feel bad enough to go to the dr. I told him I wasn't anxious to see that guy. He said, I told you when you first said you weren't ever-joyed with him that we should have changed then and you said you would get used to him. Well, I haven't and it's too late now, because either I just peed my pants or my water broke and I think it the latter. Clarence ask Joyce, if she was going to be all right with David and she told him, of course, they had become great buddies, haven't we little buddy? David came running to her and jumped up in her lap. She was holding a sucker over her side that only he could see. Clarence said, I leave my walkie-talkie here with you, so I can keep in touch or vice-versa. He showed her how to work it and out the door they were. My contractions were starting up already. I said, do you realize that unless I have this baby in the next four and a half hours, we are going to have a little April fools baby. So, he said, and at about 5 0'clock the next morning I finally had a beautiful little girl. I was so happy, even if we never had anymore, at least I had given Clarence a son and a daughter. After going to the nursery to hold her for a while, he came in to see me and see how I was feeling? I told him I could already tell that she had his heart now. He told me, I would always be his best girl. He asked if I had thought of a name and I told him as a matter of fact I had, I just didn't want to jinx it by saying a girl's name before knowing. So, what is her name. I said, Janet Lee. Clarence said you and your movie stars. I giggled and said I had loved that name when I heard it, He said, I knew that because you didn't say anything. See how well I know you, by beautiful wife. That's it then, correct. I said, do you like it and he said he loved it too. On April 1st. we had our daughter, Janet Lee Rader. 6 pounds and 13 ounces and 19 inches long. Clarence couldn't resist a joke. He said, she started out with a bang and ended up an April Fool. But then he, added she will be nobody's fool.

Joyce couldn't have come at a more perfect time. She was such a big help keeping David happy. He loved his new baby and wanted to hold her all the time. He seemed so big now with this tiny little girl to compare him to. It's like I went to the hospital and left a baby boy and came home two days later and he was a little boy now. Amazing how a tiny baby changes everything. Within a few weeks, David was so good with her. He would just come up and touch her head so gently. I felt like the luckiest woman on earth. A husband who I loved more than life itself, a handsome little boy and the most beautiful baby girl ever. Life could not be better. Joyce was asking if I had any idea where she should start looking for work and I told her that I would have Clarence ask his boss, because they knew everyone around within forever almost. When Clarence came home, I asked him if he thought Mr. Foster would know if anyone in the area who might need help. He said he would call and ask him. So as soon as we finished dinner, he called Mr. Foster and before he asked, I heard him say, yes, they are wonderful and thank you for asking. I was just calling to ask you if you know of anyone in the area needing a woman, for some kind job. Yes, Stella's sister has been here with us for a few weeks and she is wanting to find a job. I think she is tired of sharing a bed with my, 2 year old. Mr. Foster told him he would ask around the next day and let him know. So, the next day I got a call from Mrs. Foster asking if Joyce would be interested in helping out a good friend of hers who had several young children and they also had a small store on their farm, so she stays pretty busy. She said that she would need someone willing to live-in if possible. I ask Joyce and she thought it sounded perfect. Within the week, Joyce was working for a family which owned a very large cattle ranch called the Grimes Ranch. I drove Joyce over to meet the woman for an interview. The woman was just about the nicest lady I'd ever met, except family members. Her name was Marion Grimes and the had 4 young children, which seemed like a lot, but since Marion said, she would always be there, but she only had two hands and two eyes, and once in a while she was needed out in the store. The house was a gorgeous mansion to us. I mean it was nothing like the one of Mrs. Peterson owned, but it was a very different kind of elegant home, and Joyce and I both loved it. Joyce had only talked with her a short while when she decided she would love the job, if Marion was willing to take a chance on her. Marion said, that the Foster's had said that the Rader's were wonderful people, so that's good enough for me. Marion asked Joyce when she could start? Joyce looked to me and said how long before you can be without me. I told her I was fine now, So Joyce said I guess anytime you want me. Marion said you can start today, how does that sound? Joyce says well all my clothes are at Stella's. Marion, which by the way, is what we were told to call her as soon as we introduced ourselves, said she could have someone drive Joyce back over to get her clothes, later on, when the kids were down for their naps.

So, I got up and told her how happy I was to meet her and I hoped we would be great friends. She said she felt the same. I wasn't sure how this drive was going to be, but I just told David to sit real close to his sister and make sure she doesn't slide off the seat. I laid Janet down very close to me and told David to stay real close to her and help mommy. He felt very big, I could tell. It was only about a forty-five minute, drive and we made it just fine. I told David how proud mommy was of him for his help He was just as proud of himself. I fixed him lunch and he sat and ate while I nursed Janet. I loved being a mother. I felt this was what I was born to do. After David finished his lunch he scooted off his chair and went over to my little knic-knac stand, which he had had his little hand swatted more than once for getting into Mommy's things. I help kept my eye closely on him just to see what he would do, knowing I was busy and couldn't jump up. He looked at the things and then he looked over at me and saw that I had my eye on him. Then to my surprise, he took his one hand and gently slapped his own hand and said no-no. I couldn't help myself, I laughed so hard he came over to me and laid his head on my lap. I said, get up here on the sofa with Mommy and your sister Janet. He crawled up and sat close to me and snuggled his precious little head up against Janet. I was so happy at this moment, I just didn't see how life could ever be better. As soon as Janet had nursed on both sides, I changed her and put her down for a nap. Then I sat down and told David to come over to me and let me give you hugs and kisses. He came running over to me and jumped up on my lap. I took him in my arms and rocked him with so much love in my heart, I felt like I was going to cry. From Happiness, of course. In just a few minutes David wiggled down from the sofa and I got up and said, let's go lay down and take a nap sweetie. He was such a good boy, he knew he was tired, and came right into his bedroom. Within a minute, he was sound asleep. I went in and laid down also. I figured I might not have too many minutes like this in the next few months and I really was tired.

When I woke up, David and Janet were both still sleeping and it had been almost two hours. I opened David's room to make sure he hadn't woke up, and snuck outside. All of a sudden, I felt frightened just thinking about it. I knew I would have heard him, but for just that instant I was in a panic. He was just starting to squirm and I pulled the door almost shut. I wanted him to feel like he could entertain himself and enjoy his toys by himself. In just a few minutes I heard him making car noises. He was playing with his cars and making the engine sounds. It was so cute. Then I heard a car pull up and I got up to see Joyce being helped out of a very nice car by a handsome man. He had got out of his side and almost broke his neck getting to her side to open the door for her. She sat there like a perfect lady and waited. I wonder where in the heck she learned that. She certainly had never dated. Oh well, I guess she is just smart. In a minute, they were at the door, quietly knocking. I guess she knew the babies might be napping. I must quit calling David a baby. I went to the door and Joyce and this man came in. She introduced him as Randall Grimes. I said, oh, you must be Marion's husband? He laughed a low laugh, and I could tell I had embarrassed him. Joyce said this is Marion's brother-in-law. Edgar is Marion's husbands name. Randall just offered to bring me over to get my clothes and things. I apologized and he said no need, it was an obvious mistake. Joyce asked if David was awake and I told her he had just woke up and was playing with his toys. She said she would run out to the storage area and get her suitcases. Randall jumped up and said he would help her. I had to laugh to myself. I mean how heavy are two empty suitcases going to be. He opened the door for her when they came back in and he was carrying both suitcases. I thought it looks like someone has a crush and Joyce wasn't minding one bit. By then, David had heard the talking and came out to see who was here. He ran over to Joyce and she picked him up. I said,

I think he is going to miss you and she said she would miss him too. Randall was standing there holding the suitcases and I said please sit down Randall, I'm sure it will take Joyce a little while to pack her things up. She sat David down and told him she had to pack her clothes up. He looked at her like what's that? She took the bags and went into his room and he followed right after her. Randall says it looks like this little guy isn't wanting her to go. I said, oh he'll be fine in just a little while, he adapts easy. His sister is only two weeks old and he acts like she's been here forever. As soon and Joyce had the biggest bag packed she was tugging it out of the room and again, Randall jumped up and said, let me get that, it's way too heavy for you, He opened the door and went out to open the back seat of the car. Joyce said to me real quick, isn't he cute? I said yes, and you don't waste any time. She said he had come over to Marion's earlier today about something and had stayed talking with them for the rest of the afternoon. Marion asked him if he would like to drive me over to my sisters to get my clothes and he said, sure I would love to. On the way here, he asked me if I would like to go to dinner with him some night. I said I would have to see what night Marion would think it was okay. He said any night was okay with him. We just talked and talked all the way here. He asked where I had lived before visiting my sister and I told him I had lived in so many places, I had lost track years ago. I didn't go into any details, of course. Don't want him to know we are from white trash. I told her that mama was not trash of any kind. As he was coming back in. she said you know what I mean. I thought to myself that Joyce had always worried so much about what other people thought. She wouldn't go to school after they called her a prune-picker and other things like that. She went in to finish packing and Randall asked how long my husband had worked for the Foster's? I told him for only about 6 weeks now, I think. I really don't remember exactly what the date was. I was so pregnant, and with that and watching David, I'm lucky to remember my name some days. I told him towards the end of the war, Clarence had worked as a foreman for another Dairy farmer who Clarence had gone to College with. And then Northrop Aircraft needed him to come and work. He is an Engineer and was just helping Alan train a new Foreman. Now, Northrop is slow again until this war thing gets all settled and they are going to call Clarence back to work as soon as they get new contracts. The Country is in such a mess. Randall said it certainly is. Joyce said I am almost finished Randall, I just need to get a few of my things out of the bathroom. He told her to take her time, he was fine. I asked him if he was married, just to make conversation and he said, oh no mam, I have never met the right woman yet. I had the feeling he was thinking he had now. He couldn't keep his eyes off Joyce. I said, do you live on the Grimes Farm? He said, no he owned his own farm, but part of the Grimes farm belonged to him and all his brothers and sisters. He was really trying to impress me, like maybe I would be Joyce's guardian. When Joyce finished packing up everything, Randall carried her suitcase to the car. Joyce said, well do you like him? I heard you asking him personal questions. I said, well I need to know my sister is not dating a flake. She slapped at me and said he is the sweetest man I've ever met. And you've met so many, I said. We both laughed. She gave me a big hug and said she would let me know when her day off was. I told her that would be great and I would miss her. Then I told Randall how nice it was to meet such a nice gentleman. He said it was nice to meet Joyce's sister. When Clarence came home I told him about my day and he thought it all sounded rather fast to him. I said yes, like it took us so long to know how we felt. He said, you've got me there.

It was about a week before I heard anything from Joyce. She said she had gone to dinner with Randall twice and she also went to church with the whole family. I didn't think I had anything nice enough to wear to church, so Marion gave me some money and asked Randall to take me into town and let me pick out a few dresses for church. He came over and picked me up and we went over to his farm after church. He wanted me to see his house. It's a big two story white house with a big barn and its own gas station pump and everything. I told her to take a breath and let me have a minute to ask something. She stopped and I asked when her day off was. She told me she was off on Sunday and whatever other day I want. Marion is just the best. I just love her. It's like having another big sister. I asked her if she planned on staying here on any of her day's off and she said I'm not sure yet. Randall wants me to go to Portland with him one day and show me around. He said it's a very big and nice town. Sounds like you two are getting pretty cozy, oh Stella, how many days were you with Clarence before he proposed. I told her that was different, we knew immediately that we loved each other. Does Randall tell you he loves you. She said, not yet, but I think he will soon. I asked her if she loved him, I mean do you really love him? She answered that she had never felt this way before. She couldn't wait to see him and as soon as she did her whole insides were just doing flip flops, like I am dizzy all over inside. I've never been inlove before so, all I know is I can hardly wait until he's back again as soon as he leaves. I asked her what Marion thought about her spending so much time with him. She said that Marion was just thrilled that Randall has finally woke up. She said he was always so quiet and usually, it was like trying to pull a tooth to get a conversation out of him, she would ask him to come over and have dinner with all of them, because he spent so much time alone and now he is here for some reason all the time, then she winked at me, like I was the reason. She also told me he was a good Christian man and never missed church. And that over the past ten years or so there had probably been at least five or six girls that were just crazy about him and he would just ignore them. They would come to her and asked what they were doing wrong and she just told them that he was a quiet man and all he did was work his farm, and that's all she knew. She said he has been over here more in the past week than she had seen him the whole time she had been married to Edgar. And she also said, it sure wasn't to see her or the kids. So, I would think he loves me, wouldn't you? I told her I was only worried about her, being on her own for such a short while and maybe she was just glad to be away from daddy. She said, that's not true Stella, its being around him makes me feel so complete. We talk and talk and just enjoy being with each other. And when he kissed me for the first time, last Sunday over at his house, it was liked I was just going to melt. He never tried to get fresh or anything like that, he just put his arm around my waist and gently pulled me towards him and kissed me a long sweet kiss. I told her it certainly sounds like a man in love to me, but I only talked with him for a few minutes. Joyce said I feel like I love him, how else do I know? I told her she would know if he told her he loved her, and she immediately wanted with all her heart to tell him she loved him right back. Oh Stella, pray for me that I know what I am doing, because my heart tells me I love him. Then I guess you have your answer. She said I will call you on Monday, for sure.

When Clarence came home from work, After, kissing me and picking up David and giving him a kiss, then he had to go get Janet out of her crib and nuzzle with her and talk to her for a few minutes. Then I finally told him about my conversation with Joyce. He told me that Mr. Foster had come out to the milking barn and talked with him today. I asked him what that had to do with Joyce, and he said Mr. Foster told me this afternoon that he had known Randall for his whole life and known him to be a quiet and honorable man, and he had heard thru guys talking that Randall was a different person these days. They say he is humming and singing to himself all the time this past week. And he is usually at the farm making sure everything is getting done as it should be. Now he is gone half of every day. Clarence said it sounds to him like there is a wedding coming up, in the near future. I told him he was kind of rushing things, didn't he think? He pulled me close to him and kissed me with all the passion I knew he had in him, and then he said, now I'm not calling you a chicken, but you are sort of acting like a mother hen. He said, do you really think if we had been free to do what we wanted that we wouldn't have married before I ever left to go to California? I certainly wanted to take you with me and I was going to ask you to leave with me, but I got that note that you were gone the next morning, so I just went back to our original plan. It almost killed me waiting to find you and know you were all right all those weeks, I didn't know where you were. We would have married the next day if we could have and you know it. I told him if he didn't quit holding me this close, the kids were going to need to be tied up so we could go to our room. He kissed me again, and said, this is to be continued right after the kids are asleep. We both laughed and he said what do you need me to start for dinner. I told him I had a chicken in the oven roasting, so he could peel potatoes if he'd like. After one more long kiss, he said it was his second option of what he wanted to do, but he was on it.

After nursing Janet, I changed her and helped Clarence fix dinner. David was getting bigger every day it seemed. He knew it was dinner time and he crawled up in a regular chair and sat at the table. Clarence went over and kissed the top of his head and said, it looks like our big boy here is ready to eat. I said everything is ready to go on the table. Now we sat down and I filled David plate with some chicken cut up and some mashed potatoes with a little gravy over them and a good size amount of green beans, because they had been his favorite as of lately. He bowed his little head as we were about to say the blessing and it made me tear up that he was growing up so fast. As soon as the blessing was finished he picked up his spoon and started feeding himself, with no help at all. I was so used to him being right close to me in his high chair, that I was amazed that he was just changing before my eyes. Clarence had pushed his chair up to where he was real close, but still he needed to be higher. I asked him if he wanted in his high chair and he said, no I big boy. I teared up and Clarence said, Sweetheart you know he has to grow up. Is said, yes, I know, but it's too soon. He leaned over and kissed me and smiled. We all talked and when David's plate was empty, I asked him what he wanted now, he said more beans and I gave him more and some more pieces of chicken, because he didn't seem to be interested in milk anymore so I wanted to make sure he had plenty of protein. Clarence said while we were watching him eat so good, that he might decide he wanted his bottle again at night next week. He will probably change lots of time. I said I wanted him to stay my baby a while longer. About that time, we heard Janet making noises and Clarence said, I think our little girl wants her Daddy. I laughed and said, I'm almost positive that what those noises meant.

I cleared the table and washed the dishes, all the while I kept turning around to watch my beautiful family, David had gone to his room and brought a few cars and had them all lined up. I looked at this scene of Clarence with Janet sitting up against his legs facing him and he was just carrying on both sided of their conversation and David so content sitting next to them playing cars. I thought no one else in this whole world could ask for a more, happy content family. David had accepted Janet into the family just like she was supposed to be there and never once showed any jealousy. I loved this picture. I wish I could save it like this for ever. When I was finished in the kitchen, I went over and sat on the sofa, next to Clarence's chair. I asked him if he was as happy with our family as I was, and he said of course, but I would love to work on extending it. I laughed and said soon. Then I asked David if he was ready for his bath. He jumped up and ran to me and I pulled him onto my lap. I asked him how he liked his baby sister, and he reached over and put his hand on her arm and said his new baby. I was filled with all kinds of emotions. David said bath, I told him to take his cars to his room first, I was trying to make sure he knew to keep things in the place where they belonged after playing with them. Clarence laughed at me. I leaned over and kissed both him, then Janet. I said, isn't she beautiful, he agreed. David had his bath and got in his pajamas and was already yawning. He had had a busy day and had not even had a nap. So I said are you ready for bedtime. He went over and kissed his Daddy and headed for his room. This was just all happening so soon, I couldn't believe the change in him just the past week or so. I went in and said it's time to wash this little girl daddy, he said okay if you must take her, right in the middle of a deep conversation we were having. I was just telling her she couldn't have any boyfriend except Daddy until she was at least twenty- one. I laughed and said, and what did she say to that, he said, she said okay, daddy. After Janet was all clean and smelling like a you could just eat her up, I sat down and nursed her on both sides for about fifteen minutes. Clarence read the newspaper while I was feeding Janet. Then I made sure she was still dry, then let Clarence kiss her goodnight. After she was all snug and cozy in her crib, I told Clarence I thought a bath sounded like a great idea, he was up out of his chair and followed me into the bath discarding clothes all along the way. I said I was just telling David to keep your things picked up. He laughed and said, later I have other things on my mind right now. I had the bath water running and Clarence was definitely ready. I looked down and he was using his penis as tie rack. He said I hung my tie. We both stepped into the bath as we were kissing and longing for each other like it was our first time. I guess it was, since Janet had been born. We had messed around and got close, but I had been a little to tender so we never finished the job, but I knew I was ready now and I had the most handsome husband who was really ready. We washed each other, our usual ritual, as Clarence teased the heck out of me. He kept soaping up my breasts and the rinsing them and giving the gentle little nibbles each time. I said I am ready tonight, I am sure. I didn't have to tell him twice. He pulled me up over his legs and I gently took his penis and guided it to where I was ready for it. We both climaxed in a matter of minutes and it felt as good as it had the very first time. We lay there soaking for a few minutes, then got out and dried each with our favorite fluffy towels. The ones that said Mr. and Mrs. We were definitely that. When we got into bed we laid there talking about how wonderful our life was, and before long we were making love again. We fell asleep in each other's arms so content with our perfect life. Nothing could be better.

Sunday night, fairly late, Joyce called and said Randall had asked her to marry him and she said yes. She said I love him so much, Stella. I can't wait to be his wife. I told her I was very happy for her. I had talked with Mrs. Foster and she told me the Grimes family were just about the nicest family she could be in, if it happened. She said Marion just loved her already, like she was part of the family. So I was very sincere when I told Joyce how happy I was for her. Mama and Velma came to visit for a while and they wanted to come back for the wedding, but didn't know if Daddy would let them. Velma said Daddy had become meaner than ever and yelled at her constantly. She said she had never felt so lonely and afraid without Joyce being there to help protect her. I told her how much I wish I could help her, but I had no influence over daddy. He hated me, and especially still hated Clarence for helping me run away. So, Velma and Mama went back to Red Bluff where they were living. Mama was so worried about the boys being so young and without her that she just couldn't relax and enjoy her visit. Velma wrote after they got back and said they were all picking prunes and making good money, but it didn't do them any good. Daddy took all the money and either drank and gambled it all away, but she said they were living in a tent under a big oak tree and the had all the fruit and nuts they wanted to eat, which was great for kids who hardly ever had enough to eat their whole lives. My heart broke for them, because I had lived exactly like they had lived until I met Clarence and he saved me from all that. We had always done all we could for them, but we also had a family now to care for and money wasn't that great in the dairy business. Clarence could hardly wait until Northrop called him back. He made sure they had his current address.

Joyce asked me to be her maid of honor, and she wanted Velma to be a bridesmaid. She was going to write and beg for Daddy to let them come, since she would pay for their way there and back. Randall was paying for the wedding, since they were so active in the church, plus knowing everyone in most every town near them, it had to be a big wedding.

He had bought Joyce the most Gorgeous wedding dress. Of course, he didn't go with her to pick it out, as he knew the groom wasn't supposed to see the bridal dress until she walked down the aisle. It was a beautiful satin material with a really pretty train. She wanted Velma to be a bridesmaid so badly. She said, maybe if we went down to Kingsburg, Ca. where they were staying she could talk Daddy into letting them come. So, I talked it over with Clarence and he agreed the it might help and he really wanted Joyce's wedding Day to be as nice as ours had been. So, Joyce and I took the bus there and only planned to stay a day or two at the most. We checked into a motel, because I didn't want David and Janet to be around Daddy a minute more than necessary and the five of them were staying in a tent, so there wasn't a place for us to sleep anyway. For some reason, Daddy just didn't seem to hate Joyce as much as he did me. But we took a cab over to where they were and told it to pick us up there in about 3 hours. As soon as we got out of the cab, Velma came running out to meet us. Mama was right behind her. They both asked why we had come, even though they were so happy to see us. Joyce said she was going to see if she could talk Daddy into letting her be a bridesmaid. Velma said, good luck, he had been on the worst drunk I've ever seen the past few weeks.

Garner and Kenneth were happy to see us too and loved playing with David, who having a ball running around all the trees and playing with their Uncles. They didn't pay any notice of the baby, but Mama thought Janet was the prettiest little thing and such a good baby. I told Mama I had been blessed with three good babies, but for a reason

I didn't understand yet, he chose to take Ronald from me early. Finally, Daddy drove up, driving like a complete idiot. I knew he was drunk and wished I had waited back at the motel. Joyce just walked right up to Daddy with no fear, and calmly asked if Velma could go back with us tomorrow and be a bridesmaid. She said she was marrying a really wonderful man who owned his own farm and they were having a really large wedding because he knew so many people it had to be big. She said he had two brothers who were going to be ushers and she really needed Velma to be her other bridesmaid. Daddy asked why he wasn't invited. She told him because she knew he would come anyway. I don't know what she would have said if he said he wanted to go too. But I guess she just figured she'd call his bluff and it worked. He finally agreed to let Velma go back with us. So, we had won that battle, now to see if he would let Mama come up too, later on. He said, he would think about it. Joyce promised she would pay her bus fare both ways. But Mama said she was not going to leave Garner and Kenneth for another week or longer. There just wasn't anyone she trusted to watch them. I really think she just didn't trust Daddy that long alone with him knowing he had to have someone to be cruel to. So Mama agreed she would come up the day before the wedding and go back the day after. Daddy said Velma better be coming back with her or he would be up there and they wouldn't like the scene he would cause Joyce and her new high class family.

So, that is how it went. Joyce bought Velma and I really pretty dresses for the wedding and she bought mama a real nice suit and a cute little hat to wear.

CHAPTER 28

Joyce marries into the Grimes family

The wedding was really quite the affair. So many people and the wedding cake was so big and so pretty. The whole wedding was just perfect. I talked with Marion for a while at the reception and I said, I sure bet you had no idea when I brought Joyce over that day that she would be your sister-in-law in just over six months, plus losing your helper. Marion said that Joyce told her she would still come over and help her every day after they returned from their honeymoon. After the reception, Mama and Velma came home with us and spent the night. I knew mama loved being in all these nice places and liked being dressed so nice. She especially loved the church and how religious the wedding was. She had not been in a church in all the years she had been married, and she had loved it. I hated to see them go when I drove them to the bus station the next morning, but none of us wanted to take a chance that Daddy would go through with his threat. I put them on a bus back to Red Bluff.

CHAPTER 29

Clarence was called back to Northrop

A few months later Clarence got a call from Northrop and they had got several new contracts and needed him as soon as he could get there. He told them he would have to give his current employer a two week notice. They said he wouldn't be the man they knew him to be if he hadn't. So here we were packing again and going back to California. I hated leaving Joyce, but she was very happy with her very large new family. She had just found out she was expecting their first baby, and that's what I hated to miss, but I loved the fact that we were going back to California. I wondered how long before we were in a place to stay for a while. But, nothing mattered, as long as Clarence and I were together with our beautiful sweet family. We were so happy together and so happy with our family. We found a nice little house to rent in Gardena, Ca., which was just a little further from Northrop than our Inglewood house, but Inglewood just didn't have anything we could find to move into right away. I had called Ruby Lee and they had moved to another town called Wilmington, so we were still going to be able to visit each other and watch our Children grow up together. She came over and helped me unpack. It was so good to see her again and the twins loved having David to play with. And vice versa. Life was getting back to normal and I loved the feeling of being back where I felt like I was at home.

Only a month or so passed and we received a letter from Clarence's Brother, Oscar. He had married and they wanted to come and visit us if it was okay. Clarence called his Mother and told her to tell Oscar and his wife Willie Mae, they were welcome to visit anytime. I had forgot about Oscar being deaf mute, and I asked Clarence if Oscar had married a woman who was also deaf mute. Clarence said his Mother said she was really a deaf mute, whereas, Oscar could hear slight vibration noises and he could feel the beat of music. He had been quite a character. Very nice and funnier than heck. He loved just acting silly and I knew the kids would love him. Clarence said his Mother didn't have much to say about Willie Mae, so that lead him to think she wasn't overly crazy about her. But we would see, maybe we'd love her. I hadn't met anyone else named Willie Mae, except my aunt. Clarence helped me at night after the kids were asleep to learn sign language so I would be able to at least communicate a little while he was at work. He said Oscar always carried a notepad and pencil in his pocket, just in case and also, when they were traveling they needed it to order food at places they stopped to eat or get gas. I thought how hard it must be, but Clarence said Oscar had the best attitude and the happiest demeanor of all his siblings. I had only met him one day when we were in Oklahoma. He had been at some training school most of the time. He needed to learn an occupation to support the family he hoped to have one day. I guess he had found the most important part. Couldn't have much of a family without a wife. Clarence said Haha, so you think you're the most important part, huh? I said, well, and before I could finish, he said of course you are the most important part of my life and we sure wouldn't have a family without you. Oscar and Willie Mae should be here any day now and I felt like I was becoming pretty good at sign language. Clarence said, it was because he was such a good teacher. I said it was because I was such a good student. I also got a book that showed sign language by showing how each letter was formed. I thought it helped, but Clarence said most deaf mutes were just so much faster and had short cuts you needed to learn to keep up.

The next day right after Clarence got home from work, they showed up knocking on the door real loud, and I was so thankful he had been here. Before he got to the door he quickly told me they don't realize how loud they are being, because of never being able to hear. Also, he said really quick before he opened the door. Oscar can read lips pretty well because of so many siblings and so much practice, but he had no idea about his wife. He opened the door and motioned for them to come in. Oscar introduced Willie Mae, and they both asked about where the kids were. I said David was in his room and Janet was asleep. He was anxious to meet them. I called David and Willie Mae let out the most scary noise when she saw him. Oscar said, she said how cute he is he. Her hands were moving twenty miles an hour. I would never learn this so fast. Clarence said, sweetheart, don't worry, they won't expect you to learn everything in a few days. I could tell David was frightened by Willie Mae, but Oscar was so sweet and gentle, they were buddies right away. It was so funny, it seemed like every time some of Clarence's family showed up, I was frying chicken. You'd think it was all I cooked. I asked Oscar if the liked fried chicken and he mouthed out chicken and actually said it to where you could hear him. Clarence said he was pretty good with a few words. Chicken had always been his favorite, so after so much practice, he had learned to get his vocal cords to work with certain sounds. Like baby, he can also say pretty well. When Janet wakes up, he will probably be so excited because of his love for babies. Clarence was where Oscar couldn't see his face, but I could. Clarence said he had always felt that if Oscar had been able to go to better doctors, like in a big city, like Oklahoma City, that they could have done something about his hearing and his voice, but when he was little no one knew about all this new technology that they have now, and probably had back then, had we been able to get him there, but who knew. My parents sure didn't know, he was just accepted the way he was, and they never bother to get help for him. But at his age, he is used to being this way, so everyone just accepts it. I thought to myself, how very sad that he could have been helped, but because of so many children back then, even before the 1920's, people in small towns just accepted so many things that could have been helped if only they had known. Even my sister Birdie, she was such a pretty little thing, but we were always so poor and ignorant, back in little towns, plus Mama having so many babies in such a short time really, Birdie probably could have been helped, had they taken her to the right kind of doctor. But I didn't blame mama, it was daddy's drinking away all the money all of us kids, made for him and we lived like poor homeless people. Well, actually we were, homeless except for places we picked cotton and the farmers always had little shacks for the cotton pickers to live in. Almost all my life living on dirt floors, I couldn't remember ever in my life having a decent place to live in, until my wonderful Clarence saved me.

When I think back to my life as a child, which we all were never given much of a childhood, like being able to just play and have fun like little kids should. When I think of all the money, just us kids made, we could have owned a home or at least found a nice place to live, but every penny we slaved for went to Daddy' whiskey. Oh, how I hate that man. I think of poor Velma now, and how he treats her, and it won't be long before sweet Garner and Kenneth will be getting the same terrible treatment. I must quit thinking of all this now and get to entertaining, as best I could, Clarence's Sweet Brother Oscar, I already loved him and I'd only been around him one day before, when David had been just a year old and, even then, Oscar was so sweet that David just clung to him when Oscar had picked him up. I was determined I would get through this while Clarence was working, even if we had to go through a whole note pad to communicate. We would get through it together. I said I had to go get dinner going before they all starved. I had potatoes peeled in no time and put on to cook, then I floured the chicken and got it on to cook in my biggest cast iron skillet.

Like clockwork, it was time for Janet to wake up and eat before our dinner, but usually Clarence was always in here to watch whatever was cooking. When I heard Janet starting to make herself heard, I called for Clarence to bring her to me and a clean diaper, please. I changed her in the service porch, with her squirming all over on the washing machine, then I sat at the table and fed her some baby food so she would be good during our dinner and just sit in her high chair. I was almost finished and it was also time to turn the chicken on its other side. I didn't want Janet to get splattered with hot grease, so I called Clarence again for help. He came as soon as he heard my call. I started to explain that I couldn't turn the chicken while feeding her and he stopped me immediately, and said, Listen Sweetheart, quit thinking you have to do all this by yourself, Janet comes first, before any chicken and that for sure. Now, let me turn the chicken and you just worry about keeping our beautiful little daughter happy and her tummy full, so we can all eat when this is finished. He said he knew Oscar's favorite was green beans, and David loves them too, so he opened a big jar that Joyce and I canned ourselves when we lived in Oregon. I was really going to miss them when they were all gone. Maybe I'll try to go up there every year or so, just to see her and help during canning season. So, I finished feeding her really quick and then took her into the living room to show her off. Oscar and Willie Mae both just went crazy over her. Oscar first, held out his arms to hold her, I was a little frightened over the passing her around thing, but I just couldn't say no, so I handed over my little daughter to her Uncle Oscar. He held her amazingly well and bounced her on his knee. Then Willie Mae held her arms out and made a couple of those awful loud sounds, and Janet started crying. Willie Mae reached over and took her from Oscar and tried to hold her up to face her and this didn't set well with Janet at all.

She started Screaming and Willie Mae didn't know what to do, so I reached over and took her in as nice as way as possible. Once she was back in my arms, she settled down almost immediately.

Clarence called us all into dinner, I motioned for them to come, after realizing they hadn't heard Clarence's voice. We bowed our heads and said the blessing, then started Passing things around. Oscar was like a kid in a candy store. His eyes got so big when the platter of chicken was handed to him. I had cut up two chickens, because of not knowing how big of eaters they were. Oscar mouthed out chicken and made the correct sound. I just couldn't see how he could say one word and not others. I was just as convinced as Clarence was that he could be taught to talk or maybe just need a simple surgery. We all ate till our bellies were full. I didn't know where Willie Mae put her dinner, because she was as big around as a pencil. But I felt happy they enjoyed dinner. They talked back and forth so fast that there was no way I could keep up. So I just ate and made sure David was eating all of his. He loved green beans. I swear he could eat so many and still want more. This tickled Oscar. David didn't seem to think much about all the hand talking. I guess he wasn't old enough to notice. He was just barely three. Janet sat in her high chair playing with several little toys I had given her. She was such a good baby. I didn't have a thing for dessert but ice cream. They all loved ice cream, so that was a good thing. We showed them David's room and said they could take their suitcase in there, and we would put David on a little pallet on the floor in Janet's room. He wasn't sure he like that idea, but we told him Uncle Oscar and Aunt

Willie Mae needed his bed and Janet needed him to keep her company for a few nights while they were here. So, he finally warmed up to the idea. Everyone was tired so we showed them where the bathroom was and said they could use it first, then we would shower after them. I laid out a couple of fresh towel and wash clothes for them and in no time at all they were finished. David had already fell asleep and Janet was sound asleep also, so it was time for Clarence and I to bath. We were both really tired, so that's all we did in the bathroom and then headed for bed, where I fell into Clarence's waiting arms and we made love so beautifully I always thought in my mind. It was always so wonderful and satisfying. I think the lord made us for each other. I couldn't imagine life without him and I knew he felt the same about me. He told me regularly that I made him complete. We had the perfect family. I was hoping I would be pregnant again by now. I had though four kids would be perfect, but time would tell.

The next morning, we woke up to Willie Mae making the worst noises so loud it scared me to death, I thought someone was dying and it woke Janet up and frightened her also. She never woke up crying, but she sure did this morning. David slowly woke, but I don't think he heard the noises, he just heard us all up. I was holding Janet who was starting to calm down and I went into the kitchen to see what Willie Mae was squacking about, she was just making some toast and Oscar was sitting there and hadn't heard a sound. It's hard to know what to say to them since we know they can't hear the awful noise she makes. I knew very soon why Mom Rader wasn't really happy about Oscar's choice.

Clarence fixed breakfast and I got his lunch ready. There was plenty of chicken left so he had three pieces of that and some fruit and a couple of rolls with butter to go with the chicken. He said that was plenty. He thought he was getting fat. I said no that's me who's getting fat and I don't know why since I eat the same and I'm running after the kids all day long. He told me I looked perfect and to quit running myself down. He was happy with me and that all I cared. After breakfast, Clarence said, he had to hurry because he had never been late to work and he sure didn't want to start now. We started trying to talk in sign language, but soon it was just notes back and forth. I said I was sorry I couldn't sign well enough for them to understand and Oscar wrote, don't be silly, you're doing great for a beginner. I said thank you, but it was sure a long day. David and Janet both seemed cranky with all the confusion. But finally, it was time for Clarence to walk in and here he was. You could set your watch by him. He never varied more than a minute. He loved his family and couldn't wait to get home every day. He kissed me first and while nuzzling my neck he asked how my day went? My back was to Oscar, so I said, very hectic and it's the first day ever that David and Janet were both cranky all day, I guess they feel the tension. I told him David Adores Oscar, but every time they were having a good time, Willie Mae came up to them and she is always making those awful noises every time she is talking to him ninety miles an hour. I try to be really nice to her and I am always smiling, but I feel like she is uncomfortable around me.

Clarence just hugged me tight and said he would have a very nice talk with Oscar after dinner and see if maybe he can get it across to her without hurting her feelings that she is really loud and it frightens the children. He won't say anything I tell him not to, I know him well and he is honest beyond words. If he says he doesn't think she will understand, then he won't say anything. I felt a little relived, hoping that Oscar would feel okay talking to her. After dinner, Clarence said Oscar was going to run to the store with him. I said okay, and they left. Willie Mae wrote, asking if she could take a shower now. I told her that would be great. I didn't usually bathe the kids until after dessert and that is what Clarence and Oscar went after, I think. I laughed real big and said Clarence thinks he is fooling me, but I know him too well. About twenty minutes later, they came carrying two sacks full of groceries. I prayed that there was some dessert in there. Clarence didn't disappoint me, he pulled out a delicious looking pie covered in whipped cream. He said it was a coconut crème, my favorite. So, Oscar went to check on Willie Mae and I asked how it went and then also really quick told him I had said I thought you two went after dessert. I hugged him and said, see how well know you?

He kissed me again and then picked up Janet and said, how is Daddy's girl? She put her finger on his nose and said, "honey". He laughed and said she still just calls me, honey. I said, it because that's all she hears me call you. He said, its cute I love it. I told him I had thought it was very cute myself, but what did Oscar say? He said he would take her for a long drive around the Ocean and very discreetly tell her he thought the kids were cranky around her, because she makes loud noises when she is talking to him and to try to just talk with her hands and not open her mouth and make noises. He said he was going tell her, that he could hear the noises because of the vibration they made and then he could see the frightened look on the little one's faces. I am sure he will handle it, because he said it was true that he could feel vibrations from her noises, but didn't realize it was that loud to people and he thanked me because, he said now he understands better why people at the places they stop were so unfriendly after a few minutes. So, I know he will let her know after they have gone into somewhere for lunch or something and then she would know it was him and not us complaining.

After we had dessert, Willie Mae said she was going to bed because she had a headache. I took David and Janet in to bathe them. The older they got the more they loved bathing together, they learned how fun it was to splash each other and especially mom. I got them dried and dressed in their pajamas and David ran in to get kisses from Daddy, like he always did. He also got a few kisses form his Uncle Oscar too. Oscar came and gave Janet some kisses on her neck. She was warming up to him also, when it was just him, because he was so darn sweet and likeable. The next morning after breakfast, Clarence was getting ready to leave and he asked Clarence to explain that they would be gone most of the day, because he had promised his wife that he would show her the ocean today. I smiled and said okay. They went into their room and came out dressed in different more casual clothes. They waved goodbye to us and both David and Janet waved to them and said Bye-Bye. My day was normal and I was able to get a nice roast on to cook and put potatoes and carrots and onions all around it. Clarence loved it this way, so I hoped Oscar would also. They got back shortly after Clarence came home, and Oscar smiled and looked at Clarence and gave him a sly look that said, done. We all had a great night and everyone loved the roast and even Janet could eat the potatoes and carrots because they were cook so tender. Oscar said that he and Willie Mae were only going to stay one more day because. Willie Mae had some cousins she wanted to go and see up in Northern California. Clarence told me what they had just said and I acted a little disappointed, and I really was sad to have Oscar leave. He was such sweetheart. I was sure if they came again sometime the kids would be old enough to explain, she couldn't help the loud noise she made because she couldn't hear. The next day went great and I was sorry I had ever complained, I always wondered now if they really were leaving that soon, but Clarence assured me that Oscar would have told him the truth, he was sure. I felt guilty anyway, because now that thing had calmed down, they were really enjoying David and Janet and Willie Mae would sit and hold Janet until she would want down and she would just wiggle down off her lap. Willie Mae seemed to really be enjoying the kids and the liked both of them a lot. David was crazy about Oscar, he kept taking him by the hand and showing him different things and Oscar would just act so excited. They both enjoyed each other and I was sad to see them leave the next morning. I wrote them a note and told them they were welcome anytime. They both smiled and hugged us all and said Thank you for the wonderful visit.

The next few months were very quiet and normal for us. We were in our own little routine and life was so good.

Joyce had written and said she was pregnant again and her and Randall were thrilled. I was looking forward to a visit next summer to do some canning and to visit, of course. I received a letter from mama and she was so worried about Velma. She said she just sulked all the time about something and her and Daddy fought like cats and dogs. She said she kept thinking he would get old enough and become a nicer person, but that sure wasn't happening. She said he seemed to just get meaner. He cursed and talked so filthy to Velma and to the little guys. Even though they weren't that little anymore, they still seemed way too young to be hearing all that bad, fifthy language. She just didn't see why he had to be so mean and nasty. She closed saying J.E. had written and said he had a 30 day leave and was going to come and visit for part of it, as long as the old man didn't give him any reason to take off. I guess he wrote to Lola to see where we were now. I'm so glad she knew. It's been so many years since I've seen him. It's just not right that a mama can't see all her kids regular. I wanted to write and tell her she probably could if she would leave that good for nothing man, but I knew it would do no good. I told Clarence I felt so bad for Mama that she was so trapped by that man. He agreed, but said it was her choice and I said not really, she had been made to believe you had to stay with a person when you married them, no matter what. And I just couldn't believe no matter what the bible said, that God would expect mama to live like she had all these years, and her children all being beat and whipped constantly for no reason. Clarence said there is never a reason for a man to treat his wife or kids the way he did. I agreed about that for sure.

I got a letter from Maxine and she was pregnant also. All my family were having babies and Mama would not be able to be there for any of the excitement. I suddenly remembered how happy Hazel had been going to help her daughter with her first child. Mama should be able to do that with her kids, but that old man wouldn't let her get far from home. I was still surprised that Daddy had let her come to Joyce's wedding for the whole three days she got away. A few months before mama and Velma had come for a whole week, but Mama didn't enjoy herself at all, because she knew what he was capable of when he was on a drunk and Garner and Kenneth were so little still and she worried about all that was coming in their later life and it she just wanted to keep her two baby boys okay as long as possible. Oh, how I hated to get my mind on all this when there was nothing I could do about it. I had my own perfect little family to keep happy and I needed to have a happy mind to have a happy family. I was convinced of that. How I wish my family were like Clarence's family. They were all so close and Mom and Dad Rader were the sweetest couple. We had a letter not long ago from them and Ellen had met a very nice man, who was also a school teacher, and Mom said he was just about the prettiest man she had ever seen. I couldn't stop laughing when I read that because Mom was rather quiet and reserved, I guess you would call it. And Dora had married a man who had a horse ranch, so they all seemed to be doing very well. Clarence said he knew Orce would never get married. He just couldn't keep still long enough to be a good husband, but he was sure a great brother. I said I though he was a great brother-in-law too. I was looking forward to a visit from him again. He hadn't seen David or Janet. Of course, none of the others had either. Mama had just saw Janet when she was a few months and know she was all over the place. One of these days I would have to break down and visit Mama again before David started Kindergarten or it would be so hot going back on a bus with two little ones. It was just too hard on them, being that cooped up for almost a week, I had heard the bus lines were getting faster, but I'd have to see it before I would believe it.

Clarence came home from work and said he had received a whole dollar raise. We were thrilled and decided to go back to Inglewood and have dinner at our favorite café. We had not been there since moving back to California. Sally would love the kids. We had a really fun night and the kids loved the way they could run around in there, because it was just so at home and casual. They both ate good and then while they were playing over in a corner fixed up for little kids, Clarence and I had a piece of Apple Pie. It was so good and we got it all down without the kids ever noticing. We were trying to keep them from eating too much junk, like we did. Great examples we were. It was Friday and Clarence didn't have to work the next day, so we decided to drive over to Wilmington and see Ruby Lee and her beautiful Children. That little Ila Jean was really going to be a knock-out when she got older. She was already a beautiful little girl, but you could just see all those gorgeous features turning into a very pretty girl. When we got there, no one was home. It was silly to drive all the way over there, not knowing if they were home or not. We should have called first. Oh well, I will take you to work and go visit her one day next week. But we had a really fun weekend. We took the kids to the zoo and to the park to play and just enjoyed out wonderful happy family. Life could not be any better.

Clarence went to work Monday morning, and I decided I would get in touch with Ruby lee and see what day would be good for us to come for a visit. She said she was sorry they had missed us Friday. They had been to school for a Teacher-Parent conference. She said thank goodness, the report was good, because I guess from what a few things she had said way back, that Lawernce could get really mean too. I thought, what is wrong with these crazy men with wonderful wives and great children and yet they just had to show who was the boss. I felt like the luckiest woman alive. Clarence was so perfect, I couldn't ask for anyone better, ever, ever.

CHAPTER 30

Velma shot Daddy

The phone rang again and it was Lola, she said that Velma had just shot and killed Daddy. She said J.E. had said he would have taken the blame for her, but he knew he would go to prison for the rest of his life. He felt so sorry for the kid and all she had gone through in her 16 years. Way more than any little girl or boy should have to go through. He said he knew from experience how horrible life was with the old man. Ruby lee said she could watch the kids for week or even two, if it took that long, so not to worry, she would take really good care of David and Janet. So not to worry at all about them. Clarence could come over for dinner a couple of times and visit them. I finally agreed, because I had to get there as fast as possible, so we decided to take the train because it was so much faster and Joyce and I wanted to get there as soon as possible. Joyce and I arrived at about the same time and J.E. picked up both up from the train station. He looked so good. I couldn't believe how he had changed, even though it had only been a few years. He had aged, but still looked great. It had been so many years since I had seen him and Preston, J.E. said that they had found Preston, and W.K. and were sending both of them home immediately, and Maxine and Lola were already close by. He said it had been so awful. The little guys both seeing the old man blood dripping from his head. He said it was the best he had ever looked to him. After all the things daddy had done to him and to Preston, I couldn't blame him for feeling that way. So soon all of Mama's children would be home together for the first time in more years than I wanted to count. Actually, more than had, ever been together at the same time, since Garner and Kenneth had not even been born yet when Al, J.E. and Preston had all run away from home years before then. On the drive to the house, J.E. told us all about what had happened. He said Velma only cried when Kenneth looked at her like he was frightened of her. She held out her arms to him and told him, she had done it for mama, and for him and Garner, so they would never have to live the way all the rest of us had. Then he said mama told him to go to Brownsfield, and get the Sheriff. Velma sat in the car while I went in to tell the Sheriff what had happened. When the Sheriff came out, he had Velma and I ride back to the house with him. And Mama, Velma and I drove back to the Sheriff's office with him and Garner and Kenneth rode back with the coroner. Then he almost looked like he was going to cry, when he told how they took poor Mama in a room and kept questioning her and Velma and he had both been in a separate room's being questioned. He said they just kept after him to admit he had done it and was letting his little sister take the blame. I guess they were trying to get mama to admit the same, but finally, I guess we had all told the same story, so they had released Velma to Mama until the trial next month. I thought I can't go home without going to the trial and I certainly didn't have the money to come back again. Who was going to watch my babies? Clarence called and told me not to worry, stay as long as I needed to and he was picking the kids up every day as soon as he got off work, so they could sleep in their own beds and getting up early enough to get their breakfast and take them to Ruby Lee's. She tried to tell me it wasn't necessary that was doing so much driving, when she had plenty of room and help from the older two kids, but I wanted them with me. I was still worried with knowing that Ruby Lee's husband could be mean too, but I really didn't think he would hurt little children. Still, I asked Clarence to ask some of the neighbors if they knew of someone that could come to the house during the day. Then he wouldn't have to drive that much. Clarence called me the next day saying he had found a really nice girl going to college at night and she really needed some extra cash to get through, and sweetheart, you know I would never leave them with someone who I had no references from. And she came by and met the kids and they seem to really like her.

After Preston and W.K. both arrived, we had Daddy's funeral, for Mama's sake and the two little guys, as J.E. kept referring to Garner and Kenneth as. Mama just kept crying and asking, how could this have happened? She knew, it was just a thing to say, I guess. Velma said, when she saw daddy in his casket, that it was the first time in her whole life he looked clean and didn't stink of whiskey and worse. He actually looked like someone that could have been a real human being if he had tried.

CHAPTER 31

The Trial

The court gave Mama her choice whether she wanted to have a six man jury or let the judge decide. Mama chose the six man jury. Aunt Nita and Uncle Hoyt came and hugged us all and hugged mama for several minutes. There were a lot of people at the trial and even a couple of Daddy's Sister's showed up, and they acted like we should all be hung. I couldn't understand why they would all be so mad at us, when they knew nothing about our life and horrible living standards and the way daddy had beat mama daily and every one of his children had run away because of these conditions. It was literally unbearable watching mama being abused, both with constantly being spoken to with filthy language and slapped to the ground more times than I could ever count even in my 16 years of having to live like that, but I am getting ahead of myself. Back to the trial, each one of us were called up to the box to testify. We were sworn in on the bible, and said we swore to tell the truth and nothing but the truth. Al first, gave his full name and told of the daily beating to himself and to his mama. If he tried to get daddy to leave mama alone, he got it worse with a belt and whip or whatever he could get his hands on. Then he would go at mama harder. It was a non-stop horrible life, which I could no longer bear anymore, and ran away at 15, to work on a farm a hundred miles or so away. Anywhere that daddy could not find me. I always found a way to get word to mama so she knew I was okay. Working on these other farms was really hard work, but I was used to that, at least I was never hit, even once and I got my fare pay at the end of each week. Then J.E. was called and was swore the same. He stated his full name John Edward, then said, I don't know why I was the one to get stuck with his name. What a curse on me. Thankfully, I was always just called J.E. He told of the time daddy had hit his knuckles so hard with a huge wrench, just because he didn't turn loose of the pipe like daddy yelled to him to do. He said I was crying and told Daddy my hand was frozen to the pipe and I couldn't let go. So, he took the wrench, and hit my knuckles so hard that my hand turned loose, but every knuckle was broken and I had left most of the skin from my palm on the pipe. Mama tried her best to wrap my hand, and put what medicine she had on it. Mostly just some salve like you put on cow's udders and wrapped with clean flour sack material, which mama tore into strips. She saved every bit of any material she could get her hands on because she had to use anything just to make various things. I had to continue to work doing whatever daddy told me to do, regardless of the pain I was having. He held up his hand and showed them to the Jury to show them the condition of his knuckles, because of the way they were never able to heal straight. And the scars on his palms He said, he endured things like that from the time he was old enough to remember. He then, said that he and Preston and run away at the ages of Fifteen and Thirteen years old.

Preston was called and sworn in. They asked him to give his full name. He said, Carl Preston, but I've always been called Preston. He then went on to tell of his life, basically the same as the rest, except, he told of the time he and J.E. were just goofing around in the barn where they were living at the time, he said, daddy came in and caught us not doing the work he thought we should have had done by that time, and he picked up a large piece of heavy wire laying on the ground, then made me take my shirt off, and started whipping me over and over till there were so many open wounds on my back that the blood had ran down and soaked my pants, and he walked away, saying, I'd say you better be getting your work done. He said, J.E. helped him clean-up as much as possible, and put some of the udder salve on his back and wrapped it with clean pieces of flour sack material that mama had saved in the barn in a big clean flour sack. J.E. snuck in and gave Stella a note, telling mama we just couldn't take it anymore and we were going to join the Army and anything would be better than living like this, in a constant state of fear. We told Stella that we were both tall and looked older, so we were going as far away as we could get, then we both are going to lie about our age and join the Army. Stella was crying so hard when she hugged us goodbye, never knowing if we would see each other again. It was a very hard thing to do, but I've never been sorry a day since except for missing my mama and sister's and brother's left behind to live this life. Guys thought boot camp was so hard, but J.E. and I breezed through it like we were at a party. Compared to home life, it was. He unbuttoned his shirt and turn a full turn slowly to show everyone the scars on his back from that last beating.

Next it was my turn, I was sworn in and testified to all that I had heard from the other to be true and honest. Then I told about how many time daddy had beat me until I was bleeding in more place than one, but the worst, being the time he was beating mama so bad and he had her down on the round threatening to kill her. I jumped on his back and pulled him off her. He stood up, took ahold of my hair and slapped me as hard as he could more times than I could keep count. He then threw me across the room where my head struck something and it spit and blood was gushing. He came over and leaned down and kept beating on me. mama was so afraid of daddy, she never dared to open her mouth if he was drunk, but she was sure he wasn't going to stop until I was dead. She saw a hammer laying on the table he had carried in with him, she picked it up and in a hurry hit him over the head, forgetting to see which side of the hammer she hit him with. The claw of the hammer stuck into the back of his skull and he passed out. Mama yelled for W.K. to run as fast as he could and find the Dr. that lived nearby. When the Dr. got there he came to me and started fixing and sewing up all my wounds and sent someone for the police and had daddy arrested. We were the happiest we had been for a long time, probably since the previous time he'd been thrown in jail for some drunken brawl in a bar or something. I had no sooner healed than some jailer let daddy talk him into releasing him. He couldn't remember why he had been thrown in jail that time, thankfully for mama's sake. He would have killed her for sure had he known about the claw in his head. Anyway, we moved out to yet another place to pick cotton while daddy was in jail, but Mama was worried what he might do if he thought they had run away, so she went to the jail to see him. We all begged her not to, but she was afraid, and none of us would go with her, except for Velma and Garner and they were too young to argue. He tried his best to sweet talk her into getting him out, but she said she couldn't. But that was the happiest time in my life, not only was Daddy gone, but we were in a tent next to a bachelor who I immediately feel in love with and vice versa. My husband, Clarence Rader, proposed to me not long after, but daddy got out and came home, so I hid my ring until I could get it back to Clarence. I knew if daddy found it, he would quickly make whiskey money out of it. Clarence and I met in secret places after we knew daddy had gone into town to get drunk. Clarence said he was going to California where he could make better money and send me as much every week as he could until I had enough to run away to California and we could marry as soon as I got there. He was sending the money to my Sister, Lola. I had written to her and explained. The rest of this story has no bearing on this trial, but I can guarantee you that any of the rest of us kids would have done the same, had we had the chance. He certainly deserved it. Maxine and Joyce were both up next and said that they were so frightened of daddy that they stayed away from him and never uttered a word to him unless asked a question. They both said they had seen what had happened to me because I was so spirited and just couldn't keep quiet when he started hitting on me. So, daddy never did too much to them, but they had witnessed many beatings to J.E., Preston and Stella. The other were long gone before we were old enough to know what was going on. All we knew is that we were always hungry and cold in the winters. There were never enough blankets and not nearly enough food ever. We were all hungry most of the time. The first time we had any candy and gum and some good groceries was when Clarence had the tent next to us and would take us into town when we got paid each week to buy groceries. Then daddy had to go and spoil everything and get out. We were used to working hard, but not to being able to buy real food. Before that, daddy would collect all our salaries and bring home a big bag of beans and a sack of potatoes. Once in a while, he would feel generous and buy flour or cornmeal, so we could have bread or cornbread. We were lucky, I guess that not only were beans healthy, but also most of the farmers didn't mind us milking the cows if we could catch one, and W.K. and Garner were pretty good at that, for little guys. That actually got a little bit of a laugh from the courtroom, which were mostly all crying.

When it was W.K. turn to testify, he stated his full name, William King, then just went on to tell stories about the same, except he said, daddy seemed to hate him from the moment he could remember because he was short and always kind of sickly, like I could help it. He would walk into the room and knock me down with his fist and then say, what, you too much of a wimp to fight back. He would constantly tell me I would never amount to anything since I was the runt of the litter and should have died in birth. After a while the attorney didn't ask as many questions, because he knew they were all the same. He just hated that I was never as big and tall and strong, like the other boys in the family who I barely remembered. I just always felt unwanted and definitely unloved. Mama would try to give me extra love when he wasn't around, but if he happened to walk in early, she would get smacked around for wasting time on a good for nothing kid. When I was fifteen, I couldn't take it anymore and ran away and hitch-hiked to Los Angeles, where I knew from a letter mama had received from Stella, that She and Clarence had moved there. They kept me long enough to get me healthy and fattened up, so I could join the Navy. I knew the war was going on and they really needed guys, so Clarence swore that I had been living with them and I was 18. Even though I was short, they didn't care as long as I passed boot camp. Which I did, I have been in the Navy now for a little over 5 years and doing very well. So, I did amount to something, you old bastard, he said as he looked towards hell, fighting to keep from crying. He was dismissed by the judge. I had always felt so sorry for him because of all of that had been done and said to him by daddy, almost worse than the beatings I constantly received. His spirit was broken from the time he was little and that's just as bad as the beatings I had received.

Next it was time to call Velma, she was sworn in and stated her full name. When her attorney started questioning her, she had to take a deep breath to keep from crying. He asked her a few questions and she told of how he treated her like she was a huge man, the way he expected her to do so much work and run the tractor and fix it when it broke, even if it took until midnight. She said he had been on the worst drinking binge she had ever seen him on and there was so little food for them to eat, until J.E. came home on leave and bought some things. He didn't have much money after buying his ticket to and from the army, for his leave. Unfortunately, he got the drinking habit too, I would have thought after seeing daddy all those years, he would never touch the stuff, but still, he was so good to us, but as soon as daddy would get home, they would fight and he would take off to somewhere. On this night J.E. had gone in the other room to take a nap. I was helping mama fix dinner. He came in and said we were moving again. I thought to myself, oh God in Heaven, when is this moving ever going to stop? He was watching every move I made as he sat down at the table and finding fault with every single thing I did. He kept cursing and talking that filth he always did, not any of it good for writing down or repeating. Mama would wash my mouth out with soap if I'd ever talked like him. He was the dirtiest talking man I ever saw and he was always bragging about his Irish decent. He had a very red complexion and a huge belly and his pants were always down below his belly with his pants hanging down. And he always smelled of whiskey and pee. He was so disgusting. As he ate his dinner, he kept spitting on the floor and then in his plate, saying things like this food wasn't fit to eat. He was the nastiest and most stinking man I had ever seen. And my mama was always clean and smelled of soap. I couldn't see how she could let him get into bed with her and touch her. We were all in the same room most of the time and just because it was late, didn't mean we couldn't hear his ugly grunting. He just kept spitting and calling mama names. He finally pushed back his plate and fell over with his stinking drunk head almost in his plate. A dog would have had have better manners at the table. Mama went outside to tell Garner to go to the field and fetch some cotton sacks so she could start packing. I picked up a comic book to read and under it lie a 22 rifle that the boys had borrowed from our boss to kill some birds that were getting into our garden Mama had tried to start, hoping we would be there long enough to have some good vegetables. I walked in to look at daddy laying there passed out drunk and I went back in and picked up the 22 and found some shells for it. After I loaded the gun, I walked backed into where daddy was passed out and put the gun to his head and pulled the trigger. He took a breath and gurgled and the blood was running down the oil cloth on the table. His arms came out from under his face and hung to his sides. I never thought about what would happen to me, I just knew I would never have to walk into a room and see him hitting my mama or smell his dirty whiskey soaked body. I wanted to cry and jump up and down, I was free. I knew at that moment that I would never fear another walking human being again. Fear is a terrible thing, and hate is even worse. It can wreck a person, brain, mind and turn life into a living hell.

Mama came running into the room from outside and she couldn't see Daddy, but she had heard the gun. She said, child, what have you done? I very calmly said, I shot Daddy. Mama began crying and ran to him, J.E. was in the room by then and he picked up Daddy's head by the hair and the blood was running out of his nose and mouth. J.E. said, Dad, can you hear me? Kenneth came running in and saw the mess. I thought, what a terrible thing for a little boy of seven to see. Kenneth ran out to Garner and I stepped out on the porch and heard Kenneth say to Garner, Velma shot Daddy, Garner said, WHAT? And Kenneth said, "yes in the head". Garner dropped his arm load of sacks and ran into the house. He never said a word as he passed me, but Kenneth looked at me like I was a wild animal about to attack. The look on my baby brother's face made me cry. I held out my arms to him pleading for him to come to me, I said, don't you see, I did it for you, Kenneth, and for Garner and Mama. He jumped into my arms and squeezed me so tight it nearly chocked me. I went back into the house and Mama was saying," get a Doctor quick". I said, No Mama, he's got to die or if he doesn't he'll kill me for sure. Mama said, hush child, then told J.E. to go into town and tell what had happened, and she said, he'd better take Velma with him. And you know the rest, sir. I would never tell another girl my age or any age that this was the right thing to do, but then, no one else lived the sixteen years with that pig, like I did. I only pray the Good Lord forgives me.

There was not a single dry eye in the courtroom, including the judge. and when the defense rested, the district attorney said, No Questions.

After a very short time the jury came back with, "NOT GUILTY" The trial had lasted one day.

Epilogue

At the beginning, Henry and Lola had come forward and asked for custody of Velma, the jury had been told it would be up to them whether she should be sent to the Gainesville, Texas state prison for women until I was 21, or be released to Henry and Lola. Lola had chosen not to testify because of being too upset and emotional and wouldn't be able to talk without crying. In the beginning, the opening statements the district attorney had tried to get the jury to send me to State's Prison. He tried to brand her "just another juvenile delinquent" The jury was only gone what seemed like minutes and came back saying I should be released to my sister and her husband. The judge gave me a good talking to and told me to be a good girl for my sister and not give them any trouble. When the judge told me I was free to go, I ran into Henry's arms and buried my face in his chest and cried. He took me by the hand and almost pulled me over to the jury box, and he shook hands with each one and so did I and we both thanked them. When they walked out all the family was there and hugged and kissed her. Everyone I could see was crying. I don't think there was a person in town that thought an injustice had been done to society.

Most had probably seen Daddy around town drunk, and everyone knew what he brought in groceries to feed a family of five. But like we had all said, at one time or another, there was always plenty of money for whiskey. When asked to give a comment for the paper, she simply said," I am not proud of what I did, I just hope someone learns a lesson from it. Take your troubles to the law and don't be afraid to ask for help. You have more friends than you think you have."

She went to Ft. Worth to live with Henry and Lola and their two daughters, Glenda and Joyce. Mama, Garner and Kenneth came to California to live with Clarence and Stella. She knew they would be alright, because she remembered what a wonderful man Clarence had been to us when we first met him, and then when he came for Stella and their baby, David. All the enormous amounts of groceries he had bought and cooked for us. We ate like kings and queens that week. And he was always there and his look to daddy had said, just try something, buddy and see where it gets you.

When I called Clarence immediately after the trial and told him the outcome, he was over-joyed. I asked him about bringing, Mama, Garner and Kenneth back with me? He said, Sweetheart, you know me better than to even ask that. Your family is My Family and it's about time David and Janet get to know their grandmother and uncles. I wished I could go through the phone and kiss him, but later.

All, is well now, and some of you might not think this is a happy ending. But you didn't have to live the way we all did. Just be thankful and count your blessings one by one. And also, my mother got to go to Church every Sunday and every

Thursday and Bible Studies at different homes on Tuesday nights and also Sunday night and she taught my Children Bible verses in bed every night. And, she was able to sing her heart away until she died at 85 years old. So, I feel that's a pretty happy ending.

Written by Janet Lee
Daughter of Clarence and Stella Rader
The Best Parents Ever.

ABOUT THE AUTHOR

Janet, and her husband Bill retired in 2000, moved from California to Tennessee. Janet loves to bake and keep her home clean. She loves to draw house plans, if she were younger, would consider becoming an architect. She has drawn the plans for their last three homes. Janet loves flying back to California to visit their two Sons in Northern California. A Fire Department Captain and a Wine Salesman. She has two Brothers and two Sisters. She loves going to Church and Sunday School. Above All, God is Number One and Family is the very Most important thing to her.